William Howell

The Two Worlds, or, Here and Hereafter

An epic in five books

William Howell

The Two Worlds, or, Here and Hereafter
An epic in five books

ISBN/EAN: 9783744726450

Printed in Europe, USA, Canada, Australia, Japan

Cover: Foto ©Thomas Meinert / pixelio.de

More available books at **www.hansebooks.com**

THE TWO WORLDS;

OR,

HERE AND HEREAFTER.

AN EPIC IN FIVE BOOKS.

BY

WILLIAM HOWELL,

Of the Bristol Grammar School.

London:
SIMPKIN, MARSHALL, & CO.

Bristol:
W. MACK, 38, PARK STREET.

1865.

PREFACE.

Courteous Reader,

Sometimes when more than enough is given it is discourteous to the receiver. There is an apparent instance of this in our title-page, at least to subscribers. The explanation conveys an apology. "Here and Hereafter" was the advertised title of this work, but when the letter-press was far advanced, we learnt that a work—not a poem—was already in existence bearing the same title. Hence the change to the present title.

Commenced as a pastime, there was not at first a remote idea of ever publishing what at length became a volume. Its existence at all is owing to my kind and humble-minded friend Dr. Bell asking my supervision of some manuscript poetry of his; this cut into a vein that had been overlain by the cares and business of life—the public will assay the metal. I am not in any way deprecating criticism: no one has a right to trouble others with thriftless diligence or aimless effort, neither of which is the vice of the following pages.

A grateful spirit demands that another dear and valued friend should be mentioned here, the Rev. W. Leask, D.D. It is from his kind and encomiastic notice of the MS. that the public are challenged for their opinion. Dr. L. took the trouble to read—which he is pleased to call "a rare pleasure" —and then pronounced a judgment which, however sustained by those who read, characterizes a heart devoid of disparaging thoughts towards others, as it is filled with warmth and sympathy for one "unknown to fame."

If the author seems to have a low opinion of his race, he forgets not that he is a unit of the same—"tua res agitur, paries cum proximus ardet." His regard for mankind, however, is deep, remembering that for them the Eternal God has given His all;—"He that spared not His own Son, but delivered Him up for us all, how shall He not with Him also freely *give us all things?*"

If man's follies have been laughed at, his sorrows have been pitied; and the remedy is set forth in no vain manner, nor doth "the trumpet give an uncertain sound."

One prevailing thought has energized throughout the whole exercise—that God may be glorified, being vindicated, feebly but earnestly, in all His dealings with man, and from man's aspersions of His governmental character.

The work is entrusted to the public, which always values what it esteems, by one who desires to have nothing better said of him than, "after he had served his own generation by the will of God, he fell on sleep."

THE AUTHOR.

Clifton, May 24, 1865.

CONTENTS.

PROEM ... ... page 1.

BOOK I.
THE ARGUMENT.

An excursion of thought into ethereal space. The heavenly bodies—the Sun, the Planets and Comets. Apostrophe. The Earth and its concerns, spiritual and temporal. The Seasons. Apostrophe. The miser. The rich man. The successful tradesman. Our neighbour. The drunkard. The adulterer. Lovers of pleasures. Fashion. The garden. The farm. A coal mine. Geology. England's capital. Self-Will. Diseases. Theft. Charity. The harlot. Attempt of human wisdom to account for the present state of man and things. ... ... page 8.

BOOK II.
THE ARGUMENT.

Wisdom stays the rash surmisings of an enquirer with some unfolding of God's ways: commits to Revelation the work thus begun. The enquirer is sent in retrogression of thought to Eden to see man in his primal state, and make a record of what he sees and hears. Revelation resumes for a while, and sends the enquirer again to hear Adam and Eve's colloquy. On his return Revelation commits to the enquirer the written Word of God for the full unfolding of God's will and ways. Its reception and use. Cain and Abel. Adam and Eve's lamentations. Discourse on Death and Life. Progress of sin. The flood. ... ... page 61.

CHAPTER II.
THE ARGUMENT.

Egress from the Ark. Noah's drunkenness and curse. Slavery. Noachic laws. Nimrod and Babylonish idolatry. A fancy sketch. Abrahamic covenant and history. Israel in Egypt, and deliverance. A glance at the progress of the nation of Israel. Babylonish captivity. The four kingdoms of Daniel: the fourth identified with the last great foe of God and man: his doings: his end. The final consummation. ... ... page 125.

BOOK III.

CHAPTER I.—REDEMPTION.

THE ARGUMENT.

I.—THE PRIMAL CAUSE—THE LOVE OF GOD.
    i. Irrespective of the creature.
    ii. Therefore not afterwards affected by it—
        a. By the creature's goodness.
        b. By the creature's naughtiness.

II.—THIS LOVE, AS FAR AS WE KNOW, WAS SIMPLY WILLED, OR SELF-EXISTENT, FOR THE FOLLOWING REASONS:—
    i. Because God is not the subject of emotions, though anthropopathically said to be so.
    ii. Allowing that He is, there was nothing existing to effect this love.
    iii. Nor could it be called forth by foreseen things, for these were antagonistic.

III.—THIS LOVE IS IRREVERSIBLE.
    i. Because God is unchangeable, though
    ii. This love has sometimes this appearance.
    iii. It was unconditional; though
        a. A condition is laid down, but
        b. This condition is secured by God's purpose.

IV.—THE TERMS OF GRACE IN PROMULGATION ARE LIMITED TO NONE; BUT THE RESULT IS A PARTIAL ACCEPTANCE, BECAUSE—
    i. The present condition of man is hostile, and an enemy can only resist.
    ii. God has not met this by an express intimation that He will use more than a reasonable and natural appeal to all.
    iii. A partial reception is secured by a supernatural influence.

V.—THE REASONS FOR THIS DIVERSITY OF RECEPTION.
    i. Two diverse races exist,
        a. The seed of the Evil one.   *b.* The seed of the Holy One.
    ii. The limit designed.

VI.—GOD'S PARTIALITY IS NOT UNJUST, FOR—
    i. Man is dealt with according to his demands, as a reasonable being.
    ii. Justice has its due in all—every sin is expiated.

page 189.

CHAPTER II.—THE REDEEMER AND THE REDEEMED.

THE ARGUMENT.

I.—THE INCARNATION.

    i. Its nature.   ii. Its prophetical indication.
    iii. Its fulfilment.   iv. Its purpose.

II.—THE ATONEMENT.

    i. How available, not in the sense of a human substitute merely.
    ii. The extent of its application.
    iii. Its results, different
        a. On those who receive. *b.* On those who reject.

III.—THE OBJECT OF THE ATONEMENT—THE CHURCH.

    i. In time.
    ii. In eternity.   ...   . page 208.

CHAPTER III.—THE WORK OF THE SPIRIT.

THE ARGUMENT.

INVOCATION.

I.—THE NEW BIRTH.

    i. What is it?   ii. What is its design?

II.—THE NEW LIFE.

    i. In what does it consist?
    ii. How does it bear on its counterpart—the life which is to come?
    iii. How does it exist Godward?

III.—THE GRACES OF THE SPIRIT.

    i. Faith, Hope, Love.
    ii. The results of Faith—virtue, knowledge, temperance, patience, godliness, brotherly-kindness, love.
    iii. Of Hope—patient waiting.
    iv. Of Love—an abiding in light, self-denial toward God and man, freedom from fear, with perfect confidence and boldness before God.   ...   ... page 227.

BOOK IV.

THE MILLENIUM.

THE ARGUMENT.

Introduction. The King of nations. Character of the Millenium. Relation of man to man. The walk of Pleasure. Duration of life. Natural changes. The arch of Heaven. Regions of the air. The regions under the earth. Inhabitants thereof. A conclave there—Satan, Beelzebub, Apollyon, and others. Despair breaks it up. A subsequent meeting. Results. Final committal of evil spirits. Time's close.   ...   . page 251.

BOOK V.

THE ETERNAL STATE.

THE ARGUMENT.

Introduction. The New Jerusalem. The earthly Jerusalem. Jacob's dream fulfilled. Heaven's harmony. God all in all. Hymn.   ...   . page 299.

HERE AND HEREAFTER.

PROEM.

NAY, tuneful Nymph Pierian, cease thy claim
To lead, as rightful guide, our measured thoughts:
Go, hie thee to thy own unchallenged haunts.
Soft-nursed in shady groves, or bred in glades
Of sunny warmth—Parnassian habitudes:
There let thy modest limbs, but loosely draped,
Press at their careless length sweet Nature's couch;
With coverlet of green, arched in by boughs
Of intertwining growth, where zephyrs sport.
Or, visiting Aonia's favored climes,
Or Pindus' sacred heights, or gushing springs
Of Helicon; or, sipping daintily
Castalian dew, thy mission fill.   There strike,
Ye bright Enneades, the mythic lyre;
There gaily sing of unsubstantial things;
Provoke and, graceful, lead the airy strain
That dreamily recites heroic deeds,
Brought on the stage of life by vagrant thought.
Gay nymphs whom Fancy, always teeming, bore
To brisk Invention at the limpid font,
Where leaps inspiringly the crystal lymph:
And in its flood immersed, were there surnamed,

As each had presidence of science, art,
Or poetry, or roll historical.
So *Clio*, laurel-crowned, a trumpet holds,
A lute as well, and plectrum, trilling sweet
Historic lays, recording men and things.
Euterpe, chiding melancholic mood,—
Her open brow, with flow'ry chaplet wreathed,—
Breathes in the liquid flute her magic art.
Thalia too, enrobed in simple dress,
All unadorned, with shepherd's crook appears,
In careless, leaning attitude; a mask
Her right hand holds: she iterates her name
In pastoral lays, light-hearted comic strains.
Melpomene, arrayed in glittering garb,
Advances buskined leg, with dagger poised,
In solemn state, and meditative air,
Premising awful, bloody tragedy:
Her sceptred hands grasp crowns as well.
Terpsichore moves trippingly along
To tuneful cadences and lyric strains;
Her head surmounted with a laurel crown.
Voluptuous *Erato*, the tender muse,
With roses crowned, and myrtle intertwined;
Her right hand grasps a lyre, a lute her left;
And, lighted at the glowing shrine of Love,
The marital flambeau.
And *Polyhymnia* too, her right hand raised
With grave, impassioned air rhetorical.
Veiled Nymph, in purest white, harmonious Muse!
Her left hand with a queenly sceptre filled,
Her classic head a jeweled crown adorns.
Calliope, her brow embayed with wreaths
Of laurel twigs; her hand a trumpet holds,

And books, significant of deathless fame,
Heroic deeds, and earnest eloquence.
Urania, rapt in meditative mood,
Surveys the dome of heaven, the concave heights.
An azure robe falls o'er her graceful limbs,
And stars begem her crown.

   Not such as these we now invoke—vain myths !
For plain reality, severe, forbids
The classic muse to celebrate her song.
But if ye will intrude, ye gentle Nine,
Our courteous ear shall catch your dulcet strains,
And give them note and currency; and they
Shall plead your cause; invalidate your claims,
Or otherwise. Forced company sustains
The host's immunity; be this our plea.
If in our theme ascriptive speech occur,
Let words correlative to him who speaks
Define his thoughts, nor thread dim mazy lengths,
And picture aught abrupt from things that are.
Far more seductive winds the invious path
Of Fancy, leading through her charmed abode,
Laid out by cunning skill and subtile craft;
Where spring indigenous, balm-yielding plants,
Shrubs odoriferous, with gorgeous bloom,
The air all redolent with spicy yield,
Released mature from pregnant nectaries.
Where vaulted groves, alive with choral mirth,
Invite prone limbs, supine on grassy pile—
Nature's soft velvet, well inwrought with skill
Of master hand; king-cup and daisy interspersed:
Where streams, meand'ring imminent, impose
A spell of drowsy power. There amorous lays,
Illusive songs, and deeds of heroes, join

With feathered songsters' notes—outbursting joy
And melody. There Naiads visit; there
The fav'rite haunt of Hamadryades,
And sylvan gods: celestials too found there
Attractive charms, and gave a countenance
To errant love, voluptuous ease, and mirth.
Let such as list survey th' enchanted ground,
Invoke Mnemosyne and all her choir;
And Phantasy invite to lead the song.
Our way is in the beaten track of Life,
That now is strangely circumstanced; awry
With Time's endowments, varied and profuse.
There trav'lers throng, there perils crowd; there youth,
With eager hearts, brunt dangers, covet more.
There manhood smiles, with confident resource
Of ways and means. Old age, with broken heart,
Or hopes forlorn, creeps on. There wailing babes,
Just introduced as wards of Time, send forth,
To those advanced along life's varying course,
Complaints of helplessness, solicit needed care.
　　How long the time of pupilage, ere man
Has learnt the art of caring for himself !
Trite observation; not on that account
Less weighty. Is it not designed to teach
Man's mutual need, and check the foolish thought
Of self-dependence? Not as brutes, that soon
Have learnt their needed lessons, and at once
Appear well furnished for their term of life.
Nor as so many gemmules, severed from
The parent bulk, that claim no further care.
Each needing each, so each should minister
His meed of common good, his part enact.
This life is limited by thought, a wide expanse,

An opening vista of projection vast.
Material things man scans, and lengthens out,
In mental range, their probable extent.
Analogy he frames, and so infers
Laws of a sim'lar kind to those of sight:
As thus, the Earth and Moon, analogous
In many things, may be analogous in all.
If both have mountains, dells, and outstretched plains,
If both an atmosphere—denied by some—
May not the both then be inhabited?
E'en thought is limited; but yet it breaks,
At times, its narrow bounds, and spurns amain
Prescription's law; mere fancy then prevails,
And wild conjecture conjures up, at will,
What ne'er exists, that cannot rightly claim
Affinity to thought legitimate.
Fair field of thought is found in all the eye,
Unaided, searches out; or telescope,
Or microscope detects; deductions thence.
Thus Science springs, and makes alert advance,
By aid of subtile Art; each aiding each.
The mind instructs the hand; the hand the mind.
The simplest thought conceived, the hand is prompt;
An instrument is formed—the Telescope.
The eye now traverses its range: how much
Is learnt through this artistic scheme!
The mind makes fresh demands; the hand replies:
An instrument appears, surpassing far
The first, as that the naked eye surpassed.
Twin helps throughout God's marv'lous scheme appear:—
The Brain impregns the Blood with vital power,
And vigor for its ever circling course:
The Blood, in turn, supplies with nourishment

The wasted Brain, recruits its languid strength.
Mysterious links exist, enyoking mind
With matter; yet the strictest search is foiled.
So intimate the bond, that ablest men
Declare their ignorance, and fain admit
The cause, effect; th' effect, in turn, a cause.
The stomach feeds and strengthens all the frame;
Itself must be sustained for healthy work;
And so requires nice care from other parts,
In just secretion; lest its roomy cell,
Eroded, cease to act its proper part.
The Rain descends, and percolates the ground,
Again appears in springs; hence rivers rise,
Their flow the sea receives; again it mounts,
Through exhalation; clouds ensue therefrom,
And rain again:—which cause, and which effect?
A circling immortality endures
Till the Almighty word shall stay its course.
So man himself, in species thus designed,
Continuous lives; the individual dies,
Bequeaths his life to others like himself.
So herbs and grasses yield their fragile life,
When they have perfected the future germ.
In morals too the same set law appears:—
The kindly act increases in the heart
The kindling glow—soft kindness there; and then
This kindness warms to multiply the act.
Sin and Remorse the same: Sin breeds Remorse;
Remorse re-acts and fouler Sin repeats.
So Hatred and Revenge: the former broods,
Warms with the fire of Hell, with which it glows;
Revenge is hatched—augmented Hatred thence.
So offices of life: the Husband, Wife;

The Parent, Child; the Master, Servant; each
The other sways for good or ill; and all,
In just return, receive the same: if each,
Considerate of each, the other serves,
Then happiness results: so each a cause,
And each shews in himself a glad effect.

But is man satisfied with all Time's gifts,
However great—or does he long for more?
Unless the intellect, debased, ignores
The creed of after state, man cherishes
The thought that he shall live again.
Of old sages have told their tales of hopes
And aspirations of a mind, conformed
To brighter issues of a world to come.
They speak of future disembodied joys,
In sweet companionship with those they knew
And loved below. Yet none had told them aught
Of other state, of resurrection life.
They fondly mused of spirit intercourse;
And robed their thoughts in ardent words, but based
On nought beyond the longings of their hearts.

BOOK I.

THE ARGUMENT.

AN excursion of thought into ethereal space. The heavenly bodies—the Sun, the Planets and Comets. Apostrophe. The Earth and its concerns, spiritual and temporal. The Seasons. Apostrophe. The miser. The rich man. The successful tradesman. Our neighbour. The drunkard. The adulterer. Lovers of pleasures. Fashion. The garden. The farm. A coal mine. Geology. England's capital. Self-Will. Diseases. Theft. Charity. The harlot. Attempt of human wisdom to account for the present state of man and things.

WARY, yet bold, the spirit makes attempt
To soar, and pierce the blue expanse; to grasp
Enquiringly heaven's portals, look within,
Then enter there, desire its wondrous stores.
Bold, but not rash, intrusive Thought repairs
To distant worlds; holds firmly on, and thence
Projects some further flight adventurous.
Alighting there unsatisfied, still plans,
Devises still some spot unvisited;
Unchecked by aught, unless prohibited.
Daring, but not profane, where diligence
Meets great encouragement; for o'er our heads
God has enrolled His attributes of power
And wisdom infinite. So Thought mounts up
To things beyond the unsubstantial line
That bounds the peering gaze; relayed afresh,
Enwrapt in contemplation, now it aims

HERE AND HEREAFTER.

Beyond the reach of telescopic power:
Thence pushes on 'mid worlds of Solar light;
Looks back amazed; for, from the starting point,
And in direction opposite from that,
'Tis measureless as this. The sum of all
Is found: what then? The trav'ler starts afresh,
And, in unwearied toil, measures a track,
In onward course, as far as that he leaves
From where he stood at first. He multiplies
This line a million fold, and with it sweeps
The vast expanse; projects a hollow sphere,
Whose bound'ry line, so vast, slightly disowns
Undeviating course. He peoples this
With countless worlds. His Sun, a rolling Orb,
And other Suns as large, or larger still,
To sight untutored, scattered thick as dust,
Are stepping stones to Him, who framed them thus,
Though severed by unmeasurable space.
A central sun he finds, imposing laws
On circling systems; one rotation yet
Unfinished since it first began its course.
Procession grand—array imposing, vast!
Its place each knows and keeps: no jostling foul,
No fatal smiting there; nor ling'ring course,
Nor immature approach: each in its path
Imprints its Maker's law, unswayed. Should one
A little later stay, or earlier urge
Its ordered course, destruction might ensue:—
It never comes. Man speaks of one so smashed;
But in itself the evil ruled—if e'er
Fragmentary worlds, so deemed, had origin
In this abnormal way; it may be, not:—
No false conjunction marred; no quickened pace,

Or tardy step, such rude disruption brought.
Or did some cause malevolent provoke
The hand of Him who made it to descend
In vengeful mood, and so its place was left,
As though not fitly filled? Still make advance;
On—on, farther and farther yet press on:
Thought is not satisfied, nor aught repressed.
Remoter worlds are beaming far beyond,
Whose rays have never reached our nether sphere,
Though trav'ling on through space, with matchless speed.
And farther yet, th' ethereal vault enshrouds,
Through mere remoteness, blazing worlds on worlds.
Now thought, so stretched, forbears, and, in design,
Erects a barrier, circling this domain.
Outside this, what? Amazement culminates
At this vast bound. Thought aches—silence profound
Becalms the mind—reason resumes her place—
It cannot be—the phantom masonry
It tumbles down. Though vast the former scheme,
Of space interminate, this vaster still:
The wond'ring, pregnant mind yet labors more
With this abortive progeny than that.
Outrageous limit! Who its Architect?
The Infinite! thus limiting Himself!
Nay; vagrant, startled Thought had reared, confused,
This adamantine circlet, immature,
Bounding its curious search unsatisfied.
  But why not wander farther, if so far?
This mighty, hollow sphere, in wisdom stored
With rolling Orbs, defined and limited
By immaterial walls, an aggregate
Of units, round th' Eternal rolls but one
Of countless such; all these His ceaseless care—

Care without labor, watching without toil.
One Sage has forged a sounding-line, with which
He plumbs the heaven's depths; skirting along
Ethereal sands, raised high amidst; or else—
If in its course—pervading them: at length,
He finds a limit to the crowding worlds.
And is it convex there? a bound'ry line
To Orbs in spherical array? How vast!
What radius swept the main? what centre bore
The steadfast point beneath the mighty hand
That guided, through its course, the tracing point?
Or is it concave there, incurving on
The heaven of heavens, where high enthroned He sits
Who made the whole, disposed the same, each one
In safe proximity to each; order
Conserving, where, to rustic sight, confusion rules?
This limit reached, beyond deep darkness holds,
Impenetrate. Is this th' effect of light—
Of uncreated light, God's dwelling place?
Light unapproachable, to creature sight,
Through telescopic aid, seems solid night.
Dread throne of God, centre of all His works!
Infinity around, peopled with worlds,
Swells out from thence; mute courtiers there attend,
Some luminous, and some opaque; these fill
The limitless expanse; recipients all
Of God's created light.
Ancient of Days! thought labors now in vain,
Parturient not; for how shall words describe
The Indescribable? whose floor is paved
With Stellar worlds; the Earth His footstool, Heaven
His radiant throne. Thought, now restrained, bows low
Before th' Omnipotent; returns, and longs

To penetrate, with chastened eagerness,
Things less remote,—her handmaid Sight,—the Sun,
And his attendant worlds; revolving Moons,
That rule the night; Earth and its accidents,
In Science, Art, and all their abstract lore.
Things manifest, and things obscurely known;
Things seen and things unseen, felt and unfelt.
Sight seeks assistance, Thought enyokes its aid:
They summon Handicraft, and weld their skill;
Heavenward direct a tube; th' astonished gaze
Beholds new worlds of planetary mould:
They move at His command; their measured race
Nor hasten, nor retard their destined speed.
On nothing hung, they run their onward course;
His bidding do, who planned and made them all.
His skill devised, His plastic hand produced
Their being out of nought. His sovereign will
Confirmed their place, His law immutable.
Around they roll, with subject varying speed,
The greater light. From this, the central Orb,
They borrow lustre, shed on them, as they,
Revolving on their Axes, turn to Him
Successively their poles' incline.
Yet other occupants of errant kind,
As strangers o'er this field of vision skim;
Their mission, destiny, and kind, as yet
Have not transpired; they fill a sphere unique.
Is disobedience here—rebellion foul?
Insensate, cumbrous matter! has it owned
Influence malign—broke loose from first control—
Outraged the law of orbèd kind? for this
Condemned to wander in unusual track?
Some seek th' Ellipse of longitude immense;

The Parabolic curve is wrought by some;
Others th' Hyperbola—their course abstruse.
Whence come they? whither tend in dreary course?
Close to the Sun they move; away they roam
In dread remoteness: fiercest heat now swelts;
Anon, intensest cold locks up their frames.
Across the track of planetary Orbs
They fling themselves proclivous; still watched o'er
By Him who planned; lest, in abnormal course,
They dash, with headlong speed, on other worlds.
While some, of subtile being, have impinged
On worlds of solid make, and so received
Meet recompence—disorder in themselves.
Some faint, persistent clouds heaven's brow reveals
Through telescopic means; these Nebulæ are named.
Another tube, of build immense, explores,
Detects, and shews them stars appointed close.
Like curious scroll are some; and filament,
As though, like golden sands, they stream along
Heaven's azure vault; or pendent, as a chain
Let down of golden links, joined by their severance.
Some gleam in lurid conflagration dread;
Incension fierce consumes the doomèd worlds.
Why this? Do Heaven's archives register
The cause? Evil occurrent in themselves?
Malignant plotting from without? or fire
Engendered, always there, now profluent?
Or foe implacable, presumptive, dread?
Deep myst'ry shrouds the empyrean tale.
Others again appeared in ages past,
And had a name in human catalogues,
Record of sites once held in concave heaven:
Their place is known no more. No fame has reached

Of sad catastrophe, if burnt or rent.
Perhaps some distant mission called them hence;
Or fiat of th' Almighty, ceding them
To nothingness—whence they were drawn at first.
Others twin Orbs, in revolution fond,
As if in coy embrace; their distance great,
Yet intimate appears to mortal ken.
The greater and the less seek fellowship;
And intertwined, by some mute law constrained,
In free obedience run. There too are set
Some Stellar systems, ranged in clustered groups
Of three, or four, or more; to mortal eye,
So little space they hold, as though a man
Might in the hollow of his fist hide all.
  Amid all these the Solar disc revolves,
Resplendent, throws his rays of light and heat,
On worlds of his domain, as o'er them King.
'Mid those rejoicing, from his heat benign
There's nothing hid: heaven's end his starting goal,
His destiny the same; his ample course
Begins at every step—beginning, end.
And now thy glitt'ring pendants, glorious Sun!
Hid in effulgence bright, lo! one revolves,
But little scanned, fast locked in warm embrace
E'en to consuming; but that He who framed
And placed it there, has wise provision made,
Temp'ring the fervent ray to it supine.
Man's peering eye, by telescopic aid,
Hath late divulged one venturing nearer still;
Suspicion too affirms another there;
But whether nearer still the torrid heat
Of ardent Sol, is not premised. Fair Science
Has avouched th' existence of this stranger twin

To keep the perfect balance of her laws.

    The next for beauty famed, the Matin rules,
Refulgent 'mid the brightest; bright her show
Beyond compeers: the Solar ray e'en fails,
At times, to quench entire her queenly light:
From him indeed the chastened ray serene.
Bright in his brightness; without whom, obscured,
A darkened disc obtains, dreary and cold.
She in his glory walks, a queen confessed,
And Vesper owns the gift. But when anon
Dark midnight folds the earth, the beauteous form
Has fled; severed from him, no light reveals
Her heavenly state, her peerless form.
His neighborhood she keeps.

    The third our Earth—its theme awhile defer:
Now those hung up aloft.

    The next, supernal Orb, adjacent rolls
In fiery guise: in solitude he glides.
No moon attends, his gloomy nights to cheer,
Alone he wends his way. In mythic lore
His place is found 'mong deeds of blood, and clang
Of murd'rous arms; stern guide of marshaled hosts.
Sword, spear, and plumèd helm his savage care;
War his delight and gory plains indrenched.
The orphan's plaint, the widow's shriek emboss
His madly rushing car. The same elsewhere
Is named the mighty hunter, he who built
Proud Babel's walls, and reared his temple there.

    Next roll, as men suppose, in thick array,
The scattered fragments of a world disrupt,
In many parts; with paths dissimilar:
Commingling, just as though in judgment left
To choose and order pathways for themselves.

Each other's course they cross intent, with risk
Of rash affray. What calculation nice
This risk to shun! how deep with wisdom fraught
The counsels of Omnipotence!

Next, he moves on, whom men of pagan creed
Once worshiped King of gods, father of men:
In bulk supreme, in majesty confessed.
His light serene from belted disc, illumed
By distant rays; four moons relieve his gloom.
Magnificent he rolls: and whilst our Earth
Once fills her path, he part fulfils his course.
Twelve times the Earth completes her constant round,
Ere he has finished his.

What grand attire! words fail to chronicle
The beauty of this Orb that now rides past.
Around him flung a threefold spacious dome
Of circled sheen, glory resplendent beams;
Far distant from the Solar ray, as though,
In regal state, he weened imperial light.
What gorgeous furniture of minor spheres!
Eight satellites, orbicular, arranged
In crescent, gibbous, rounded form they shine;
Some this, some that: in bulk they rival Earth.
Saturnine globe! perfect in beauty thou!
Empyrean heraldry emblazons thee
The sire of him last sung. And art thou he,
Th' embodiment of spirit unconfined,
Throned orb of greatness fallen, estate long lost—
He, whom deep myst'ry shrouds, but darkness claims?
Thy name suggestive, Babylon its source;
Saturn, in Chaldee Stūr, her mystic god,
Which name, in num'rals read, makes up in full
That fated score, six hundred sixty six.

Sitt'st thou a god? 'mong stones of fire thy throne?
All secrets thine; in understanding, clear;
Endowments bright and wonderful.
Thy seraph-covering ev'ry precious stone—
Sardius and topaz, diamond and beryl,
Onyx set with gold, jasper and sapphire,
Em'rald of softest green, with carbuncle
Lustrous in sabled night—earth's glory these.
Tabrets and pipes thy dulcet minstrelsy
In th' holy mount of God.
Thy beauty snared thee, brightness cast thee down.
Anointed cherub! fatal gift was thine!
Thy ways were perfect; wisdom sat enthroned
Within the precincts of thy ample brow.
Ah! woe the day! corrupted by thy gifts,
Thy wisdom fell, iniquity was there.
Eden, garden of God, thy presence owned,
Irrupt by thee, broached with malign intent.
Still brooding mischief, and still coveting
The forfeit arch of heaven; say'st thou yet
I will ascend above the stars of God;
In heaven I yet will manifest and prove
Vigor regen'rate; o'er the heights of clouds
My throne I'll set? Thy Judge will dash thee down,
In ashes lay thee low; by thine own fires,
From thine own midst, consumed.*

    Next, him whom poets feigned the primal Sire;
Saturn his son, and Uranus his name;
Which name, interpreted, is Heaven.
Six moons attend and cheer his distant path,
Round him assiduous move, in adverse course;

---

* Ezekiel. xxvii, 12, &c.

His west to east, *theirs* east to west; motion unique.
Dark deeds of shameful violence are sung
By bards of old; their pages teeming gross
With records of this ancient god; his sons
And their unfilial deeds. Poets have told
How Saturn, with his crew, opposed his Sire,
Foul deeds of wickedness contrived and wrought
With rage prepense: his father cursed him deep,
Denouncing woe on him and his—his, made
By compact dire, and sympathy malign;
Cast down to hell, they say, and bound in chains
Of darkness drear and merciless. Teitans
He called them—foul, opprobious epithet,
As marking shame and blackest infamy.
Hence Satan, name bestowed on him, who works
Adverse to God and man.

Now last of all, stretched far away beyond
His Grandsire's route, moves on the fabled god
Of Ocean's depths. Two moons alone attend
His path remote; if more, not yet confessed.
Here pause, and grateful tribute pay to them
Who labored much, and urged their patient search
With abstruse symbols, formulas of art,
And transcendental algebraic skill.
Some sweep the heavens, survey the spangled dome,
And map the outspread empyrean plains.
Such had not found, at least not marked, the track
Of Neptune's march: the eye had seen his disc,
But, unsuspecting, gave him common place
Among the crowding stars, as one of them.
Two men,[*] whom Science owns among her sons

---

[*] Leverrier and Adams.

Of brightest fame, had, independently
Of each, resolved to reconcile, what they
And others had observed of perturbation
In the path which Uranus had trod.
What data had they for this arduous work?
Disturbances themselves as to amount
And character; these screened them from
A dreary, hopeless search. Behold these men,
Reclused from outward things of joy and grief,
Committed to the toil of many days,
Immersed in deep analysis, surcharge,
With confidence, the heavens with one world more
Than they had yet made known.
Sagacious men! their calculations nice
Sustained their theory; and these, in turn,
Were justified by others, who observed
The parvenu, through telescopic aid,
Just where directed by the keen pursuit
Of Calculus refined. There now he rolls
And adds his meed of balanced order, fixed
By Him who placed him there and all besides
Which deck the ceiling of this world of ours.
So distant is this last discovered world,
Far in th' unfathomed depths of space, that sight
Seems yet defective to descry its train
Of worlds attendant, or of other things,
Adornment serving, or more solid law.

 O grand entablature! writ underneath
With skill divine, punctured by glyphic art
In Heaven's mute signs—lay bare the head!
A God we see; invisible Himself,
But in His works th' Almighty Godhead speaks,
And His eternal power. Here He appears;

His temple—Nature's range. No speech is heard,
Nor language framed in mortal tongue; yet deep,
Impressive utt'rances are on their way
Unceasingly; symbols in silence print
The lesson, so that all may read, whose eyes
Admit no prejudice from hearts debased.
There God hath set the warrant of His power,
His wisdom, goodness irreproachable.
Man has deciphered this; in ignorance
Has framed a nomenclature for a creed
Of pagan vanity, and symbolized
His monstrous deities by planets, stars,
And all the host of heaven—pantheon foul
Of gods and goddesses, frail like himself.
Ah! shame on thee, thou creature of a God,
Who framed sweet Nature for thy residence!
 Things huge and things minute; things far and near;
That which no sight could reach; and that which near,
Yet hides itself in very littleness,
Reveal to man their hidden habitats.
Size, distance, and presumed design of those;
Of these, their size contemptible, but that
Perfection buds and blooms in them, as in
The monarch of the woods, fowl of the air,
Or man himself. Though microscopic these,
Yet God has fitted them with heart and lungs;
And veins wherein the circling blood fulfils
Its ordered course. A point's a world to them;
In this they roam, disport, with ample range,
In teeming myriads. Earth's subjects these;
To this we turn, contemplate what it yields—
Its occupants, its products, varied ways
Of man, its wayward lord; pry into things

Of time; attempt Eternity—its state,
Award, and occupation there, where it
Unfolds its secrets to the wond'ring gaze
Of those who go to dwell where Light prevails,
Or where dread Darkness shuts light out.

    Earth takes its place, assigned in path prescribed;
And there maintained by law centrifugal;
Oppugned, but not delayed, nor pushed aside
By force centripetal. In concert, these,
By law immutable, construe the course
Designed. Its pond'rous swing would bear it off
In course disastrous, risk collision foul
With other spheres; but, checked by gravity,
No broil ensues; no discord, but acclaim
Of Him—Heaven's glorious Architect.
Again, this latter course centripetal
Convergent bias gives; and prone, would make
All others seek with speed precipitate
The central sphere. Harmonious discord here!
This fatal haste is shunned; adjustment nice
Unites opposing laws in bland accord,
And medium state resolves. The greater light
By day illumes; the lesser light by night.
Sun, Moon, and Stars perform their part assigned;
Obedient fill their place; their destiny await.

    The year take up when Spring is young: the Sun
In Aries found, gives equal day and night.
The pregnant bud, advised by vernal warmth,
Puts forth its strength and, lab'ring, strains its husk,
Which, hauberk like, had sheltered it secure
From rude assaults of stormy wind and cold.
The verdant leaf unfolds; the meadows smile
All carpeted with grateful green; inlaid

With burnished gold.   God maketh small the drops;
Water in tardy mood descends thereon.
Distilled in Heaven's alembic, tender herbs
Receive His dew in beads of crystal wealth;
Refreshed thereby, revive in close of days
Oppressed with heat; the greater this, the greater that.
God's fiat was, Let earth bring forth its grass:
Its bosom, heaving warm with teeming growth,
Anon is redolent with leveled sweets;
Reft by the keen attack of sharpened scythes,
The field has yielded up its spoil: now boys
And merry girls delight to toss about
The new-made hay; but better still to play
At hide and seek, amid the heaps made there
By older hands and graver skill.
The welkin rings with joyous caroled praise;
Now on the bough, now soaring up aloft,
Fowl of the air give out their simple joy.
Meanwhile maternal cares detain the mate
At home, not loath; she, filled with quiet hope
And happy instinct, patiently awaits
Young strangers there; or else, already come,
She seeks their food, with busy, happy toil.
Purveying for their infant household now,
With joyous heed, assiduous they combine:
He stays his song to cater for his brood;
Yet interfluent notes of cheering strain
Beguile the time; she, in mute joy refrains,
Her thankful task fulfils.
   Summer succeeds.   The Sun, in Cancer now,
Glows with impulsive heat; and ripening gifts
Confess his genial power in glowing tints.
God visits oft the earth and waters it;

HERE AND HEREAFTER.

Prepares it waving corn, when place, and time,
And circumstance replete, provided, wait
His time.   No measure scant He gives, but makes
The ridges drink abundantly His rain:
The furrows settled by His care benign,
Softened with showers, the tender blade shoots forth,
In springing blessed by Him.
Anon the spike appears; and, in right time,
Full ear of mellow corn.   The sickle now
Is charged with prostrate spoil; th' advancing year
With goodness crowned; His paths with fatness drop:
His blessings thickly strew the way He takes;
Handfuls of purpose dropt benign for us.
The pastures too, and little hills rejoice
On every side; flocks dot their verdant sward,
Cared for by Him, whose constant smile is life;
They shout for joy, they also sing.*

   The Balance now receives the sloping Sun;
And Autumn yields its complement of fruits,
Congeners of the Summer store.   The stream
Of bounty then was full and overflowed:
The stack was reared, and barns with plenty filled:
Full presses bursting with new wine.   And now
The stream, not dry, still flows with normal tide.
His hand is open wide, ne'er shut, but prompt;
He hears the bleat of patient sheep, the moan
Of lab'ring beasts and fowl of every kind;
The crawling worm; the savage, prowling beast,
Instinct with sanguine rage; the timid herd;
Fierce lions roaring for their frightened prey;
The loving hind, and pleasant, gentle roe;
The slayer and the slain.

* Psalm lxv.

Now hoary Winter, grim and ruthless, lays
His icy hand on Nature's head; her blood
Runs cold through all her veins; her pliant limbs
Recoil and rigid grow; her shudd'ring frame
Shrinks from his gelid touch, as though appalled.
Zephyr, rebuked, no longer gently woos
His Flora, now assailed with rough embrace:
Her tresses fanned before with ardent breath,
Dishonored grossly by the trenchant blast,
Lie prone—inglorious spoil.
Her smiles are changed to tears; she mourns her loss—
Her exiled friend, her gems, her rifled sweets,
Her many colored robe, from Nature's loom;
These strew her tomb, and mingle with its dust,
And thence, in resurrection's hour she springs.
New life and vigor reproduce her form;
Perennial, not immortal, she exists.
Birds sing her requiem, leaves form her pall,
Soft snow her winding sheet.
Now streamlets pause, or stubborn, hide their spleen
In under flow. The Sun too slants his beams,
His heat assuaged t' excess: fierce storms arise;
The Sailor scans his nautic lore, and finds
This sign tempestuous, yet he tarries not;
The love of gain subdues the dread of death.
Aquarius next receives the fervid guest;
Then Pisces fond—so ends the year.

 The Earth has filled its course. Meanwhile, man's life
Is hastening on to Nature's final goal:
Brief space! in which are crowding entries made
Of Science, commerce, guilt and shame; of these
Discourse awhile.

 Jehovah's praise, ye circling Sun and Moon,

Ye stars of light, ye heavens of heavens; and you,
Ye monsters of the sea, all deeps; and fire,
And hail, and snow, and vapors, stormy wind
His word fulfilling; mountains and all hills;
Trees yielding fruit, cedars of stately growth;
Beasts, cattle, creeping things and flying fowl;
Kings of the earth, and all with one accord,
His praise give forth.* Fierce lightnings hurl their fires;
Loud thunders roll, heaven's ordnance peals; the air
Is resonant with Echo's strain. God speaks:
Earth's pillars shake, they tremble to their base.
God speaks to man, His awful voice He gives
In stress profound and terrible: man hears
The voice, and questions it; God's dreadful sign
He reads—interprets not—its nature, not intent.
This subtle thing man gathers, curbs, confines;
Quiescent then, till cause exciting gives
It energy. First Science claimed it, and,
To minds untaught, made it her leisure toy;
Now man's fleet messenger, outstripping time,
His need subserves; he, grossly ignorant
Of God's considerate goodness, knoweth not
His God instructeth him. With conscious power,
He opens Nature's book; her bowels rives,
Seeks there and finds hard questions solved.
With power and will commensurate, his heart
Devising, nought would be restrained of all
His deep imaginings. His curious search
The awful secrets of the spirit world allure;
And thought intrusive wrests unclean response—
Forbidden, therefore foul and perilous—
And so educing lies. A true reply

* Psalm cxlviii.

Is oft obtained to rash demands; and thus
Deception grows yet still more positive.
The victim, snared by truth's resemblance, speeds
Along his self-willed course; nor stays to think;
Nor hesitates to scan the roll of Fate:
He hurries on till darkness shrouds his day.
Not Science is this named, but Devilry.
And whence this dark communing? whence this thirst
For knowledge sealèd up? And why is man
So circumstanced? Frail man, of woman born,
Is full of toil; his days are few, as grass
He groweth up; or as the flower of grass,
Cut down as that, continueth not.
A helpless babe, embryo of future strength,
He enters on life's stage, and there he brings
Unconscious intellect—a slumb'ring germ
Of future good or ill. Time passes on,
He takes his place, intent on his own will:
One clouds his path, on errand bent as he;
They, wrathful, pause, and each demands his right:
Fierce words ensue, rage nerves th' uplifted arm,
Wrath fires th' embittered heart. Self-will requires
The prostrate form to tread upon of him
Who claims his right of way, denies all else.
Hence wars and fightings, bred of wars within,
And lust of power. Man is man's enemy,
Insatiate of spoil, on gain intent;
He thirsts and craves the blood of him who thwarts.
Thus empires grow and wane; some petty feud
Gives fair occasion, vengeful war ensues.
Embattled hosts, arrayed for bloody fray,
Lose fear in savage strife.
　　Now see that hard, keen-visaged, wretched man,

Whose bony fingers clutch his hoarded wealth;
His gloating eyes ne'er tire by day: by night,
Visions of gold illude. Has man a sense
Not yet descried—metallic? seen in some
Intense; in others, not developed quite?
Does this, in some, o'erride all else, and quench,
In them, the natural appetence almost
For daily bread? One wise in common things,
As well as in our deep philosophy,
Has said, "there's nothing better than to eat
And drink;" and so men think, and justify
This maxim to excess: but here is one
Who finds a better thing to him; and gold
He values for itself; while others seek
The glittering dust, to pander to their lusts,
Or serve the needful purposes of life.
But why this heaping up? why not increase
By putting out to usury? Some do;
Both he and they the same incitement own;
One increase loves, the other charneled gold.
Their god the same, though sought with diff'rent names:
One Mammon's serf, the other Commerce serves:
Both covetous; the one—by all confessed—
The senseless worshiper; the other plumed
And praised for early care, for sitting late
At ledger craft; a thorough business man,
He covers sins, enough to sink a poorer man,
Though just. Decry a man for diligence?
Nay, Sir; the motive, not the deed, is blamed.
Success ensures esteem; and men will praise
When to thyself thou doest well.
Failure entails disgrace; hence grossest frauds;
Hence circumvention keen; hence that wise saw,

Much praised—"Buy in the cheapest mart
And in the dearest sell."
Not half a century past, a rich man died.
"He must be good, aye sure he must," said one,
Who slept and ate, and worked, and slept again—
"He must be good : for when he died, there stood
A barrel, cushioned well—arm-chair 'twas thought,
As being fashioned so with back and sides—
Hard by his bed, with guineas filled," and thus
So stedfast that 'twas thought some carpenter
Had screwed it to the floor. When he was gone
Why it remained so long unmoved was known,
'Twas heavy with his gold.

    The portly burgher, too, with deep ahem—
Membraneous resonance—intones his thoughts.
He walks with conscious might; with air profound
He asks—you know my name? and if that name
Plebeian sounds ; or lacks anointment from
Some mitred head ; or bar sinister mars
The line of coronet—in him defiled ;
Nor warrior, statesman, patriot, sheds a ray
On him derived ; he, confident, demands,
Will not my bags of gold atonement make,
For all deficiencies of pedigree?
What if no ducal ancestor appear,
Or lord, or bishop ; sure, I've made amends.
My country house might entertain our queen,
And retinue ; replete with all that heart
Could wish or skill devise. My spacious grounds
Were bought with gains of honest trade.
No groans of slaughtered hosts betide my ears,
As, closeted with ledger, I recount
My quick returns. Most true, the prison walls

Re-echo with the curse of him immured
By my command : but then he owed me cash.
He couldn't pay? What's that to me? He bought, I sold;
Money's fair answer for delivered goods ;
He fails to pay, I take himself as check:
That's good in law; I have undoubted right.
He hadn't power, d'ye say—would if he could?
Well that's not my concern, he had the goods.
Not diff'ring much from him who dyes the plain
With blood? you lie; this murder is, I no one kill.
He pined in gaol, who figured in your books
The debtor side. Piece-meal despatch as this
Is scarce to be preferred to speedy death.
Give him the chance of running free through lines
Of flagellating fiends, who take delight
In cutting strips of flesh from off the bones—
This, or be charged with balance of account,
When struck between arrears and discount full
Of thy much vaunted charity; he'll run
The dreary risk of knotted whip, laid on
With heavy hand, and hearty will of men,
Delighted with the curl and writhings of
The tortured flesh; yea rather this than trust
The hand of him, who smooths the lordly brow
With cringing smiles and bows; but frowns away
The stricken sons of sorrow from his door:
Who will be rich, though broken hearts upbraid,
Sigh from his coffers; and his curtains shake
With threat'ning coil, as bony fingers point,
And famine struck, the costly drapery clutch
In visions of the night.
He's pledged, and nought can turn him: hearts may break,
And hearths their embers miss: the happy wife

Be widowed; smiling children pine away.
In vain their mute appeal of sunken cheeks,
Or words importunate, by famine taught;
His heart remains unmoved.
One point alone he sees; all others too
Whose lines, subordinate, converge in this,
And so conveyance make in cordial trim.
O how he loves the chink of legal coin!
No music charms like this. When somewhat fagged,
With hot pursuit of golden scheme; or books
Examined long, yield, to his eager search,
Much satisfaction, then he seeks and finds
Some relaxation in his filliped gold,
Or rustle of bank-leaves. Faugh! let him be;
If soul he have, it may be asked of him
When he is loath to give: when eager looks
And ready hand combine to seize-more spoil.
It may distract him in the very midst
Of rearing warehouse rooms of storied height,
To meet increasing goods. He disavows
Expensive routs, subtracting from his gains;
All such he views with angry, honest scorn.
Unthrifty souls are all who barter wealth,
His greatest good, for pleasures such as these.
All men speak well of him—a fatal mark—
And count him happy; so he thinks himself,
And so deceives himself, till conscience wakes,
When he is stricken by the hand of death.
Then victims of his greed stand by, look in
Upon him as he writhes in pain of mind
And body too: their spectral forms illude,
And mock attempts to fix them in a spot:
They glide, with cunning speed, from head to foot;

They fill the room ; inconstant, flit about,
And seem to mutter curses deep. Poor wretch !
My bags of gold, cries he, now bring them here,
I'll handle them again ; they'll comfort me.
No, take them hence, my ears are filled with groans.
These bags once charmed me with their cheerful look,
Quite healthy, full, and fair : but now, alas !
Their well filled sides are fallen in : and so,
Confused, he wanders on. Death presses hard.
I cannot die, he shouts, in wild dismay ;
I never thought of death—not yet prepared.
Great gulf I see—all dark this side ; beyond,
All bright and beautiful. How shall I cross ?
No bridge ! Is this my future residence ?—
Cold shudd'ring thrills the frame ; unpitying,
Death sends his dart home to life's centre, and
Thus rudely struck, the wheel of life stands still.

In place conspicuous stands the social law,
" Thou shalt thy neighbour love e'en as thyself :"
A pilloried command ! the butt of jeers ;
Curled lip of scorn, impatient, hastes to hurl
Defiance at the strange behest : himself
The god of gods with man ; to this he bends
A willing slave, a toiling devotee.
Divergent paths, innumerous, men take ;
Concentric, at the very source take leave
Of brotherhood, or else the name defile
With social bonds, of aim iniquitous ;
Or, at the best, of dubious end.
O strange, fierce lust of gold ! accursed pelf !
Earth has, of late, revealed large store ; and men,
With headlong haste, have run to catch the prey.
They will be rich, and so have snared their feet,

And plunged their souls in crimes of deepest dye:
One finds, another fails; this murders that,
And steals his glittering trash.
    Yon reeling brute, prefaced with form of man,
Presents another phase of self, despised
By him who toils in decent serfdom long,
And leaves at last, worn out in servitude,
A warning cenotaph. This muddled thing,
Finds food for self in quaffing bowls of wine;
A good abused: a little cheers the heart,
While much dethrones the intellect.
Yet what's the difference? Is he who walks
With balanced step, in eager search for wealth,
A whit the more in his right mind than he
Who rambles to his lair? O surely not!
One is a prodigal in lust of wine;
The other drowns his soul in lust of gold.
    Another loves uncleanness, filthy brute!
Eyes, full of an adult'ress, cannot cease
From sin and sensual leer, and snaring arts.
Seductive, on his victim smiles, and lures
In guise of honest love, with fair pretence,
And fervid show of guileless amity.
He not alone entraps; for, in his turn,
He falls unwept an easy prey.
Just retribution!—matched in craft by one,
Yet still more fully versed in lech'rous wiles,
Subtle of heart, bitter as death; fair speech
And flatt'ring words beguile the willing fool;
He follows, as an ox to slaughter goes;
Or as a hart bounding into the net;
Or bird, unwary, hasteth to the snare:
So, prone, he madly takes the way of death;

Not knowing, till too late, the dead are there.
    What prompts the wary burglar to invade
His neighbor's house? with misdirected skill
To make abortive, locks, and bolts, and chains?
His trade is robbery and spoil his gain.
And what his plea? My neighbor has too much,
And I have not enough—another shift of self.
Impatient too, he spurns the tardy pace
Of slow foot trade; greedy of gain, he seeks
Another's store; resisted, takes the life
Of him who owns it. Might is right with him,
But not with him alone; he drinks indeed
The wine of violence; brute force, in league
With errant skill, combined, effect his aim:
He plays the game of chance; demented quite,
He throws the dice, his life the stake.
Another seeks a safer, smoother road
To sudden wealth; finesse, his castellan;
His stronghold, creeks and crannies of the law;
His victims various—the rich; the poor;
He who, with rake of bone and sinew framed,
Has scraped a pittance for declining years;
Make him their trust: their loss his fiendish gain.
The ward, a godsend deemed, a legal prey,
With harpy claws he fastens on, devours;
Or, vampire-like, the very blood he sucks,
And lulls, with smirking face, the trusting heart.
    Lovers of pleasure some, in dubious guise,
Which men call innocent; the dog and gun
Administer to such: the faithful brute
And deadly tube help bag the favored game—
By law reserved—the timid hare, the startled bird;
In days prescribed by law these multiply,

Protected for the privileged battue—
A yearly slaughter, justified and palmed
By fair opinion, and by fairer spoil
For dainty tastes. The rod and line, with bait
And treach'rous hook, concealed with subtle skill
By fair resemblance to their proper food,
Fishes entrap; they, unsuspecting, snatch
The cruel bait; in mute surprise recoil.
The cunning barb defies release; secured,
They writhe, mute suff'rers on a hostile shore:
The hook is needed for another throw;
With stubborn hold, it spurns all tender care,
In disentanglement; the jaw is rived;
Necessity, the specious plea, is urged:
Which has the colder blood, the fish or man?
But fish is food; fair plea for netted prey,
And sport the torture gilds. On willing steed,
Some seek the dappled game, in eager chase
With kenneled crowd. O'er hill and dale—too slow!
The victim scours along with urgent speed.
The deep-mouthed dog pursues; discovering trail,
Yells dread intelligence of death. Men love,
And revel in this mortal cry, to them
Most musical; they add their own halloos.
Or hare, while domiciled in quiet form,
Is suddenly presaged with scent of foes.
And now, up hill she seeks avoidance prompt
Of silent coursers; distances awhile
Their utmost speed; for, long of limbs behind,
The ground, declivous, favors her ascent:
Thus circumstanced, secure she scuds along,
In easy flight: too soon the balance turns;
With headlong haste, but bootless speed, alas!

She rushes down the glebe; the distance shrinks;
Pursuer and pursued soon meet.
Has man a plea for this most cruel sport?
Oh! yes; excitement of the chase; and then,
He eats, at licensed ease, an oligarchic dish.
   Some on the race-course speed their earnest search;
Self craves strange things, by law conventional.
Good is imbruted; ill, provisioned high.
So food for one, rank poison proves to him
Whose nature is the same, with adverse taste.
This has been registered 'mong saws profound:
One surely finds its illustration here.
Horses are trained to run, and men to ride:
Sleek coat in one, and fair conditioned flesh,
Not full, nor spare with jutting bones amiss.
The other, temperate in all things, shews
A thrifty care, worthy of nobler aim,
To keep his jockey frame in racing trim.
Th' impatient horses start, their sinews strain,
Warm emulation feel; and, stretching on,
They grudge their neighbor half a head beyond.
Away they speed, as though themselves they please,
So eager is their zeal to reach the goal.
'Tis gained. Not sport alone attracts the crowd:
Mammon is there. And now the race is run,
They count their spoil—a losing game to some;
Others, the loss befriends. Some yield their store,
Of gold or meaner coin, to nimble skill;
Fingers intrusive find their quiet prey,
In spite of all precautionary care.
   Gay Fashion sways a num'rous, glitt'ring race
Of devotees. All classes own her rule;
Varied in kind and mutable her laws;

Her claims imperious; rigid too her bonds,
Silken indeed, but cabled silk is strong,
The more so, woven by self-will and pride.
Oh! what a sphere is here for vain display!
Fashion parades her court in dress superb—
The jeweled, proud tiara; pendents, gemmed
With pearls and precious stones; circlets for neck
And wrist, of cunning workmanship, and wrought
With curious art, urged by the magic touch
Of Mammon's wand: the bosom sighs, surcharged
With load of ornament! Nature is racked
To fill the mart of this voluptuous queen.
Her loom is ever weaving, helped by art,
Exhaustless patterns of her wealth and skill.
Plumes nod on heads of beauteous front; or wave
With lowered state. The sea gives up its spoil;
Whilst lands of sunny fame, and arctic realms
Disrobe their denizens to clothe profuse
The dainty limbs of ornate luxury.
At home, abroad, gaunt toil, well-pleased, remits
No labor to supply the vast demand;
To fill the maw of luxury and need.
And yet the cry goes forth amain, Give, give;
However boundless in supply, not less
Demand enlarges, gorged but not content.
And not the form alone is decked with art;
Its complements are great, its need is small,
It covets much. Men have their varied show,
And women theirs: some shared by both; others,
Prescriptive laws enforce, and shine apart.
Palatial domes, the rolling equipage;
The prancing steed; the stage—vicarious show;
The giddy, whirling dance. All sights and sounds

Are quarried for their sweets: the hearing ear,
The seeing eye, nor palls, nor ever tires.
Music, in dulcet strain, or martial clang,
In stirring chord or am'rous lay contrived,
Advenient joy supplies—a good entombed.
   The Garden some delights; its varied sweets
And native hues bespeak exhaustless skill,
Goodness benign, wisdom with silent tongue.
The rich Provider cares for more than need;
The eye is pleased, the air is redolent
With fragrant wealth. Art lends its cunning aid:
Arranged in figured beds, in tasteful groups,
Accordant tints are placed; dwarf plants demand
And find the foremost rank in bordered widths;
Those of more stately growth fill up the rear.
A house of glass of fairy build, with care
Conserves the tender blooms of tropic climes.
There cold oppresses not; perennial warmth
Makes them forget their genial, native glades,
The robbery condone. When Winter stalks
With rigid gait, the out-door residents retire;
Some under ground th' unequal conflict shun;
Some to the friendly tenement betake;
A few the chilly blast and frost withstand.
Behold the moss, that humble growth! it dares
The torrid heat, nor shuns the polar cold:
Yea more, when Winter throws his icy pall
O'er Nature's limbs, the mosses bloom and fruit.
The dark and noisome cave, where sullen gloom
Rejects the solar ray; the barren rock—
Or barren but for this—on which pour down
Unmitigated, scorching rays, gives these
A residence; they too fulfil their part,

As furnished lodgings for the myriad tribes
Of insect life—a sheltered home, when blasts
Of angry wind, with icy morsels charged,
Howl round; their yielding, clustering growth
Repels the fierce attack: food too they yield
In Lapland's dreary waste, for those who serve
Man's exigencies there.
   Others the Farm enjoy, endure the care
Of green and cereal crops, and lowing herds,
And bleating sheep. In former husbandry
The land enjoyed its rest; awhile in tilth,
Then undisturbed in unproductive ease:
Meanwhile recov'ring strength for future yield.
But now the ground, if arable, is racked
With teeming crops; the weeds no leisure find
To ripe their seed in undisputed sway.
Some crops exhaust the soil, others renew;
Only observe that goodly law—whate'er
Is taken thence, return.
But let us o'er the farm awhile; and note
God's bounteous hand, lib'ral, upbraiding not.
'Tis Summer eve: and now the waving corn
Is whitening, and inviting thankful hearts
To gather in its good—the staff of life.
The hay already housed, sweet-smelling still,
Impregns the air tenacious, with the charge
To give delight to nerves olfactory.
Bucolic charms around invite our meed
Of earnest praise. Mark now the browsing herd,
Intent to feed; they have no thought how thus
They minister to man: yet so it is;
All that they have, and are, and do, are his.
The nibbling sheep contribute too their stock,

To swell man's merchandize, supply his need,
His comforts multiply—a quiet folk.
The burly porker too, obtrusive guest,
No law polite subsigns. The trough is filled
With medly fare: he, with keen relish, grunts
His satisfaction full; scant welcome needs.
With eager haste he plunges feet unwashed
And muzzled snout together in his food.
A household scavenger, he fills a niche
Quite vacant else. Unruminant, his name
Is struck unhonored from the list of those
That cleave the hoof and chew the cud, and so
Were privileged to bleed for man's cuisine.
The barn-door fowl, with shrill clear ringing voice,
Or Cochin's bass, or Bantam's piping cry,
Reminds us of their birth prevenient,
Whilst yet inclosed within th' elliptic cell,
A food most delicate: their feathered selves,
Of varying age become man's prey refined.
The dairy yields its good: butter of kine,
And milk, and cream, and cheese, supply a need
Created by the rich supply itself.
Thus God doth multiply our wants, and so
He multiplies our joys: the need provokes
Our healthy efforts, and from these results
Healthy indulgence too, if not defiled
With gross excess. Bare necessaries keep
The life bestowed; comforts add to that life
Gregarious, social joys, that give a sum
Of happiness: abstract these from our store
And we begin the backward move, that strands
Life civilized on barbarous shores, where lurk
Grim wreckers of life's choicest, best designs.

The earliest state of man was one refined
With more than need demands; our walks still shew
This excellence. Drawbacks indeed abound
In all that heart enjoys; but then abound
Proofs of arrangement for response
To man's deep cry for good, to supplement
The merest cravings of his mortal state.
Soft beauties all around seem framed to charm
The natural sense: in vain they lay their claims
On those who daily plod their way in lanes,
Or o'er the sward, or through the plough-cut lea.
But do they not enjoy? does commonness
Do more than blunt current perceptiveness?
Is there not still a good derived, although
Unconsciously to him who labors on
Intent on daily bread? For this he strives,
For this he thinks, for this he always cares;
And misses much, through lack of leisure time,
To mark what others long and pine to view.
But take him, coop him up within the bounds
That towns and cities make; his heart recalls
The country's sunny glades, the friendly shade,
The air unpoisoned by the mingled fumes
That art and commerce breed: thus does he prove
That, unacknowledged, he derived much good
From sources hid to him, in that his sense
For this was drowned in over carefulness.
 Now underground awhile, and to th' emboweled earth
A hasty visit pay; glance at its tunneled depths.
There men endure an exile from the light of heaven;
There dig and disengage most precious freights,
For exportation to the realms above.
Let one suffice—a coalpit near, prefers

Superior claims; emerging thence we see
Men so begrimed, examination keen
Alone can say what fathers' sons they are.
The Arts and Sciences, our hearths as well,
Make large demands on these most ancient beds;
So ancient thought by some, that this our world
Is but a stripling, in its present phase,
Compared with this transformed concrete.
Some, twenty thousand years assign; and some,
Millions t' effect this ligneo-mineralgic change.
So deep has Science searched, enquiry urged,
Made observations and deductions thence.
Thus woods have fallen, laid by the ruthless tide,
Encroaching on the hoar preserves; the foe,
Retiring, gives the needed time for seeds
To germinate; thence spring herbaceous plants
Soon numbered with the past; inherent law
Makes this demand: trees spring again, and grow,
And flourish through succeeding years; and then
The foe again returns, and fells the growth
Which hoary time has reared. So patient years
Roll on, witness the rise and fall of woods
And forests, devastation great, to form
These seams exhaustless, carboniferous.
Others perversely urge some adverse facts
To this elaborated theory.
They urge deposits made of trees brought there
By rolling action; and not placed, as if
Laid prostrate where they grew: or, buoyed by floods,
At length, when water-logged, subside, and find
A resting place in sunken depths; and there,
Amassed, form beds of future coal.
They further urge—alas! for him who goes

Before the crowd, with well-wrought theory:
One follows, searches out relentlessly
Some flaw, drives in the wedge and splits the whole—
They mark the absence of a soil, wherein
Might grow, *in situ*, trees found there.
He, learned in geology, replies,
Denuding currents bore the soil away.
What, such as leveled forests where they grew,
And snapped the trees, but left them there to lie
In quiet bed? what nice discrimination
So to spare the floating freight, but take
And bear away the strata thus o'erlaid!
But then, the fond geologist replies,
Behold the stumps with roots; beside them there
The trunks o'erthrown. It is unfortunate,
The other says, that you forgot to fit
The trunks and stumps; moreover make your count
Of number too: and then, these roots present
A rounded form, as though, *in transitu*,
Abraded; and so short! impossible
To fix those trunks by such a length; whereas
They may have left their lengths elsewhere, and brought
Their remnants here. The Portland *dirt bed* forms
A grave, pet theme of *savans* who have searched
The geologic world. Persistent too,
The stern objector follows here as well,
And searches for himself; he finds the soil
Inadequate for trees of larger growth:
And though the parts of trunks have been applied,
And give continuous lengths; the stools won't stand,
In corresponding size, beneath these lengths.
And then—provoking coolness!—he demands
Why this elaborated scheme t' account

For such phenomena as earnest search
And geologic hammer bring to light?
My scheme is simpler, adequate, it finds
No problem having dislocating power;
But this is solved by that; whereas your scheme
Is wrenched continuously; for call to mind
How first the Permian strata claimed the right
To bound your search for quadrupedal bones:
On this you framed a geologic law;
This soon was broken by the group below—
The Carboniferous: and, later still,
The deep Devonian strata yields its store,
And sorely puzzles learned heads; for they,
With patient thought, had ruled that every bed
Had just its own peculiar occupants,
And nowhere else might these be found.
Then Man had no existence in these rocks,
Laid down, as they affirm, successively,
At periods severed by a lengthened space.
Th' Azoic term is first expended; then
Silurian rocks; Red Sandstone too, hold on
Their dreary course: to these succeed, in turn,
A gorgeous flora, source of coal, amassed
Through many thousand years. Then next ensues
The Permian, the Triassic age: to these
Next follow monsters of the deep, and fowl
Of monstrous size—huge denizens of sea,
And air, and earth. These spend some ages here,
Then pass away; to yield their tenement,
Without disruption, to enormous beasts:
These too have gone to bed, their coverlet
Superincumbent rocks of proper kind,
To tell their age. But man was nowhere found

Among the living creatures, ere entombed,
Because not with them there; rash theory!
For if some human fossils come to light,
How fares it then? Since then they have been found
Mingling with other bones. Man's bones are found
In caves; and deep in strata too; his feet
Have left their impress in the sand—the Old
Red Sandstone; thought—how fondly thought by some!—
A repertory undisputed quite
By man's intrusive form.
'Tis fair to say that others have proposed
Their geologic schemes; but all agree
To overturn the rocks, and bury there
The great Creator's works, in earlier times
Than Eden's woe; and by a greater force
Than urged the watery waste in Noah's day.
They view a tranquil sweep and gentle rise
Of creeping tide; which, though prevailing o'er
The earth, destroying every living thing,
Had no dislodging power on solid rocks.
But others see th' impetuous rush in words
Of Holy Writ; they parallel effects
To cause there named; and instance lesser floods
As bringing great disruptions in our day.
Ruthless Iconoclasts! could ye not spare
The Geologic idol, reared, by earnest hands,
On rocky pedestal? And is it so?
Is the whole temple doomed? What will ye do
With all its furniture and hard-earned spoils—
Azoic monuments; Silurian beds;
Old Red Sandstone slabs; and concrete Oolite?
Henceforth must all the Eras merge in one,
And Primary denote the place, but not the age?

If Truth demands, so must it be; though loath
To futilize untiring efforts, made
By men, who, lab'ring, sought th' advance of truth.
The mere o'erturning is no sport to us;
Still less a charming work to hint a thought
That venerable Palæozoic bones
Are not pre-Adamite. One cannot see
The tottering pillars of an edifice
With unconcern: men seem to gather round,
Admiringly exclaim;—What goodly stones!
Still our prophetic spirit views the whole
With pitying gaze; foretells its certain doom;
That not a stone of all this noble pile
Shall stay its fellow, or itself remain.
The records of the past give evidence
How one may rear a fane, magnificent,
With well-wrought stones, polished with labored skill,
Adorned profusely with the schemes of art;
And all in nice proportion framed; so wrought
That not a flaw appears. All bow the head,
And worship there, with captive minds and hearts.
At length, in rear of many years, appears
A bold Heresiarch, who gravely asks
On what the building rests; for he had marked
A sinking in the walls; expressed his fears
That weakness at the base imperiled all.
He searched and found it so: great stir arose,
Some still admired and worshiped there; others
Retired, began, *de novo*, philosophic search.
Is this just paralleled by modern zeal—
The rash erection, and th' unsparing smash;
As well reluctance to forsake what they,
And numbers ere their day, have fondly dreamed

Perfection of an art? This difference
We see indeed—and readily record—
That he of ancient date enthroned himself,
Brought Nature to his feet, and made her there
Arrange her facts, subordinate to laws
Which he had framed at philosophic ease.
Not so in modern times: our Architects
Have sought a good foundation, but have built
Too hastily; nor have they wholly shunned
To theorize on unsufficient grounds.
To adverse facts they shut their eyes and ears;
Ignored Dissent and all its claims; denied
Its allegations based on things that are;
Averred that human fossils had no place
In Palæontologic lore.
The times are changed. Man was at first shut out
Most jealously from hoar apartments, where
The Mammoth and the Mastodon appear.
The fossil man would clash with theories
Which antedate existences, that men
Of sober thought and simple faith had deemed
Sufficiently remote six thousand years ago.
But man *would* shew himself—at least his bones—
In the rude company of guests pre-Adamite.
Tables are turned. What shall be done with facts?
O modify our views, and make the best
Of awkward contretemps; abandon ground
No longer tenable; pull down old fanes
And build afresh; subject the Genesis
To further search—stricter analysis;
Ignore its claims to credibility,
If that must be; or that must fall, or we.
The Mammoth lived back in the range of time

A hundred thousand years ago, no doubt;
This we have ruled after much patient thought,
And cannot, will not now retract: since then
Some anthropoidal bones have come to light,
Mixed with remains of animals extinct.
Hence we resolve they lived together, and
Together died a thousand centuries back.
But why, says one, must these be thrust so far
Back in th' impalpable obscure, and so
Deride our grasp? Our theory demands:
If compromise were possible, we would
Just strain a point; as thus, we might advance
Th' historic Adam, say a thousand years;
Subtract as much from what we have pronounced
The fossil term; a thousand more or less
Is no amount; but really man would still
Appear a myth; and if we bring him on
Some thousand years, then we are very sure
He had some predecessors in the line.
Unwillingly, believe me, we are now
Constrained to think Genesis a romance.
May not your theory be incomplete,
Defective through defect of evidence?
May not some future revelation made
Urge to despair, and breed rash theorists?
Are you quite sure that if we learn your scheme
We may not soon be forced t' unlearn it all?
We much admire your castles in the rocks;
They have a solid look, but yet suspect
That in the Old Red Sandstone and elsewhere
Foundations are a little mutable.
The world is now in hot pursuit of men
In fossil guise, under huge glaciers, drifts,

Erratic blocks, in caves, alluviums, sand,
And under stalagmite. The Natchez man
Has had great honor paid; four cypress woods
Successional have mourned his early death.
The Mississipian delta too has claims
On your regard; a hundred thousand years
You lavishly assign to that; 'tis like,
'Tis very like the man who gives away
Another's rights. You're lib'ral to excess
With man's antiquity; if right in one
You're right in both; if fossil fauna claim
This high antiquity, so fossil man.
But what, if proofs turn up that man looks back
No further than six thousand years—too short
On which to write a geologic tale—
Will you revise your fossil code, confess
Your hastiness, and reconstruct your laws,
Delete your axioms and cotemporize
The fossil monsters with the modern man?
That would present a circulate indeed.
Oh! you have labored heartily to shew
Th' existence of a myth, to come at last
To simple verities, which one may read
Without the learned capability
Geology demands. Facts we admit,
But to the theory we must demur.
A ling'ring fondness for the fossil chair
Will still prevail; and still will issue thence
Prelections of the mighty past: ages
Receding from admiring gaze, will yet
Reveal their tortured guests to devotees.
Did he, almost the Great High Priest, fitted
T' expound the myst'ries of the creed, or fill

HERE AND HEREAFTER.

The lithic throne, sit mute when tidings bore
The sad discovery of man's remains—
No more recover from chagrin? Did he,
Too honest to reject the truth, yield up
His earnest life an early sacrifice?
No marvel if on rocks fond man engrave
A mythic science; so the stars were forced
To lend their name to crude Astrology;
And Alchemy arose, a shade of that
Which now is Chemistry. Great names hold high
The bannarol of geologic deeds.
Is there a day to come when men shall smile
And wonder at the scientific scheme,
Which long enthralled the mightiest minds?
So long have fared Astrology and Alchemy;
And so, ere long, the splendid Lithograph.

Awhile the City roam—the Capital,
Proud Britain's boast. No lack of subjects here—
Its wealth, its poverty; its courtly show,
Its abject wretchedness; its large supply,
Its pinching need; plebeian sickness, nursed
By pitying charity in princely wards;
The haughty peer, defiant commoner;
Riches ill got, spent in no better way;
Here lordly mansions, squalid huts hard by,
In close attachment, much as if they clung
In bitter taunt and mute derisive scorn.
Ill-balanced state! ill-omened mien! yet not
Because that one is high, another low;
That one is rich, another poor; not so,
Nature displays diversity throughout,
Disparity as well; yet harmony,
Except where discord flings its madd'ning gage.

The scavenger is intimate with that
Which would defile the man of gentle birth,
Did he but touch. The honest artisan
Dons a frieze coat as most appropriate;
The king his purple robe and royal crown;
The judge his ermine and his flowing wig;
The peer his coronet and robes of state;
The beggar too is most at home in rags.
Let some mischance this order disarrange,
What ludicrous wry looks would peer beneath
Th' averted eyes! The cottage room would blush
To own the tapestry of courtly halls.
He argues ill who claims equality:
This cannot be; effort and strength of mind
Subserve advancement; yawning indolence
And minds of weak intent are retrograde:
The one to rule succeeds, the other serves.
Abuse of good will taint the issuing stream,
The fountain still conserves its primal good.
Yet not that rule is ill, or service shame;
He serves who rules, if justice yields its due;
He benefits who serves, if faithful found.
There is a service hard, and grim its lord;
Not servants simply, galley-slaves he holds
In galling chains, and loathsome servitude.
Self-Will his name—proud, domineering, harsh,
Exacting, fierce, and vain: his prison doors
Are ever shut; glad liberty denies
To all his slaves. No neighbor clouds his hearth,
Nor warms his heart; pretentious, in his den
He lurks, and plots, and circumvents; too soon
He drags his victim to his net. Such owns
His country seat or house in town: sometimes

In lordly guise; sometimes in fustian found.
Both high and low, both rich and poor; he roams
Quite multiform. Not Moloch's fires, nor car
Of Juggernaut, such numerous victims boast.
  The tolling bell peals out its solemn sounds,
The sable hearse with nodding plumes plods on.
The King of Terrors here holds much his court;
A grisly band attends and courtiers grim.
Hot Fever wasting slow, or raging fierce;
Of Proteus' form, as yellow, bilious, black,
Or scarlet, typhus, intermittent; wide
Its cruel range: no age exempt; or youth,
Or bending age his ruthless torch inflames.
Consumption, blighting sad the hopes of all,
Except the victims of its cruel scourge:
Sometimes the very day of the last sigh
Is mapped with schemes of earthly good.
Paralysis, that subtle foe—Palsy,
Its trembling form. Impatient Gout, and Rheum:
Spasmodic Cholera with horrid Cramp.
  Here thousands roam, profess no trade but theft;
In this proficient, they instruct the young
To filch in quiet way; and, wary, plumb
The depth of pockets fondly deemed secure.
In whining plaint, with tale of sore distress,
The streets abound with pleaders, who exact
Soft hearts' most willing toll; for, true it is,
Midst all the hard pursuits of struggling life,
Much tenderness remains, and sympathy
For woe-struck forms; not caring to enquire
If real need, or feignèd want, prefers
The urgent suit: the heart believes the eye.
  Of all the monuments this country boasts,

Not one aspires so high; nor sinks so low
Its strong foundations in the masonry
Of poor men's hearts, as that now nobly reared
By hands of charity. Yes, charity—
Say not that this degrades both them who give,
And who receive. It is the brightest gem
In every crown, the goodliest jewel hung
O'er every hearth. This grace imposes not
A tax repugnant to the generous heart;
But, as a priv'lege, claims to drop a tear
At sorrow's moan; nor ceases then, but throws
Its portals wide to crowding visitants;
Nor obligation lays on them, but counts
Itself obliged that they should take its dole.

  The Harlot walks—poor blighted, short-lived thing—
In gloomy prowl to search for willing prey.
Full fifty thousand wand'rers swarm the streets:
There, shameless, flaunt their meretricious charms:
Thus lure the simple to their unclean haunts.
Of all this tainted host, how many lured,
How many lure—how many pand'rers snare,
And barter others in this loathsome trade?
How many neither lure nor lured, but trapped,
Their prison first the lap of luxury,
With gay attire and careful tendance served?
Atrocious care! Oh! doubly damned the wretch
Who panders to base lust, and makes a gain
Of others' woe and foul pollution too!
Oh! let their chilly hearth be never warmed
With cheerful fire! their table never spread
With wholesome fare! No medicine assuage
Their pains, till bitter tears repentance tell!
Is murder there? Who knows? The Registrar

Nor birth nor death records of these abodes,
When so it suits the inmates to conceal.
The snared and snarer sometimes fall a prey
To sanguine rage. The gloomy suicide,
Despairing, seeks the murm'ring surge to close
A loathèd life; or courts the fatal noose
With desperate hands. O deadly fatal haste,
To take a hurried leave of all that heart
Once fondly grasped! And whence this frenzied rush
To Death's embrace? and why this shrieking plunge
In unknown depths beyond? this blind assault
On future's secrecy? Is it t' escape
A burdened life; or, maddened, quench the smart
Of conscience' venomed sting? Poor bruted wretch!
Sure Retribution's scourge awaits its time.
Thy wrongs shall tell their tale: not thine alone;
All their account must give: conscience shall wake
With fearful strength, and mem'ry's lines, deep cut,
But now o'ergrown with Time's effect, retouched,
Shall then disclose, to shrinking, frightened gaze,
Deep damning guilt. Hell's depths themselves will seem
A refuge to unshriven souls—a welcome screen
From Heaven's high Judge—His awful frown.

Can man no measure frame for man's estate,
No remedy for patent ills deplored?
Are all his varied plans abjected quite—
None meetened for the stress of social need?
One presses Education; confident,
Proposes schemes to elevate the mass,
So deeply sunk in ignorance and crime.
Knowledge is good, and ignorance the source
Of sorrow, guilt, and shame. Fair premises;
But ignorance of what? What knowledge helps

To work this happy change? Shall we redeem
The intellect alone from sterile grade?
We have convincing proof of failure here:
Nay, more than failure shames this vaunted cure.
The more man knows, the greater power he wields—
The heart untaught—to work the greater ill.
Who plans the largest schemes t' accomplish good?
That man-who moves appliances of skill,
Of learning, and of morals framed and wrought
By wisdom's code. Who brands his caitiff name
With lasting infamy, by treacherous wiles,
And lies, and monstrous fraud? He, who has sat
In learning's hall, and stored his ample mind,
But left his heart untaught.
Another boasts that he has found a cure:
Imperative enjoins—Touch not, taste not.
But is not God's great law imprinted deep
On all created things, that He has made
A gift of all to man? not for excess,
But use: excess entails mad drunkenness
And other ills; a thankful use secures
The greatest good. But it is manifest
That man is ill; a deadly sickness racks,
Enervates all his frame; yea, mentally
He pines, desiderates some better state.
The problem yet remains unsolved, how he,
A guilty, ruined man may be restored.
But stay: how came man so? was he at first
This sickly thing? How came he here at all,
How introduced into this world of throes,
This dreary tenement of blighted hopes?
Or has he changed from good estate to bad?
If so, how brought about—himself the cause,

Or did some other rule his destiny?
Or was his Maker baulked? Could He not keep
The thing He made? Endowments wonderful!
Were they for ill designed, or did some foe
Of both, ruin devise? And if a foe,
Whence he, and whence his power to work for man
Such potent mischief and such utter wreck?
O hapless man! the dreadful truth remains;
Whether some foe without, or traitorous scheme
Of thine own heart, thy early ruin planned,
Thou art not what thou wert; nor can thy heart
Devise a remedy, so that the source
May no more pour its poisoned stream.
Is there no clue to this? no influence
To clear all mists away? unravel threads
Of this dark myst'ry? must he wander on
Forlorn, through this dark, dismal labyrinth,
And close at last the very best of lives,
It may be, with the very worst of deaths—
A forward, downward plunge, in depths unknown,
Of darkness, thick, impenetrate?
Man has indeed essayed t' investigate
These shrouded secrets, seek his origin,
His state at first; why now so obdurate?
To break the seal of hidden things: as thus—
Creation's source—eternal or derived;
And how—as formed, or in a shapeless mass?
Inert or self-impelled? devoid of sense,
Or self-endowed with sentient powers? stubborn,
Intractable and wild, resulting hence
The product Man; divulging plain his source?
Or else putrescent, and thence springing Man,
As if by exhalation foul, inept?

Or matter good at first, but mutable,
And variable, and prone thereto, and thus
Man has a base inheritance of lusts,
And broils, and appetites of base intent?
Or matter not derived; a Demiurge—
Sprung from the Deity supreme—met this;
And by inferior skill moulded and wrought
Its present form? This Æon, weak in power
And necessary knowledge for the work;
Or wanting goodness, fatal mischief framed,
And evil indiscreet; whence sprang profuse,
Intensive malady and detriment?
Or water, source of denser form, or air,
Or fire, by revolution in itself,
Or fiat of th' Almighty will?
Or Spirit underived, unchangeable;
Parent and Author of all good, supreme;
Efficient cause of all we see and hear;
Of all imagined things, objects of thought;
And mind with all its store of subtle gift?
Or else, from matter crude and void, arose
The heavens and earth, organic residence
Of Gods and men; displaying skill in plan;
With soul infused, instinct and rational,
Pervading all the universal scheme:
This universal soul at first secerned
Demons and gods invisible; thence too
Man had his individual soul from what was left?
Or one of subtle craft took plastic clay,
And with it formed a man and woman too,
Stole fire from Heaven and gave it life?
All this and more man, in his lab'ring mind
Revolving, has proposed. How manifest

That man, left to himself, must ever fail
To find out God, or how He works!
A man of subtle mind, with giant grasp
Of intellect, and conversant with creeds
Of men; and mighty power to search and make
Deep inquisition of all Nature's state,
Sent up this wail at last—
"Into the world I foully came; anxious my life:
Troubled I leave it, Cause of causes pity me." *
Though such, with curious skill, have made deep search
And fathomed all the depths of mortal mind,
Yet still the cry ascends—Who will resolve
This lengthened doubt; dispel this thickening gloom,
This burdening weight? Still the demand recurs—
Who gave to man his being, who conferred
His furniture of thought and skill; his power
To work, to meditate and plan vast schemes;
To be awhile, for ever pass away—
Then whither gone, and does he still exist,
And how? his fellows see his body droop;
Like beasts he lieth down, dust to the dust;
O'er them has no pre-eminence at last;
They die, so dieth he; together drop
Into the grave, commingling dust with dust.
Is there no diff'rence then? do wise and fools
Depart alike—the virtuous and the vile?
Must he who, living, sought his country's good,
Imperiled life; forgot to build his house
With public spoil; sank under weight of care
For others, not himself, rot in his cell,

---

* Aristotle. As he expired he is said to have exclaimed—
"Fœde hunc mundum intravi, anxius vixi, perturbatus egredior, causa causarum miscrere mei."

As he who forges chains of slavery
To load the limbs of fellow men; or he
Who liberty defiles, tramples her fires,
And rears a monument of wrong?
Is the reward alike? and do they lie
Mingling forgotten dust in Fate's embrace?
Not quite: their ashes rest in common state,
But Fame enrols respectively their deeds.
Their generation speaks the praise of those
Who loved their race, and sought their country's good;
And makes fair record of their patriot worth,
With registry of honor's rightful meed.
Impartial Hist'ry notes the course of him
Who marshaled hosts with guilty zest of power;
Her pen, with faithful stroke, records the spread
Of ruin, famine, death—dread visitors,
Attendant on the steps of him, who scorns
To stay his route, because of others' woes.

And is this all? is man used up? the grave
His final bourne? no immortality?
His fervid hopes closed with the mortal touch
Of Death's foul sting? No after state of thought?
Has he thus sped a life of cheerless toil
In fruitless search? Did such his heart append
To daily toil? No future—no hereafter!—
But if there be, must wild conjecture frame
Its normal state and occupation there?
Are all his ties rough severed and for aye?
Is Time a fragment—does a counterpart,
Sundered afar by Death's cold flood, exist?
Or hath this cheerless coast, washed by its waves,
No view of realms beyond the narrow belt;
No hopeful sight of happy plains, where roam

Enfranchised souls in disembodied state?
Hath Hope, so rudely stayed, no sequel there
Of brighter days? has Joy no fond appeal
To future spheres of boundless, rapturous life;
And not the risk again of breaking up?
  Oh! why these longings? why this fev'rish grasp—
This fastened hold on things unknown, unseen?
May one retain, with sure and certain hope,
His fond attachment? know that *now* expends
A moment in his course? that Time is short,
Though lengthened out e'en to a thousand years?
That God will gather up and bring to light
All works, all words, all creeds, all thoughts of men?
Shed light on all, and manifest, at length,
His Godhead underived; man's marv'lous frame
By Him devised, endowed with living soul?
Yea, God o'er all, most blessed evermore,
And close this Time in dread Eternity?
  O for some heavenly gifted Visitant,
Some guest awhile to silence doubts; to shew
What man can only think: to lift the veil
And give a glance of things beyond; and shew,
In part, what heart, and mind, and spirit seek,
With earnest toil! Must all await Death's overture?
And not till then the awful myst'ry pierce?
Is this God's way? The Just and Holy One,
Has He .   .   .   .

BOOK II.

THE ARGUMENT.

WISDOM stays the rash surmisings of an enquirer with some unfolding of God's ways: commits to Revelation the work thus begun. The enquirer is sent in retrogression of thought to Eden to see man in his primal state, and make a record of what he sees and hears. Revelation resumes for a while, and sends the enquirer again to hear Adam and Eve's colloquy. On his return Revelation commits to the enquirer the written Word of God for the full unfolding of God's will and ways. Its reception and use. Cain and Abel. Adam and Eve's lamentations. Discourse on Death and Life. Progress of sin. The flood.

STAY, sinner, stay thy madly rash demands;
Thy God is just. Couldst thou but comprehend
All He has done, silence would seal thy lips;
Or thou wouldst speak admiringly of Him,
Of all His works. I, Wisdom, will make known
All that thou seek'st, more than just satisfy
All thy conceits; unfold deep mysteries;
Divulge God's thoughts, so great, so marvelous,
That man, or brightest seraph, durst not give
Such thoughts, if formed, encouragement of birth.
   From everlasting, when as yet the heavens
Were not, nor earth, nor fountains of the deep;
Before His works of old, me He possessed;
Then I was with Him, daily His delight.
Now therefore hearken and rebuke thy heart;
For life and favor wait for him who hears
My words. To Revelation I commit
This work of grace. See, God has reared on high

His glorious tablet; there things visible
Declare the things invisible of Him,
E'en His eternal power and Godhead underived.
But this suffices not for more or less
Than unfallen man; for thou art not
What first thou wert; then holy, innocent,
Well satisfied; now guilty, vile and lost:
As craving more than need requires, not just;
Thus needing more than nature gives or can assign.
And now, with ear attent, and heart disposed;
Eye hath not seen, ear hath not heard, man's heart
Hath not conceived the things prepared of God.
Thy ardent thoughts restrain, but not repress;
As learner seek, awaiting daily at my gate;
Presuming nought; but, humble, hear my voice.
Counsel is mine and strength; by me kings reign,
And princes rule, justice decree by me.
My ways are pleasantness, my paths are peace.

  In the beginning God, th' Almighty, made
The Heavens and Earth: formless and void appeared
The Earth at first, and darkness brooded there
Drear on the deep. Unfurnished then it rolled,
Upheld by Sovereign power: He laid deep down
The Earth's foundations firm, and covered them
With hoary depths, as yet sealed up, congealed
In thick-set ice, no warmth as yet had thawed.
On these the Spirit moved, and energized,
Resolving thus a normal fluid state.
God said—Light be, and there was Light.
God saw the light, pronounced it good; and while,
As yet, no Sun appeared, glad harbinger
Of day; nor did the Moon, reflective, shine;
The Day and Night were there—God's first day's work.

Then—Let a firmament appear, and clothe
The Earth as with a garment; in its folds
Suspended floods, severed from floods below;
And so it was: God called this Heavens, the work
Accomplished on the second day.
Now—Let the waters under the whole Heavens
Be confluent, and let dry land appear;
And so it was: this He called Earth, that Sea.
And this was good. God said, Now let the Earth
Bring forth her tender grass; the herb yielding
Its seed; the fruit tree yielding fruit: God spake,
And it was done; He saw that this was good:
And hence the third day's work.
Then in the Firmament He placed great lights—
The Sun to rule by day, the Moon by night:
These seasons serve, and signs, and days, and years.
Likewise the Stars He made—the fourth day's work;
And this was also good. And next God said,
Now let the waters teem abundantly
With moving creatures having life—great whales,
And other monsters of the deep, and fish:
And in the firmament, the Heavens, He caused
The fowl to fly; and God endowed them both,
And bade them multiply—the fish to fill
The waters of the sea; the fowl, the earth.
All these were good: and such the fifth day's work.
Then the command—Now let the Earth bring forth
Cattle, and creeping thing, and beast of every kind;
And so it was; God saw that it was good:
But God would yet appoint a head o'er all
That He had made—o'er all His handy work.
Let us make Man, God said, bearing the stamp
Of our divinity—our image wear,

And in our likeness rule o'er all our works—
O'er fish and fowl and cattle, creeping thing,
O'er all the earth, and all that moves thereon.
So God made Man, and Woman out of him;
And gave to them viceregal power on earth.
For food, seed-bearing herbs, fruit-bearing trees;
To other living things, every green herb.
This was the sixth day's work, and very good:
The seventh God rested on, and blessed, and sanctified.

   Thyself, O Man, Jehovah formed of dust,
Dust of the ground; into thy nostrils breathed
The breath of life, and thou becamest hence
A living soul. God found thee work to do,
To occupy thy time, and exercise thy limbs.
A garden, planted by His hands, was placed
Eastward in Eden, there He put the man
To dress and keep this blooming ward; and there
He put trees of all kinds; the trees of Life,
Of knowledge good and ill—peculiar growth—
Were there. One tree alone man might not touch,
Or touching it he died—dread penalty!
Yet no way disproportioned to the breach
Of God's command. God saw man's lonely state;
No mate for him throughout creation's bounds
Had yet been found: so God induced deep sleep
To fall on him, took from his riven side
A rib and closed the flesh instead thereof.
Jehovah moulded this, a Woman made,
And brought her to the man—these two are one.

   O man! in thought revert to this glad time;
Away, and mark this pair from God's own hand;
Record thy estimation of His skill,
And goodness too: for man is not built up

To live awhile, then cease, and pass away,
And not again exist. Here is his state
If he observe the tenure of his fief;
If not some change impends, provided for
By Him for whom no casualty awaits;
And no calamity alarms: His mind,
Surprised by no event as unforeseen,
Has met all consequents of this His act:
Yea, all is His, since He has planned the whole.
Framer of agents, He encircles all;
Since He upholds while they perform; since He,
With antecedent cognizance has cast
The myriad wheels, which ceaseless work
The vast machinery; since He imparts
All energy—the power of thought, the will
To do or not to do; whate'er is done
Converges in His will. But not less true
It is that man is held responsible
For all his thoughts, his words, his ways.
Forbear to judge, thou understandest not;
Thou art not capable; but if thou wait,
God will unravel all; in His own time
Give thee to know what now thou knowest not.

One like myself I see, in feature, limb,
And general frame; but larger, happier, seems;
And one of womankind, some space apart.
Soon they each other find, with wondering eyes,
Without delay each other seek in near approach.
He, not with stealthy step of guileful plot,
Or spring of latent ill designed; no speed
Of hasty feet, shod for some mazy road,
Some errand of self-will, or rash intent.
With impulse soft, he onward frames his course,

Most willingly the subject of his willing heart.
Attraction strange he feels, and yet not strange
When estimated by the wondrous cause—
A cause efficient, answering well the end.
Beauty of form is hers, and graceful mien,
And moulded limb, bespeaking skill divine;
Glowing with youthful vigor, just emerged,
With ample dowry, from her Maker's hands;
A speculum, in which he views combined
God's wisdom most profound, and goodness couched
Under provoking charms.
No tardy pace is hers, nor dubious haste;
Yet willing feet obey the willing mind;
Gazing with pleased surprise on him, from whom
She had so lately sprung. Limbs like her own,
But cast in larger mould, attract her gaze;
Features the same, yet differing, annealed
With perfect skill: both very beautiful,
This Man, and Woman *that*.
He, muscular; she, lithe, of airy build;
Swart-featured he; she, fair with glowing tint;
He, of large stature, tow'ring high, robust,
Of loftier reach than sin has left to man;
She less, becomingly; her head attains
His shoulders' height—whence now we often see
The eye, in melting love, upturned to gaze
On him much prized; whilst he looks down, entranced—
Her radiant tresses hang in lavish length,
In playful curl bespread her snowy neck,
Her shoulders clothe, stray o'er the swelling bust,
Nor stay their course, but wander gaily on,
The body half conceal.
He too, in graceful length and bushy growth,

Displays a front of raven locks, resting
Profusely on his brawny chest, and there
Delayed, and clustering with the fertile growth
Depending from his chin, continuing on
The loins embrace. A pair of noble kind,
Unlike, and yet how like! God's praise proclaim.
And now, at length, in sweet assailment met,
Both own the sanguine bond, and both conceive
The genial law of mated kind; entwined,
Together walk, discoursing fond awhile
Of mutual ties, and God's design.
 First Adam spoke, assayed the wondrous gift.
What tones of voice, sonorous, musical!
Majestic swell, or cadence soft prevailed,
As varied theme, or avenue of thought
Occasion wrought. No huskiness, as now,
Impeded harsh the full clear sound, which flowed
Impressive of itself; but when surcharged
With earnest, weighty truth, how eloquent!
His other self, all ear, deeply impressed;
Her eyes, in liquid softness, yield assent
To his inspired discourse: and thus at first
His Maker's praise his tongue engaged :—
 Praise Him above, ye host of heaven—ye Sun
And Moon; ye Stars of light; ye heavens of heavens!
All here below your Maker praise; His praise
Exalt, cedars and fir of towering height;
Ye oaks and chestnuts wide, with multitude
Of pregnant boughs; far-spreading banyan, filled
With occupants of agile limb, and tribes
Of nimble wing; rooting thy progeny,
They yet appended to their parent frame;
A parent each, yet each descended from

A common stock, so nourishment supplies
Through veins not severed, bearing sap to all.
A type of all our race, from me to spring
And thee, fair Eve, progenitors.
Obedience, claimed from us and them, ensures
Resulting happiness to all, in bonds
Of love, and joy, and peace. For us and ours
No measured gift, no pittance from His store,
Gives thought of grudging on the part of Him
Who gave this present life; and with this life
All other things to satisfy our need— .
Herbs, bearing seed; trees, bearing fruit, for food:
Sweet-scented flowers our ravished eyes delight,
In trailing form; or climbing, they adorn
The highest trees, or spread the verdant ground
With varied tint. One tree we may not touch:
This is no bar to perfect bliss; in this
We see how little God exacts from us—
No code of laws that, having many parts,
Might be forgot; no worship stiff with forms;
No service hard, conditioned with mere will,
Apart from good. See thy assignment, Eve!
It is my part to dress and keep the ground;
Refreshing labor! yet monotony
Might dull perceptiveness of good; so thou
Dost add a charm. I look on thee, and breathe
More joy. It is thy part to help; meet place
For thee, so slightly framed. For though we dread
No harm from occupation such as ours,
Yet strength is mine; so trees of larger growth
My hand shall trim; thy gentler skill and taste
The creepers guide, the varied flowers arrange:
Near me thy place maintain, and both near God.

Thus worship, not so much an act, as state
Of mind and heart, pervading every act,
And word, and thought, will make us intimate
With Him who gave us common life and joy.

Then Eve—her ears delighted with the tones
Of Adam's rich full voice, her buoyant heart
With glad accord, and understanding clear,
In silvery voice, and joyous accents sweet,
Of higher key, mellifluous, her tongue
First found. O how attuned my heart
To speak my Maker's praise, that He, benign,
Hath made me what I am, thy joyous help!
Meet for occasion, linked to thee, my life,
By a mysterious bond, well recognized,
But not advised in understanding yet.
Nor need I know more than the will of Him
Who made us both—thee out of dust, and me
From thee; bone of thy bone, flesh of thy flesh:
The same as thee inwrought, the same in me.
Though two, in form distinct, and body framed;
In spirit one, and in intent of mind:
Pursuits and aim the same. To be employed
Is well; and to be near thee, my delight.
Whilst we, rejoicing, do our Maker's work,
Accepted worship occupies our hearts.
How large our Maker's gift! One tree alone
Of knowledge good and ill we may not touch .
In Him we live, and move, and being have.

To whom, with gladsome heart of love, to her
Whom God had made out of himself, and clothed
With flesh like his, but softer, delicate,
And rounded into shape of smaller size;
From jutting lines, robust, of muscle free—

To her, admiring, Adam made response:
For thee, fair Eve, my bounteous Maker's gift,
My heart gives thanks to Him, and cleaves to thee.
Unsought, unthought of, undesired, because
The mind, with conscious void, could entertain
No faint conception of so rich a prize;
But now my joy, my life.
No lack of due allegiance to my God,
My Maker, institutes these love-born words,
Objective epithets, so duly His:
For His indeed we are, and all we have;
Well said by thee at first, by me rejoined.
With full intent nought to withhold; and nought
To thee apportion which to Him belongs;
Nought to abstract, nor faintest thought project
Of aim apart from Him, who thee endowed
With beauty, me with strength; whilst each, in these
Surpassing each, has yet his proper share
Of that which eminently the other has.
Thus then, a due admeasurement of strength
According to thy slight conditioned frame
Is thine: I beauty have, of other kind,
But answering well th' intent of Him who gave.
Enough for thee to view well-satisfied
Is mine: but this is not the secret power
Attracting thee to me; nor does thy charm
Lie in thy strength. Whilst I behold and gaze
With wonder on the lovely, loving gift,
My heart grows warmer; bounding joy prevails
Through all my frame. Thee other power assails,
Assured to thee by God's creative mind:
I love the lovely, thou the lover lov'st.
O subtle, gentle force! my heart from thee

No sev'rance bears; and thine with mine is twined
In fond desire; impulsive, yet not rude,—
Intensive, yet not fierce.

    Again, with swelling bosom, Eve replied:—
Within I feel responsive to thy words;
My heart makes glad assent, and praise I give
To Him who made me thus, my joy fulfils.
No votive seasons call away my heart
Divided, caring how to please the one,
The other leave in short abandonment.
The spirit, framed by faultless skill, admits
No adverse claim; but loving both, and both
Attending, sweetest care my spirit fills,
My time employs. No idle moments craved:
No such demand can rise, where every wish,
Ere yet expressed, is met. No future good,
Amerced by fond anticipation now,
Affects the balance of our daily joy:
Sufficient for the day the present good avails.
Enough to know that He, who portioned us
On this our bridal day, has for each day
Its good supplied. That tree alone, profuse
With luscious, mellow fruit, He has denied.

    Then Adam spoke, in happy mood, and yet
With quickened glance, from Eve to tree just named.
I mark the glowing tints of that fair fruit;
I own its power to please. My God, and thou,
Fair Eve, His gift, my heart engage; His work,
My hands: for though this work is mine to do;
His to expect; and thine, as gladdening help;
Toil He prevenes, by gracious deed of gift,
Made in creative power, considerate skill,
And goodness all combined. Labor is good

For thee and me: no weary limbs recline
When day its evening brings; no yielding couch
Awaits their stretch. My mind, prophetic, looks
Through time's appointed course : our progeny,
Bending with toil, crowd through the varied ways
Of life: labor, still good but deeply soiled
With disaffection, wears the garb of ill,
Its aspect wasting, wan; and not as now,
Medium of quiet praise, our Maker's claim.
I see diverging int'rests too, set up
By adverse claims, in ignorance of Him
Whose claim they, impious, disavow.
I see the consequence; embroilment, wrath,
And strife, and bitter fray: factions arise ;
The weaker fail, the stronger rule; at first
In small domain, till clashing claims renew
The contest faintly hushed: oppression's hand
Laid heavily, provokes; and, as before,
The weaker rise, resist, the lower fall,
Succumb, and yield their portion to the grasp
Of mightier strength. Again, dissatisfied,
New quarrels spring, again their strength they prove;
One sinks, the other triumphs and forgets,
Demented quite, his brother's loss is his.
Thus kingdoms rise, thus empires aggregate.
My spirit makes essay, but fails to find
The cause of this. Nor can I now feel aught
Of sorrow or of burd'ning dread; for nought
Of kindred cause with them my spirit pleads:
Yet let us both His gifts enjoy: thankful,
His will perform, His presence keep; and both,
In loving concert, occupy our time.
That tree avoid: no good comes out of ill;

The spring corrupt, so is its flow: that day
We taste its fruit, that day we taste of death.
No doubt this is some fearful punishment;
But meet award for disobedience foul.
I have no wish to know the full extent
Of evil lurking there; not in itself,
But in conjunction with some sentient thing.
Our Maker's single law this matter clears;
When I, or thou, or both, outrage that law,
Then grievous ruin falls on us and ours.
Is this the prelude of my lengthened gaze,
Extended through the onward course of time?
Almost it troubles me to think, that we,
Now happy, may ourselves initiate,
Somehow, this woe-commissioned state.
Keep near, for thee I need, thou needest me;
Complete with thee I move, and thou with me :
Apart we miss each complement, and risk
We know not what. Suspicion may not work;
No guilt, as yet, affords it proper sphere:
But caution well becomes, th' occasion craves
Avoidance of this tree. Ere God had framed
Thee out of me, He gave me solemn charge—
"But of the tree of knowledge, good and ill,
Thou shalt not eat, for in the very day
Thou eatest it, then dying thou shalt die."

 He ceased; then Eve replied: Oh! could I slight
This loving care, this fond solicitude!
My heart is thine; yet not the less I give
Due reverence to Him, who gave thee me.
My all is His, my Maker, Sovereign, God;
Yet not the less entirely thine, by gift
Unasked: abounding goodness, that demands

A subject heart in thee and me.
That tree is fair to look upon; to me
It seemeth good for food. . . . .
Thee I believe, and thou believest God; I both.
Now let us to our welcome task, to dress
And keep this Eden, garden of our God.
Thine the direct assignment, made by Him;
And I thy steps attend. One law alone
Our gracious God enjoins, of light demand.
To shape our course, one law pervades our life—
For thee I live, and thou for me.

   Thus they discoursed, rejoicing in themselves.
And finding each in one another all
That each could wish or fondest heart devise.
No fading leaf was there; no lurking snake
Prefaced with horrid hiss its fatal coil;
No roar of rav'ning beast; nor, hov'ring o'er,
Fierce bird of prey, with cruel scream, induced
Its victim's dread. No rending thorn was there,
Nor thistle, marking nature's saddest curse;
No blighting wind; nor insect, injuring foul
The tender plant; nor sudden, biting frost,
Destroying quite last evening's budding hopes.
No ruin marked the track of stormy wind.
The keeper and his help—no weary toil
Their frame sustained; though nude, no conscious blush;
No mauve or fuschia tint; no color rare,
Or gaudy dye, waved in the playful breeze,
Or decked the tainted limb.
O happy pair! no need but every tree
Or plant supplied, because no adverse will
To your Creator's had as yet a place
In this fair realm. . . . . .

But what? O what was that which so appalled?
Deep darkness fell at once, as if to hide
Some fearful thing. Whilst I in spirit viewed
The primal scene of bliss, where beauty smiled
In earliest youth—man's state of innocence,
And all th' attendant joys of that sweet time;
A ghastly shroud fell over all the scene.

To thee, O Revelation, I return;
Wisdom gave thee t' unfold these mysteries;
In part made known ere, wrapt in reverie,
I strayed to that fair spot, and listened there
To tones and speech, of more than mortal kind,
Judged by our rarest, sweetest sounds.
My ear attent, my heart disposed, thy words
May clear the awful gloom that lowering hides
The deed in drear uncertainty.
I fear the worst; some dreadful act, perhaps,
Whence springs the woe of all our race.
Earth felt the deed; trembled, and shudd'ring, paused,
And to its centre shook; the poison coursed
Throughout its frame; its ruin owned.
The heavens, astonished, trembled, as it seemed,
At God's reproof; and, horribly afraid,
Sad mourning wore.

I, Revelation, now resume my place,
As thy instructor; sorrowful indeed
The tale of Eden's woe, and man's sad loss.
The guileful serpent, subtle beast, was there—
Let not thy heart prejudge this single fact:
What could his subtilty avail, unless
A corresponding subtilty gave tone
To his address? I thus anticipate
Communications thou hast sought; nor rash

Is thy request: for man in ignorance of God,
And of his own intemperate desires,
Has charged God foolishly; himself discharged
From proximate reproach.   This subtle beast,
By God's decree, was subject to the man,
As federal head: he broke from this, received
A foe more subtle still, who wrought, through him,
Most fatal mischief for thy race.
Here thou mightst urge objections, seeming fair,
To this precursory step in man's decline.
Thus, thou mightst ask whence flowed the ill,
Which, mediate, wrought on man; and whence, at first,
That bitterness which sought his overthrow?
Why was God's creature turned to be God's foe;
And what gave him his potency?   Forbear;
Satan, urged on by his own will, devised;
The serpent wrought, met by a kindred thing;
By that inspired, seduced th' unwary one.

   And thus the serpent, "Yea, hath God so said,
Ye shall not eat of every tree that grows?"
This to the woman, and she, answering, said,
"We may most freely eat of all the trees,
Their fruit enjoy; one tree alone is marked
By God's express command; we may not eat
Of this, nor touch it, lest we die."
"Ye shall not die," he said, "for God doth know
That in the day ye eat thereof your eyes,
Now dim, discerning nought, shall be relieved;
Then ye, as gods, shall know evil and good."
And when she saw that it was good for food,
And pleasant to the eyes, and also much
To be desired to make one wise, she took
And ate; and gave her husband, and he ate.

And now indeed their eyes were opened wide;
They saw their nakedness, and were ashamed,
And sought to clothe themselves, and hide from God:
Thus Adam fell through Eve, God's choicest gift.
The man was not deceived, the woman was;
She, blinded, took; but he, with uncered eyes,
Preferred his Eve to keeping with his God.
With him the whole creation also fell—
Fell with its lord; unfallen, supreme; supreme
Now fallen; then in his happiness, now woe
Enrols him first: for, sentient, he has power
To know and taste; and, as a connoisseur,
To judge, expatiate on the depth of guilt
He wrought; the woe his guilt entailed on all.
With him sank down, in vanity, his fief;
Creation's groans, attesting this, break forth,
A sore expression of her pain till now.
Thus entered Sin by one, and Death by sin;
And so on all men penal death has passed.
From Adam death has reigned; e'en over them
Who have not sinned in Adam's type, but born
Corrupt; for how can any thing unclean
Conceive a clean and holy thing?
Thus is the problem solved of man's estate.
Go, seek them not where Nature dropt her veil
O'er that sad scene of disobedience foul;
Bifarious too, for she who took the fruit,
Beheld it through beclouded eyes; her mind,
O'erwrought by subtle art, gave glad assent
As to a greater good than she had known:
But he, who took from her was well advised
Of all the bitter issues of his act, yet took;
Received it from her hands, a fatal gift,

Well knowing how his conscious act would work.
   Thus Eve: O Adam, had I heeded well
The warning of thy words, this ne'er had been.
Had I repressed at first the weak desire
To gaze on what was fair, and checked the wish
To know its fatal power, we still had been,
As then—happy in each, and each in God.
Oh! must I leave thee! happy, happy scene
Of innocence, of joy, of fond employ?
And blissful, no more reap the glad award
Of thy kind smile, O Adam? for through me
Thy ruin came: for thou wert not deceived,
But I, th' enchanted listener, gave ear;
And in that moment lost my rectitude,
And set the snare, unwittingly, for thee.
Had I but thought—and Oh! why not?—that thou,
As lord of all, hadst more the mind of God
Than all created things—not ignorant,
But too oblivious, when I needed most
Heaven's panoply—Oh! had I this recalled
I had escaped. Deep sorrows now recoil
On thee and me—on me, for my esteem
Of that foul tongue; on thee, through thy fond heart
For me: alas! such pref'rence was thy guilt.
Thy fall was not as mine, in ignorance:
I knew not; or, imprudent, I discharged
All wariness; or, self-confirmed, I left
Thy watchful care. Thy sin—this I avow
For thee and all our future progeny—
Thy sin it was to hearken to my voice.
Seduced by me—or rather by thy choice
To be with me, in saddest banishment
And wreck of all our hopes—thou didst receive

The offered spoil: thus thou didst leap, whilst I,
Led on, slipped o'er and fell. But whence is this?
How could this creature speak? how find a tongue
For language framed in our vernacular?
How did he learn at all our God's command?
How dare he raise a doubt that aught but truth
Could issue from his Maker's lips?

    To whom thus Adam—not as in life's morn;
Alas! his Sun had now gone down at noon—
Thy questions, Eve, are sad remembrancers
Of our bad exigence—thy fall and mine.
Was he, our enemy, the only one
Who entertained a doubt that aught but truth
Could issue from our Maker's lips?
Two are required to give a lie its strength.
If he, in open taunt, gave God the lie,
Who listened to that lie; and parleying, closed
With evil when presented speciously,
In fullest contravention of our Maker's law?
God made us upright both, and free from taint;
No poison wrought, nor evil from within;
Yet evil came, but whence a mystery.
Not we alone stood fair, but all was good
That God had made: the firmament alone
Had not this eminence. And was it thence?
Did our Creator's silence this portend,
When He refrained to call that good where now
The feathered tribes disport—the great expanse?
Did He then first call thither evil ones,
Ere this located somewhere else? if not,
Were they there pre-existent fallen ones,
Inhabiting their place assigned? perhaps,
Malign inherently, infuriate more

Through happiness beheld in us, brought near
And settled in proximity to them,
They hence, with cruel promptitude, resolved
To plot against our Maker and ourselves.
The evil came, and sought, and found in one,
Inhabiting with us this earth, called good,
A fitting instrument, a mediate thing,
Of deadly woe to us. Didst thou not mark
Our Maker's grace? He cursed not thee or me;—
Sadly contiguous indeed we stand
To that which is accursed, and for our sakes;
Now toil is ours, and weariness, and pain:—
God's heaviest curse fell on that wily thing
Which brought us harm; in cursing that He blessed
Both thee and me, the guiltiest agents there.
He gave no stringent law, as at the first,
And with that law, unmitigated curse;
But now, in ruin's hour, His goodness shines
Ineffable: good at the first, when He,
From me took thee, bone of my bone; and brought
Thy form, resplendent from His hands, to me:
Then goodness flowed to sinless ones, but now
To those who no excuse could plead, but such
As fear and conscious shame propose—
To me, who blamed His gift, irreverent; to thee
Who blamed the subtle snake—to us God made
An indirect disclosure of His grace.
Ah, fallen indeed! for each has minished power
To fill the other's heart—less in ourselves,
And less through all around, languor invades
The sated mind; the toiling limbs seek rest:
Sated, not satisfied, but craving still
What we have lost. Regret now fills my mind

That I received thy gift, thy fatal gift:—
And yet what could I but thy ruin share?
Together fall? so we together rise.
This hope our Maker's words convey—"Her seed
Shall bruise thy head, and thou shalt bruise his heel."
This to the serpent, not to thee or me;
Becoming reservation, inasmuch
As we, intelligent, had closed the door
Of happy fellowship; estranged our hearts
From Him who, though displeased, retained His grace.

Then Eve, in sorrow's plaint, replied: Thy words,
Still kind, are not embossed with early love;
Why not? The answer none can give as I.
Then no effect of sin's foul taint could mar;
Nor leave its slimy trail, nor love efface;
Nor stamp, with bitterness, the heart, the ways,
The words, the thoughts. I the effect now prove;
Yet no reproach do I advance on thee,
Though thou art changed—thy aspect, words and tones;
All, all are changed. A cloud hangs o'er thy brow;
Thy speech is thickened, and thy words have lost
Th' impress of God; thy stature, nothing less,
Is weakened in its port; thy step, less firm,
Not tott'ring, yet avouches weak intent;
As if the mind and body schism made,
Or wrought apart. O Sin, thy bitter fruit!
Is it perennial? has it firmly fixed
Its poisoned roots in this sad, darkened world?
And has it reached the Sun? for that seems dull,
As if that too had shared in our decline.
All nature droops and sighs: the lion stalks
Away in sulky mood: the eagle soars
With hasty flight, as if to shun the guilty pair.

And is it so? doth Death already move?
Is this poor quiv'ring dove its first essay?
Struck by the falcon's swoop, its fall close by,
Yea, in our very front, premonishes
Our own sad doom, and in the very guise
Of Death's affront on us—mute sufferer!
Again, the lion's roar, the eagle's scream:
O dread remembrancers! no voice of joy;
No utt'rance of delight. That horrid hiss!
My tempter's altered speech; in sinuous path
His way he takes. No long delay occurs;
The bitter curse its sorrow heaps on all.
Not I alone who, maddened, made the breach;
And that slim, subtle snake that lied to me;
And thou, who, conscious, took th' avenging spoil:
Creation sinks, dragged by its failing lord.
Already groans fall on our burdened ears;
Our sorrowing eyes their tribute pay.

 True, Eve, our sin has fallen, with reflex power,
On all Creation's frame: not we alone
Who, sentient, fell; but all around with me,
Th' appointed head, henceforth my sorrow share.
Beast, bird and fish, and creeping thing; yea, all
That God has made, insensate matter too,
Gives forth its piteous groans, assailed, oppressed
By sin's foul blight. No longer nature wears
Its proper robe; no longer swells its veins
With native blood; its visage now is marred.
Unnatural now are all relationships;
E'en ours are changed—our speech bewrayeth this.
The threat'ning roar, the startled, urgent spring;
The worrying pounce, the scream of prey escaped;
Are sad mementoes of our hasty crime.

HERE AND HEREAFTER.

This has its term: again a vista clears;
In time's far onward flight I see restored
This tarnished thing: its mute appeal ascends.
Ages shall roll away, its sorrows grow;
But one at length, thy seed, shall bruise
The serpent's head. Six days creation's work
Was on our Maker's hands—symbolic time.
Six thousand years God's mystery shall work.
Then more than primal bliss shall be restored:
The head at first, man shall be head at last.
Not then, as now, one fallible; but power
Innate, and wisdom underived are his,
In whom incarnate dwells the mighty God.
Our enemy shall sway our mortal race,
And rule this ruined world, its tyrant god.
These things I see, and more, less manifest,
But understand them not: yet do I think
That with this glorious one, many shall rise
Above all earthly good, and wear with him
Some other nature than the one now lost;
Recov'ring that, but made intact by Him
Who, in due time, shall come, and as thy seed
Shall here fulfil all God's decrees.
My altered mien, fair Eve, which thou hast marked,
Has parallel in thee. No longer graced
With innocence, thy charms have other power;
Weakened, but not effaced, in thee they shine,
On me they work, infuse within my veins
A stranger guest—a passion unadvised.
Conscious that thou art less than in the morn
Of our sad loss, to me thou seemest more.
Dissatisfied, I crave I know not what;
Yet drawn to thee, I seek my need with thee,

And, doubtless, thou with me:—a mutual charm.
Our Maker's image now is gone; our own
Usurps the place, with sin's own impress there.
These charms—well praised, when they, so praised, educed
Our Maker's praise as well—will prove, alas!
A fatal gift to those who spring from thee:
For sons of God will seek daughters of men,
Will leave their principates, repeat thy sin;
Take a forbidden thing, because 'tis fair,
And introduce a mightier power of ill.
Hence giants spring, men of abnormal race,
Bold sinners steeped in guilt, these God will judge.
Now to our toil; first let our search obtain
A resting place, where we may lay our limbs.
The poison works; and from my face now drops
The sweat of toil; sad nature's tears obtrude:
And thus we earn and eat our daily bread.
As at the first, thy part is still the same:
Relationships are changed; but not annulled;
Changed, inasmuch as each that holds a place
Is changed; for sin, pervading all, has wrought
In every one mischief most foul; and thus,
In time to come, rebellious hearts and words
Of jarring sound will challenge right of place.
We still have need to watch our constant foe;
Within he works, invisible; he needs
No form of beast; our ingrate hearts now give
The centre where he plots—dread vantage ground!
'Gainst thee he moves me, as the heedless cause
Of all my ills; thee he will urge and tempt
To spurn me as thy head. Thus pride, and rage,
And envy strike their roots in venomed soil:
No place had they—sin's brood—till hearts attaint

Gave entrance there; now there they work malign.
Their end I see: Creation yet, renewed,
Shall send her praises up, in Him embraced,
Who, KING of kings, and LORD of lords, shall reign.

  Not joyous, as my wont, then Eve replied,
For all my frame bespeaks the latent taint;
Yet surely still I know my place; that place
I mean to keep. Can I forget thy woe
By me procured, and fail to minister
To all thy need, my own pass by, at least
Defer till thine is met? Now let us seek
To meet our common wants; intent to place
Each other first, and each prefer in care:
Our Maker still our grateful worship claims.
Here is a spot of circling, branchy trees
Arched by our Maker's hand; and underwood
To intertwine; thus fenced, our weary limbs
May seek repose; or in the day retire,
When fervent heat constrains to seek the shade.
Hither my hands shall bring for pleasant food,
Or gay delight, seed-bearing plants, and trees
Of smaller growth, such yielding flowers and fruit,
Laden with goodness provident and kind.

  This do, her husband said, whilst I repair
To harder work. Our cares will multiply:
Our sorrows spring not from ourselves alone,
But those whom God shall give will bring their meed;
Our image they will bear; and some our shame,
In more intensive force, will reproduce.

  Then Eve rejoined: I dread that hideous snake,
He, as a beast, no longer moves, but crawls,
A reptile, or ascends the trees, and thence
His voice he sends to scare me, and remind

Of joys now gone. I must devise some means
Of guard and safe defence. I feel deep hate,
And long to crush the foe. He hates me too;
I know this, from his deadly lurid glare
And threat'ning hiss: time will intensify
All hostile purposes—both his and mine.
   Again, O Revelation, now I seek
Thy further aid. Man's present evil state
Is well explained: such cause might well produce
Such sad effects. But did he see aright?
Is there yet hope for any of his race?
Or did mere phantoms of the sense illude?
   He saw aright; but indistinctly mapped
The course of time. Man's day suffices not,
Its light is dimmed, discernment thus is weak.
Now take this book, God's gift, wherein is found
All yet made known, far more for thee to learn.
Thy questions all are met: the past is there;
A faithful chronicle records man's ways,
And how grace meets the rebel in his guilt:
God there unfolds to man what He will do.
Read and record thy thoughts if so thou wilt;
But, subject, let no thought or word of thine
Betray elate self-will, and glorying vain;
As though thy own presuming mind had found
Something original, not thine by gift.
There depths exist profound, which none can plumb;
Unsearchable His ways, past finding out,
Yet off'ring free research, and great success
To minds intelligent and humbled hearts.
If thou art well assured that man is now
An utter wreck, lodged in a ruined state;
Yea, all creation sunk with him, and dragged

A helpless train; corruption intimate
Embittering all with groans, and pain, and grief,
And travail e'en till now:—if thou assent
And search with chastened heart, then thou wilt find.
If further, knowing well thy state corrupt,
Thy lost condition, as derived from them
Who, in their wilfulness, preferred their will
To His, who formed them and their lot contrived;
Then search most confident, God wills it thus.
This book, the Bible, clears away all doubts,
All exhalations of a mind diseased:
For it is framed to meet the need of man.
There he may scan the past, and gather hence
His future doom; deliverance as well:
And more than this, intelligence of that
Which Wisdom infinite alone could plan—
Man's introduction to a higher sphere
Than he has lost, for ever and for ever blest.
Go search: the gift is great, and great the grace:
Beware lest, confident, thy search is vain.

O wondrous Book! my longing soul will gaze,
My earnest mind, delighted, con it well;
Deep inquisition make; its sacred store
Subject to careful search; deep study give
And meditation grave.

Now Cain appears, the eldest born of man,
A tiller of the ground—the ground accursed.
Of this Cain brings an off'ring to the Lord,
The labor of his hands—his own device.
Jehovah frowns on this, respects it not.
But how is this? Was not Cain's industry
Acceptable to God? Or were these fruits
Intrinsically bad? Observe the curse—

"For thy sake *cursed* is the ground": this bars
Acceptedness. The curse must be removed
From man and all created things. On all
That God first made the blight of sin has fallen—
On beasts, on birds, on fish, on creeping things;
But *indirectly* these sustain the curse—
Unless the sentence on the tempting snake
Included them. Not so; their curse results
From *Adam* fed'rally; the serpent holds
A bad pre-eminence; as such, is cursed
Especially, and so *above* the rest.
Not *theirs*, through *it*, but by a common fall;
A fall not theirs, as willing actors in
A common act; unwillingly they fell,
Depressed through others' guilt; hence, as uncurst
And sinless, they might furnish from their ranks
A sacrifice, correctly typical
Of Him, the sinless One. In very deed
The lamb sins not, yet bears sin's penalty,
That all creation travails with till now:
In death, no moan rebukes the violent hand
That takes its life—"it openeth not its mouth."
 Thus Cain imperiled all by this one act—
Not as a sin, but as a sacrifice.
He brought a thing accurst, to satisfy
God's claim; that is, to have the curse removed:—
A monstrous act, bred by a monstrous thought.
Abel, the second son, brings to his God
The firstlings of his flock: Jehovah smiles.
Was Abel's too a bloodless sacrifice?
Nay, mark these words—"and of the fat thereof."
Then must a life be given, and blood be shed,
To meet man's need, to rectify his state?

Yes, Abel sheds the blood; blood is the life.
The type prefigures One to come; by faith
A sacrifice more excellent than Cain's
Was offered; and by which Abel obtained
Witness from God of righteousness: and he,
Though dead, yet speaks to all the power of faith.
Thus sad occasion sprang for bitter words
And fatal strife; for nature spurns the rite.
Here let imagination stray, and give
The substance of their then presumed discourse.
But yet, demure, let Fancy dip her pen
In the deep well of truth, pourtraying each
As each might be—one in fallen nature's garb,
The other clothed in righteousness obtained.

Thus Cain irate, with clouded brow, and glance
Of scorn, fallen countenance, and taunting sneers:—
Abel, thy bloody hands bespeak no gentle work.
Could the poor bleating lamb not move thy heart
To spare its life? See! hither trots the dam
Upbraiding thee as murderer of her joys.
Religion sure demands no cruel rites.
Has God delight in blood? does He thus claim
An outrage at our hands, to take a life He gave?
I do not doubt our severance from God;
Our parents tell us this, and shew it too,
In them; in us, as sprung from them; through them,
In all around the dismal work appears.
Our God requires, no doubt, some sacrifice,
Acknowledgment becoming, of our state:
And as He gives all we require; so we,
In thankfulness, should make return to Him:
Confessing thus that we exist in Him,
And by Him are upheld in life.

What more can we perform? how satisfy,
If He demands all He might claim from us?
Impossible! for this would be to make
Return equivalent to all His gifts:
And nought can equal these but these themselves.
God claims, and well, to be our creditor;
I am content, so let it be: I brought
Fruit of the ground, an off'ring to the Lord,
- The best expression of my loyalty.
What could I more? yet it was not received.
No groan of beast oppressed, or plaintive moan,
Their pain bespeaks. My heart rejects the thought
That blood of beasts must flow to meet my sin.
I own that sin: our parents' sin is ours,
As sprung from them; to this we add our own.
 No disobedient hand, my brother, wrought
To take away the life of lamb or kid.
Blood is the life thereof, and blood alone,
As life, can meet our need, our life redeem.
Thy tenderness of heart becomes thee well;
And I would learn of thee, as elder born.
In this, and other things, I arrogate
No place of teaching thee by word or deed;
But rather, as thy younger brother, learn;
And subject, yield thee def'rence, as is meet:
Both subject to our God, who gave us life.
I may not learn; nor wouldst thou, conscious, teach
The thing that's adverse to His Sovereign will.
Not suffering merely—though that too must be—
But death for forfeit life He justly claims.
Our life is forfeited; and in His grace
God substitutes some other in our stead.
No lamb or kid can satisfy the claim,

Or reconcile the sinner to his God;
But typical, a shadowy lesson give
To humble learners what, but dimly taught,
They yet believe. Thus is God's justice met;
Not by this bloody rite, but as it points
Onward to One, the woman's seed; a man,
But more than man, who, yet to be revealed,
Shall bruise the serpent's head. My act is nought
But as through faith in Him who cannot lie.
Faint glimmer only meets my eager gaze;
Enough for faith, which deals with things unseen,
As visible; unfelt, as palpable.
Faith saves not, but attaches us to Him
Who saves, with this condition, all our race.
   Right eloquent, my brother, is thy tongue;
No teacher thou, but learner, well confessed.
My place I take, in humble guise; abased,
Sit at thy feet, and learn of thee; for thou,
Spite of thy modest disavowal now,
Hast store of learning, gained in gentle mood,
And occupation scant. My hardy toil
No leisure leaves for meditation grave.
Such themes become thee well; thy way pursue;
Another time I'll prove more apt to learn.
Briars and thorns their wholesome lesson teach;
They teach my flesh; my docile spirit, thou.
So still go on, more knowledge glean:
When next we meet, may I, with readier mind,
Avail myself of thy divinity.
   His scowling face no answer sought; and, stern,
Forbade the soothing word in Abel's heart,
To find its utterance. In gloomy state
He moved away, a prey to jealous thoughts.

Again they meet; Cain, wrathful, makes pretence
In subtle mood, and feigns the lowly mind;
As list'ner waits, invites his brother's words
Of guidance for his future course ; as if
He saw the cause of failure in himself.
Such place Abel disclaims, attempts no more
Than, unobtrusive, state what he had learnt.
He knew his Maker's will; let this define
His proper course: obedient, he receives
More light as he proceeds. God's full intent
He may not know, nor does faith crave so much.
Content, he waits till God's appointed time,
For Grace t' unfold this deepest mystery.
Thus, diffident, he still beseeches Cain
To yield Jehovah's claim; and sets his flock
To furnish victims for the sacrifice.
As when a sudden cloud obscures the sun,
And checks the light; so, omened darkness fell
On Cain's bleak face: his brow betokened ill.
No warning words escaped, but swift of arm,
With murderous aim, the frenzied blow descends.
What is it there, prone at his trembling feet?
A brother's corpse? Dead! Abel, art thou dead?
Am I the primal murderer? My blow,
Though weighted with fierce rage, was not thus meant.
Yes, lifeless there thou liest; no more to urge
My blackened blood through fevered, bursting veins.
No stranger blood defiles the ground: a brother's
By a brother's hand thus shed. O hapless wretch !
I flee; but in my flight bear shame and grief—
Not grief, I cannot grieve: nought relevant
Will go with me accurst. Ah! what is this?
What girds my brow? a cinctured brand of guilt,

HERE AND HEREAFTER.

Of infamy, of pain. I'll tear it thence: no, no,
The pain is greater to detach than leave
Where it is put—is put! who put it? He,
Who made me what I am—a murderer?
If He made me at all, or caused me live,
Then He is chargeable with what I do.
But this, if true, should free me from this load,
Which presses from my consciousness of guilt.
I would I could exist apart from Him.
Could I estrange my heart from such a creed
As that He holds my soul in life; requires
Whene'er I quit this life, account from me
How I have used this life, His providence,
His care: could I shut out this latest act
From memory's fount, erase the record there,
Or give it color of excuse, as not prepense,
I might forget my misery too—I'll try.
"Cain, whither fleest thou? thy brother, where is he?"
"Am I my brother's keeper? why dost thou
Arrest my steps, and make this strange demand?"
"And is thy memory, O Cain, so false?
Hast thou washed out the blood thy conscience rued?
It cries to me: vengeance is mine, I will repay.
Cursed art thou; the earth itself will spurn
Thy selfish care; vengeful, withhold her strength.
Henceforward thou shalt roam a fugitive,
A vagabond throughout the sterile earth."
"I know my sin is greater than thy grace,
It may not be forgiven; for thou thyself
Hast sent me forth, and hid me from thy face.
Who but will slay me, as a fratricide?"
"Behold a mark I set," Jehovah said,
"Lest any finding thee, should take thy life."

Cain hastens on and seeks the land of Nod,
Goes from the presence of His God, nor stays
To reconcile his truant heart with Him.
  O damning sin, to limit thus God's grace!
Greater by far than shedding others' blood.
Blood may for blood atone; but what can save
The man that makes God's living truth a lie?
  That shriek of woe! has Eve now stumbled o'er
Her murdered son? Ho! hither! Adam, Cain,
My daughters too—what, what is this?
My son, my Abel! has that fearful beast
Assailed thee too? is this his first attempt
To bruise the heel? What, blood! and is this death?
Abel! my son, my son .   .   .   .   .
Adam stands by; his lab'ring breast betrays
Deep agony of soul. Two like as dead
Are at his trembling feet—his son, his wife.
His grief is great; amazement seals his lips,
His utt'rance choked. Rigid with dread, he fears
That what he sees—mere death—a preface wears
To gloomier type. The frightful thought prevails
That violence has wrought this tragedy—
The violence of one who summoned death
With hasty hand and envious heart; of one
Who often had surcharged his ears with words
Of bitter wrath, and curses loud and deep.
There Adam, riveted with stiffened gaze,
Beholds the scene, accepts death's mockery.
Death mocks him in his son, upbraiding him
The cause of this: it mocks him in his wife,
With dread similitude—a long drawn swoon.
She moves; the spell is loosed, he too now moves
And first essays to help his prostrate wife.

Her mind, restored, reverts to where it failed;—
That fearful sight—is 't true? is Abel slain?
Am I bereft of him—my son, so good?
And Cain—why, where is he; our daughters too?
Our latest born I see approaching now,
Borne on with hurried step and frightened look.
O thickening storm of woe! our Abel dead,
Our daughter near, perchance with further tale
Of some dark deed and black effect of sin.
   My parents, give me breath   .   .   .
Our Cain is fled, his eldest sister too.
I knew him not; so changed a look he bore.
A fearful mark gives him an aspect strange
And terrible. His sister wife alone
Could bear his awful look. He, ere he fled,
Revealed his monstrous deed, that he had slain
Our best beloved, Abel, our gentle one:
And God has branded him, impressed his brow
With such a stamp, that, as he walked along,
The very lambs and kids, in blank amaze
And headlong terror, sought their dams.
But I, what shall I do, my Abel dead!
My brother, best beloved!
   Bereft of both my sons, a daughter too,
My mother's heart must break: thus Eve complained
As she perceived her woe. Forlorn I stand:
Our enemy was not commissioned thus—
To bruise our head: but he has gone beyond,
And left us nought. One son lies there a corpse:
Another fled; an outcast now, disseized
Of all appurtenance of good, he fails.
I thought that I had borne a son, through whom
That promised seed might come; all hope is wrecked.

What fruit of sin have we already plucked
Since I, in disregard of God's command,
Presumed to know the power and consequence
Of a forbidden act. I look at thee,
O Adam! and behold thy furrowed brow
Of care and sorrow, carved by sin's own hand,
But my device: indented lines of grief,
Sunk to the very bone they seem; thy cause
They plead: thy daily sighs, thy heaving breast,
Avengers prove on me; sad monitors
Of wrong inflicted by my hand.
I fondly hoped that Abel might have proved
Our solace and our joy through this dark vale.
For Cain was ever wayward, gloomy, fierce,
Morose, prone to resent a rated wrong.
But Abel, O my precious one! was all
That heart could wish; in gentleness, in love,
A pattern to us all: forgiving, kind,
And self-denying, seeking others' good,
His own deferring; thus securing more.

  Three children gone at once—then Adam groaned—
Oh! what a fearful complication here
Of God's most just decree! My slaughtered son!
Art thou the first to yield thy subject frame
To nature's last embrace? my eldest son
Madly to summon thus the winding sheet,
The noisome grave! My son, my son! thy dust
Must to the dust return. Thy gentleness,
Thy works approved of God, by Him received,
Provoked foul hatred and the murd'rous hand.
This was th' immediate cause; the more remote,
And procreant of this, thy parents' sin.
The ground, already soaked with blood—thy life,

Must shroud, ere long, thy body too. Much loved,
Much prized, much valued for thy gentle ways;
Must we no more entwine our love with thine?
Our toil, beguiled by thee, must now assume
A cheerless guise. These hands, already hard
With daily work, must other now perform.
 Then Eve again her doleful plaint renewed:—
My son, my son! Oh! had I died for thee!
Thy piety, thy love, my heart recalls.
Thy gentle spirit fled, no more wilt thou
Another's toil by ready help prevent;
Or strife avert by loving smile, and speech.
How many bitter wrongs didst thou endure!
How many angry words thy spirit bruise!
Yet no return in kind didst thou e'er make.
And must we lose thee—hide thee from our sight?
Is there no way by which thy loved remains
May be reserved close by, that we may come
And bear some sad remembrance of thy form,
And speak to thee though, mute, thou hear us not?
No, death is there, alas! corruption works;
We know it, though of human kind he first,
Touched by the venomed dart of death, has fallen.
Oh! harrowing thought, that we must lose thee thus!
That open, lofty brow! no guile was there:
Ensanguined now; befouled, but not debased.
Those hands ne'er grasped a weapon to induce
Another's woe; but, ministers of help,
Supplied our need: and now they helpless hang.
That tongue, so eloquent to praise our God
In thrilling song, or converse sweet, now still,
Now silent, cheers no more. That manly breast
Will heave no more, burdened with others' griefs.

H

No more the sigh of sympathy will break
For sorrow not his own. Oh! can I live?
Can trouble such as mine wish to outlive
The gloomy tomb's sad victory, and this
Death's first attempt on us and foulest blot?
O Death! now try thy new-fledged strength on me:
No power hadst thou possessed but for my guilt.
Sin gave thee birth, and I conceived that sin.
Thy power exert; rid me of life and grief at once.
 Then Adam checked these fond but sinful words.
He saw her grief was great, and knew indeed
That sorrow in a woman's heart, impelled,—
Yea, other passions too—a channel wears
With flow of words; and well conditioned so.
Sometimes we see the bloodless lips compressed
By stress of grief; the eye, with rigid glaze,
Unmoistened by the friendly tear; pent up,
The sorrow works, frets in the lab'ring heart,
So that it breaks, and sets the spirit free.
Or else, dethroned, the mind in fancy roams,
Invents a life of errant ways and means,
At variance with the calm that reason gives.—
Eve, I respect thy grief; thy husband knows
Its bitter kind: my heart makes full response
To all thy moans, thy anguished tears, thy words,
Except the last; wherein impatience seeks
To break the bonds awhile imposed on thee.
Shall we make our complaint of God's just law,
And all its consequents? Did He enforce;
Or did we act from our own wills unbound?
Had Satan power to move us to the act,
Beyond his power to tempt? He still is near,
Unfelt in apprehension, save when we,

With subject mind, our Maker's will adopt.
More sorrows yet are thine, but greater joys:
God's word must stand. Cain's impious race shut out;
Another, God will give in Abel's stead:
And thou shalt yet rejoice. Not he alone
Shall greet thy gladdened eyes; but after him—
If thou art spared with me to tread this earth—
Seven generations of our race will rise
And cheer thy longing heart. One man of these
Will stay his course midway; translated, soar
To other worlds, death's agency decline.
The seventh from us, a prophet, he will warn
Unheeding ears; denounce ungodly ways
And hard-set speech against his God and ours:
So rife, e'en then, will rank rebellion rage.
And now my wife, my daughter, let your care
Bespeak a decent shroud which nature yields.
Our Abel, when alive, was wont to place
A victim on the altar of his God:
The skin is left; this take, enclose our dead
In such; or other, as your loving hearts
And care assiduous may provide.
I go to find a place, a tomb prepare.
O fearful task! a father's hand to dig
His offspring's grave! My heart, my heart revolts;
My wounded spirit shrinks. Oh! must it be?
No other hands are near. Now let me go,
Lest weak delay work further ill to us.
The sun is hot   .   .   .   .   .

   O Adam, can we bear thy absence now,
E'en for this dread, this sore necessity?
Shall we not go and share thy desperate toil?
First let our hands their dismal task perform,

Then bear thee company. Apart from thee
How can we live! how bear the throbbing heart,
That beats importunate by every sight
Of him we loved, love still, and still bewail!
   Enough, my only ones, your plea is strong,
I feel response. My shrinking spirit shuns
The lone employ. And ye too must behold
My hideous work; and, weeping, mar my strength.
To be without you is most sad; most sad
To have you there. O hapless sire! no way
For thy escape; no friendly hand intrudes
To excavate for me a resting place
For all that now is left of him we loved;
Snatched off ere life had opened wide her strength
To maturate her plans. Oh! he was ripe
Before the normal time, and taken home,
Where hate, nor jealousy, nor rage avail.
I do not blame, complain I must; my heart,
Repining not, seeks this some slight relief.
Those fleeting years since thou didst first embrace
Thy eldest-born—what shadowy joys, what griefs
Have crowded in their span! the contrast holds,
Most sad to us, between our Eden lost
And these abodes of sin, and sorrow hence.
Now let us haste—O fearful haste!—to hide
And bury from our longing sight the dust
Of him whom we henceforth may see no more!
   The mournful task performed, they now retreat
Within a sheltered grove; there seek their God,
Pour out their hearts, and find His promise true,
To comfort them that mourn.
   Discourse awhile of Death—its origin,
Its nature, how it wrought at first, its course;

If varied, how? Life forfeited is death;
By sin that came, a penal settlement
Of righteous claims. But other may exist
Apart from sin, not penal, not educed
Through aught enacted by such agency
As may have wrought in this our distant sphere.
The will of Him, who made all things from nought,
Suffices, if in any way He would unmake
What He had made. That is not wrong, which He,
So willing, does; though wrong in other hands
Not so enjoined. Though pain, and sorrow, death,
Acutest sufferings result from guilt;
These relatives do not necessitate
The antecedent, sin: two diverse laws
May have some not dissimilar effects.
Geology may have its claims, nor clash
With aught of Scripture truth; but still may ask
Too much, and not be palpably absurd;
For it preserves most pleasing parts; presents,
So far, magnificent conceits, well drawn
From facts well registered. But may not these,
Without this labored art, be ranged as well,
Within the limits of six thousand years,
Yet not inflict an outrage on philosophy?
Huge pachyderms lie deeply crushed; mailed forms
Of prisoned monsters twist beneath the weight
Of pond'rous rocks; but these do not demand
Eras of misty age to calendar
Their doings, as they moved at Terror's beck
Among th' affrighted crowds: there is no need
To place them back, make them expound the age
Of rocks embedding them—the flood does this.
But might not death precede the fall of man?

It might, only not penal; painless too
It might exist, if pain necessitates,
In all its services, a penalty.
If this be crooked logic, let it pass
As not insisted on.   Yet death of things
That God had made did surely come to pass,
Ere man had proved the fatal power of sin;
Ere he had known this foe, fair to the sight,
Alluring to the sense, but in th' embrace
Most fatal to the smitten debauchee.
God gave the herb for beasts to feed thereon;
The ruminants would crop the grass; had that
No insect feeding there? or was that too
Seeking its sustenance upon that leaf,
Just gathered and consigned as daily food?
Did it still live in paunch herbivorous?
And so with myriads else?   Or did they die
When thus absorbed by grazing flocks and herds?
What food had birds? granivorous we know
In part; some on the wing obtained their food,
So, insectivorous, sustained their life
By others' death.   Did heedless flies alight
On viscous juice; thus made unwilling guests,
Rejoice in useless wings, and live on air?
And what when Adam quenched his usual thirst?
Was water then conditioned not as now,
With myriads, in a drop, of living things?
Was life continued to them when entombed;
And so the law digestive turned aside
To meet their fated change?   And how again
With food itself? how may we name the change
That passed on all the appetite desired?
Assimilation? what is that, but change

Analogous to decomposing law?
And what is that but death indigenous?
And fruit again, when ripe—what next ensues?
Not renovation, but through its decline.
The seed, cast in the ground, no produce yields
Except it die. No sinful cause is here,
And no effect of sin, yet death appears.
Did Adam bury living turf, while yet
No will had wrought but God's—what then ensued?
Decay? and what is that but corp'ral death?
Decay is decomposèd elements.
And why may not the flesh of animals
Fulfil this law, when that no soul sustains?
No doubt all fell with man as lord of all:
But fell from what, and into what?
Not from a state of primal innocence
To one of guilt; that were to make the brute,
Insensate matter too, accountable.
Not from a state of immortality;
Absurd the thought, already seen, for some;
And if for some, why not indeed for all?
The living soul alone could thus sustain
A living frame. Decadence lays its stress
On all created things: but man alone
Controlled this law through his peculiar gift—
A living soul; death there, the body yields,
And meets the general law: he, first exempt,
In God's own image formed, now takes his place,
Corruption's bondage proves, and all with him:
He adds more bonds, perversely forges such
For nature's thrall. Unwilling vanity
Now stamped on all, therewith continuous pain,
Are witnessèd till now: creation's groans,

Her bitter travail, utter this reproach.
The ear, attuned to nice observance, notes
The groans, not loud but deep, of nature's throes:
The eye, with close regard, detects the tear:
Her piteous wail ascends; distress is there.
'Tis aggravation then; a former law
Intensified; something appended now
To what was there before—an ill, fresh-coined.
Sin stretched her ghastly wings o'er all man's realm,
And brooded ill: cohabitation foul
Impregned sweet nature's womb, and fouled her germ;
Unnature thence prevails, a wretched parody.
Man, lord of all, in righteous rule would reign;
Affect his subjects all with glad results:
Himself, declined, would likewise burden all
With sin, and sin's default, and penalty.
So death of matter then, as mere decay,
Prevailed, ere man gave his peculiar taint.
Henceforward virulence attached; no more
Was death an ill unshunned; instinct forewarned
The fatal snare; the very leaf shrank up
From blighting touch. But of the soul, its death
Could only be a penalty; and this
The consequence of something not conjunct,
Not proper to its first conditioned state.
Freedom of choice was giv'n of good or ill;
Not wise enough to know the good from ill,
The man might choose the ill, reject the good.
Transgression is not where there is no law:
But Adam had a law; with power to stand,
He fell; for he, not ignorant, transgressed;
And, in transmission of his race, he made
Conveyance of his fallen state; and so

By law entailed, they fell who spring from him.
Self-love and vain conceit object to this.
Men plume themselves on man's nobility:
Faint observation soon dispels this weak,
This fond credulity. Where is it found—
In gaols, asylums, brothels, or the like?
Poor human nature is, at best, a wreck,
Stranded on Time's bleak coast, where wreckers roam
To foil recovery of the fragments there.
No re-construction meets the pitying gaze
On that dark shore: there the disparted whole
Its schism keeps; it may not be rebuilt.
Ah! cheerless waste! no shelter near, nor help
From threat'ning death. What shifts and projects, framed
To meet this exigence, are daily made!
Death is not baulked; he claims his shrinking prey—
The beautiful, the gay, the well-to-do,
While yet immersed, each in his heart's employ,
No soft'ning pity find, no longed reprieve.
The disappointed, fortune's cruel sport—
As men would say—forlorn, and weary too
Of this cold world, no pity seek: the one,
Dissatisfied, would crave some short delay;
The other hastens on Time's final step,
And chides the tardy pace of friendly death,
To shroud him, fainting, from the storm of life,
As, pitiless, it beats incontinent
Upon his head, unshielded by wise care
And panoply divine. The closing act
Of hoary Time—the breaking up of life,
Appals him not, who, strong in faith, views death
As slain. Death is no death to him, but sleep:
Glad harbinger of everlasting life,

Beyond this murky vale of shadowing death.
This fearful ill proves but a good to him;
This sorrow, joy; a change not sought, not shunned.
   And what is Life? is it the same in all?
Does it set forth an intimate resort
Of soul and body, linked we know not how?
And has the brute a soul? The scalpel yet
Has not discovered its retreat:—and does
The presence of the soul retain the life?
Or does what we call life retain the soul?
Or does a difference exist; a soul
Assigned to man, but to the brute mere life?
Or has man life in common with the brute,
A link between the body and the soul—
A union severed when that link is snapped?
Who shall resolve this most perplexing theme?
But is it needful? Curious search has failed.
One sage * avowed that he had found the soul
In what is named the pineal gland.
How did his search avail? Did he indeed
Inspect the living head? Or did he search
The tenement when tenantless? Vain man!
How slow, how loath t' admit his helpless case!
He fondly dreams that he has power to search,
And rifle all the secrets of his state,
And broach the book of laws inscrutable.
Some in their prurient fancy have endowed
Brute matter with set law, producing life.
Some say that matter has inherent life,
And, leaven-like, communicates throughout
Its vital power to matter organized

              * Descartes.

As for that life. Others on this improve;
To cumbrous matter give maternity,
On Electricity affiliate life.
The fundamental form this union gives
To that which issues from the senseless womb,
Is a mere globule, and inclosed in this
Another globule warms the germ of life.
The favorite matter for maternal use
Is albumen. And now, the learned say,
We know the whole, had Nature only said
How she produces albumen at first.
And then we have a problem yet unsolved—
What is this procreant electricity?
Did we but know these two, the whole were clear
Of living organisms how they spring.
Now this is good!—father and mother too
Are strangers quite; and these are sought from that
Which sprang from them—a greater stranger still.
Others have said that Nature has a power—
And some have named this Deity, but blind—
A power to multiply rough drafts of plants
And animals, of matter merely; these
Are monads: some are vitally instinct,
And with inherent tendency t' advance.
This albumen, this jelly form would have
Its varied wants, as hands, and feet, and mouth;
And these would spring. Had one a want to fly?
Behold its wings! Did other want to swim?
Behold its fins, with apparatus framed
For water life! Another needed legs
And feet; without delay they come!
Such organs were not framed to meet these wants
By some superior power—creative Mind;

But by these wants themselves:—Oh! how profound!
Man was a monad once;—well that we grant
To those who will insist—and what its kind?
The *monas termo?*—littlest of the least,
So Ehrenberg declares. 'Tis well to take
The lowest place,—we have authority
To countenance this step—and thence attempt
Some higher evolutions of this life
That man is born into: *attempt?* not that—
Submit to what is yet to be evolved—
A fated process, much at variance
With man's free-will to do or not to do.
But here we rudely shake philosophy:
One says that, "Science is prevision, and
Prevision—it is power." If this be true,
Then by the help of strict analysis
Of antecedent histories; sustained,
By wise synthetic processes, we ought
To prophesy about man's next developed form.
Let us go back a step. Man's ancestor,
Immediately—we speak of man as man,
The creature, not a specimen of such—
Man's ancestor, we say—no; *others* say,
A *Monkey* walked: how long, no record states:
At length it introduces *Man*. How strange!
For one—not in the mystery—would think
That in this process it would disappear:
But no, it lives; as if to disavow
All anthropoidal claims. We're further told
That, in disrobing, monkeyism still
Retained the caudal limb: to meet the case,
The law, that *need ensured supply*, must be
At once reversed; he wants—no tail; when, lo!

No tail appears.   But some one else asserts
That this was through effect mechanical: •
This vertebrate continuance, says he,
Through sitting disappeared.   These learned men !
How gravely they resolve such points abstruse !
Who is not pleased with such hypothesis
Of his own origin ?   A jelly germ !
And is not this far better than red earth,
To claim our common source of being from ?
And leav'ning life innate, than life inspired
By Him who formed the body and the soul ?
Or is man's pride the haughty advocate,
Removing cause without to cause within ?
This pride ! what garbage it will feed upon !
Efficiency deny, and substitute,
Instead thereof, blank inefficiency !
Enough of this.—We have a wholesome fear
Of being charged with answering a fool
According to the folly of that fool.
In spite of this, we'll run a tilt again
With one or two yet more.

   Some very learned men avow that man
Is God; yea, God evolved in highest grade;
For everything is God, they say, and man
The chief of all.   Now mark this rival god,
As seen in this precocious, potent form.
He thirsts and cries for drink, sometimes in vain;
The desert hears his moans, and there he falls,
His bones remain, mute tell-tale of his fate.
Gaunt famine too his hapless victims claims;
Nor can they hope to shun his sinewy grip,
With all their vaunted god-like powers.
Disease invades the frame; the languid limbs

Confess some foreign power, exorcised not
By this presumed anthropomorphic god.
He breaks a limb—'twas accident, he says:
And what is accident? The learned man
Becomes a fool, forgets all he had learnt,
Through injury without, or other cause;
It may be through the more than prudent stretch
Of these consummate powers of mind.
Hallucination queer conceits this god
A tripod; or some kindred thing become.
Now all dread death: why not dispute his power?
Why not evade his dart? Why not evolve—
By law of higher organism wrought
By steps consecutive—yet one step more
Above the King of Terrors, and educe
Not safety merely, but high vantage ground
Whence man may issue terms; or rectify
The present adverse laws, subjecting him,
Unwilling, to the many ills of life?
Now if advancement mark the course of man,
How do these very learned men account
For such abeyance as this progress owns
In man's development? He died at first,
He still is subject to this mortal law.
Does genius here, astute, detect no flaw?
If this development, so much avowed,
Be law primordial, who has registered
Its course, or chronicled its steps till now?
Or are six thousand dreary years, or more,
The term for this subaltern god, ere he
Emerges into yet a higher sphere?
But if no chronicle exists? then whence
This fatuous scheme? and how can one assert

That he at first was other than he is?
Empedocles—that most veracious man—
Was first a girl, and then a boy, a shrub,
A bird, a fish, and then Empedocles!
As such he lived awhile, and then desired
To know the future domicile of that
Which once had energized the bird to fly,
The fish to swim, the shrub *in situ* grow.
This vagrant thing led on Empedocles
To seek th' Etnean fires, and headlong plunge
His most accommodating frame therein;
'Twas all consumed: a sandle re-appeared,
Which told how he, a spruce philosopher,
A poet much admired, had closed a life
Most foolish, by a death more foolish still.
Perhaps he thought his next developed form
Might possibly enshrine a god; or that,
At least, some might suppose him deified.
How was development here marked? the boy—
Is that a step beyond the girl? the shrub—
Is that a well-developed boy? the bird—
Does Botany explain this curious step?
And is the fish still higher in the scale?
But last of all Empedocles himself!
Might one be free to judge—allowing now
The truth of this metempsychosis strange,
And of development as well—our thought
Is that the last was first; the rest, like dice,
Are thrown at random in to fill the list.
Pythagoras again, the Samian sage,
Was first Æthalides, who, quick and dead
By turns,—for such th' Olympian grant—explored
The upper and the nether worlds, and made

Conveyance of his stock in hand to him
Who followed next—Euphorbus, he who warred
At Troy, and fell by Menelaus' hand.
Then Hermotimus wrapt the lonely soul
In mortal bonds; impatient here, it sought
All corners of the earth, to exercise
Its rare prophetic skill, t' unfold to all
The dark futurity—its secrets broach.
Meanwhile the wife of that which lay at home
As lumbering clay, in spleen burnt it all up.
The wandering spirit rudely thus turned out,
Now found a fisherman, who lodged the soul
Through storms of land and sea, and then resigned
The fitful guest to wise Pythagoras.
Will some apologist object that these—
Empedocles and sage Pythagoras—
Held not development? But then,
If true in this our day, 'twas true in theirs;
And they have fixed the thesis on our doors,
With illustrations of the law, prepense,
Anticipative of the law itself.
It has been said that facts are stubborn things;
Now here they are, more cogent since that they
Illustrate unawares the latent law:
A law of wild vagaries as we think;
The more befitting those who now enforce
Its maudlin claims. Learning is no defence;
Much learning now makes some men mad; not that
It has perforce this tendency; knowledge
Avails for good or ill, as it is used.
The learned fool is found, a fervid growth
Of teeming sentiment, not wisely ruled.
The wise man, ignorant of science, art,

Amenities of high-born life, yet fills his place
Of usefulness, his generation serves. *
Where is th' Assyrian found, where Egypt's race,
Where dwells the Greek, or Elam's favored sons?
Have they put off, in their development,
Barbaric pomp and childish show? Have they,
In onward speed, disrobed themselves of that
Which earlier years paraded with a zeal
Intemperate? When did conviction seize
The Ninevite, or Babel's clans, that gods
Of wood and stone were powerless to avert
Their dreaded ills? Did Mizraim struggle forth,
And gain a higher eminence than when
The Persian braved the wrath of all her gods?
Or is she now among the kingdoms, base?
Her pyramids, her sphinxes, gloomy men
Of stone, which sit as warders of the past,—
Do they espouse this fond development,
Or is it retrogression they suggest?
Where is the savage in this line? does he
Inaugurate his course with horrid feasts
On human flesh of scalped and tortured foes?
Or is he fallen to that? Once civilized,
And bred to finer thoughts and higher aims,
Has he now reached the hither end, debased,
Sunk down, a sorry wreck of what he was?
Such is the Aztec, such th' Assyrian too;
Whose monuments require a stranger's skill.

---

* The mantle of the ancients has fallen on the moderns. Let Emanuel Filopanti be immortalized: he modestly tells us that he is the fortieth and last Emanuel; his spirit having previously illuminated the dust of the illustrious Newton, Galileo, and others. He practically utters again the royal *mot*, "Après moi, la fin." We should like to see Emanuel's register.

Inscriptions graven by their ancestors
Are hid from them, a hopeless monograph.
Yea, so it is; the mighty pyramids,
Though mute, yet speak in pond'rous tones to those
Who advocate development? 'Tis not enough
That theorists elaborate some facts,
And call them evidence; it may be more,
Far more run counter to these hasty claims.
No mad assertion lacks some countenance
From things that are: illusive, these sustain
The careless searcher, or deceive the man
Who knows no god but his own rebel will.
It needs a patient mind to gather, sift,
And strain facts for, and facts against; e'en then
Much danger holds, lest an inverted mode
Should bring perverted views: a theory
Should follow, not precede discovered facts.
Forbear now; press not so the impious search:
Read in God's book of nature how He cares
For every creature of His vast domain.
See how the hugest thing disports, and feeds
Out of His hand e'er opened wide; there too
The smallest gathers daily food; yea, see
The Godhead in the mighty frame, the same
In what the microscopic lens detects.
Man is religious and continues so,
Unless imbruted by his wilful lusts.
A God he sees above, around, within;
Excess of learning may benight his mind:
Extremes join issue; so his intellect,
With flick'ring glare, the grossest darkness meets.
The simple Christian has a simple rule,
He'll understand where that is feasible;

When it is not he'll just believe.
But is this reason—common sense? It is;
For who can understand Infinity?
Man's place is not to judge, but to admire,
And learn what God has wrought: much He has placed
Before our eyes most manifest; but much
Is hid by light ineffable; and much lies hid
As not revealed; or if revealed, beyond
The reach of minds debased, or immature.
God's foolish things confound the wise; the strong
His weak things foil; whilst to the lowly mind
He makes His deep things known, His counsel shews.
Learn then, O erring man, to doubt thy skill
T' unravel all God's deep designs; He yet
Retains His great prerogative to hide,
From wise and prudent men, His purposes,
And make them fully known to babes—to those
Who meekly, diffidently, learn His ways.

    Pass on some hundred years; a visit pay
To Cain's metropolis, Enoch its name,
And of his first-born too. Cain reigns supreme,
And Enoch ministers vice-regal power.
Cities have multiplied, and works of art;
Vast piles of masonry ascend; and pride
Finds great development. A common bond
Unites the growing towns; diverging views
Had yet no sanctioned channel for their flow
Political, yet individual claims
Would clash; thus love for one would seize
The heart of more than one, and hatred thence.
Some building site, much coveted by one,
Would be desired by more: contentions spring
And litigations keen; tribunals mock

The sanguine hopes of all; for policy
Forbids divided int'rests, and suggests
Some other cautionary mode, by which
To shun the certain hate a lawsuit breeds.
A brotherhood is sought, its bonds are knit
By social laws preventive of the ill,
If this be possible; repressing choice
By laws anticipative of that choice.
No idlers roam and breed disquietude,
Suggested by loose hands and unemployed.
A communism holds for common good,
The individual merges in the mass;
Not lost, forgotten not, he finds his good
Just as the aggregate attains that end.
The adventitious claims of modern times
Had there no countenance: a rising man
Necessitates some bonds on those around.
One gathers riches from the common stock,
Not culpable, still others feel the drain.
A mansion springs, hard by a hovel sneers,
And brotherhood is rived. Look on the sea,
Behold its level rest; a storm disturbs
The placid show; a heaping up takes place,
Elsewhere depression rules—the bulk remains.
So with society; upheavings here and there,
And hence some sinkings down; if one mounts up
Another sinks; and unavoidably,
Where each is left to frame at will the mode
And measure of his ways—a liberty much prized.
We may not shut our eyes, and so ignore
The issue of the thing, for here in truth
Development is found: man's very self,
Thus unimpeded, opens out, and blooms,

And in due time bears ripened fruit.
Each generation shews advance on that
Which just preceded it; restraint delays
The culminating point, until *the* time:
E'en now it looms, and with increasing power
Of size and brilliancy, arrests the gaze
Of all, but not of all alike: some view,
Admiringly, the blazing meteor near,
Foretell a joyous advent soon; some look
And shudder at the lurid glare, premise
A portent adverse to the sons of men.

   At first, and for some hundred years men sought
How they might best enjoy their good.
No goodlier way is found for this than when
Subjection rules: that liberty, for which
Men pine, and risk their lives and all they have,
Is most assuredly but one step short
Of slavery. Yes, take a model state,
Where all are free—not free to break the laws,
The laws political, municipal—
But where one may be idle if he will;
He may seduce his neighbor if he will,
And pay a penalty; he may blaspheme,
May swear, may lie, may cheat, if he but fling
The ægis of some law conventional
O'er all—observe the quietude of trade.
That liberty is foul, false-hearted, seared;
Unfeeling, makes full claim, yields none.
That man is free indeed who rules himself,
His conscience guiding him, but not as though
Infallible; for that needs much
To be enlightened from some brighter source.
He is a slave who listens to his heart;

Unless his heart is rightly disciplined,
Not by his native will, for that is leagued
To meet the inbred cravings of that heart.
Motives induce the act; the strongest rule
And dominate, though others may surpass
In urgency of call: but ears, not set
To catch unwelcome sounds, are deaf to all
That strict propriety may safely teach.
It cannot be that man is wrought upon
By that which is the weaker power, so that
The stronger is annulled by it; though some,
Discriminating not, have so affirmed;
For what is power? not that which makes address
To hearts pre-occupied and disinclined.
The law was weak, though not inherently,
But through the native virulence of that
To which it was addressed—the human heart.
If motives are without and work from thence,
So influence the will, we might admit
That oft the weak prevails against the strong.
But motives are within, and there alone
True power exists: inducements work without
Effectively on some, though they are bad:
Others reject th' alluring promised good.
Power is in each, for each has had his way;
Diverse indeed, and this proves power in each;
Therefore responsibility ensues.
 The patriarchal rule of Cain endured,
A despotism not distraught with power:
For though his will was law, experience led
The fratricide to curb the budding ill.
The aim the same as ours—the greatest good—
Was there by prompt repression much enforced;

With us development is much educed.
It is a problem for the age to solve
If ill is not developed more than good.
So ages roll; men multiply apace.
Anon some strangers visit there; in mien,
Most noble; in their carriage, elegant;
Of stature, large; in manners, most refined;
Beauty was theirs, as well, of dazzling kind;
Beauty they sought; for they had set their eyes
On Eve's fair daughters, and with them desired
The marriage bond. Some myst'ry clouds this act,
For they were sons of God, desired strange flesh, *
Having assumed the same. Did they assume
Because of this desire ? Could spirits feel
As men: or reason from the evidence
Adduced by men ? Did they behold man's joy,
The pleasure beauty gave, and lustrous form ?
Desiderate the same ? Or did they first assume,
Mix freely 'mong the sons of men; partake
With them their liability to catch
The warm appeal of beauty's charming glance ?
Impassive not, somehow they felt the power,
"Then took them wives of all they chose;" and hence
A race of giants sprang, huge-statured men.
An impetus was thus supplied, and soon
The quiet good was shelved; instead thereof
Great energy infused. The mortal womb
Was pregnant with immortal seed; hence sprang
A progeny, immortal but for this—
They took the mortal element, succumbed

* See Jude 6, 7, in connection with Gen. vi. 2—4. In the former passage the translation should be—" Even as Sodom and Gomorrha, and the cities about them, in like manner *to these ;*" viz. to the angels.

To that and fell, as mortal men around,
Before the scythe of death; and so were judged
As men. In chains of darkness bound, they wait
The judgment day; but mercy had an ear
Even for these, who, disobedient, left
Their principates, and with fair womanhood
Wedded foul sin: the Savior, pitying, went
And preached to them, in spirit, there.
Some streams are broad, but, shortened in their course,
Soon reach the ocean's depths, and there are lost.
So with the stream of wickedness; in depth,
Unequalled since; in breadth, commensurate
With man's estate. Then teeming millions trod
Earth's plains—a million millions some suppose.
God's primal curse maintained its sterile power,
So culture of the soil had no regard,
Much less pre-eminence; hence men had left
Great leisure on their hands. Inventions grew,
And works of art: devices framed t' evade
The curse of sin—to plant a paradise around,
A paradise of sensual joys; to deck
And plume humanity with courtly show;
To compromise some self-denial with
Indulgence great; the former needed much
To counteract the passions' onward course.
Wise in their day; they knew the peril great
Of bankless streams, of misdirected wills,
Uncurbed licentiousness; a barrier here
Enclosed a safer sphere of bridled lust.
But sin is sin whatever mask it wears:
The careful debauchee as surely lands
On shores forlorn, as he who gives the rein
To all his lusts: the epicure at last

Exhausts from viands all their power to please,
Still more than appetites most gluttonous.
This foul apostacy had filled the earth;
The race of Seth were not exempt, they too
Had fallen away: one man alone retained
The fear of God; before him seven had preached
The righteousness of God; and he, the eighth,
More definite, proclaimed His vengeance near.
Nor did mere words appeal to hearts suffused
With earthly good. Make thee an ark, God said;
So Noah built, and hereby testified:
For did he fail to tell them why he built?
His very workmanship announced a text;
His perseverance, sermon lengthened out.
They, disobedient, scorned his warning voice;
His long preparing, God's long suffering,
Had no effect. Their hearts they hardened more;
They scoffed and ridiculed the preacher's text
And sermon too. The end draws near: they ate,
They drank, they married wives, they built; yea all
Their hearts delighted in, they did the same.
The ark is built, the world hereby condemned.
The builder now retires, with him his wife,
His sons, their wives: of unclean beasts, by twos;
Of clean by sevens; of birds the same, and creeping things.
  Now rain descends; imprisoned waters burst
Their straining bars, and, swelling, flood the land.
Men view the preacher's work of gopher wood,
But they, infatuate still, no warning heed.
The door is shut by God Himself: too late
For any startled from their fatal ease
By patt'ring drops. Were they now first advised,
By rain, of God's great reservoir above?

A new phenomenon, how dread to them
This stranger visitant! What means this thing?
Is this the old man's threat? It ceaseth not:
All day the pelting storm; throughout the night,
The pouring flood. The second day, at dawn,
Hope set for them: encroaching waves invade
Their very hearths; and hasty rafts afford
A floundering passage to some neighboring hill.
They flee, the foe pursues; as they ascend,
So, pitiless, the water creeps; sweeps off
Relentless, with its curve, the shrieking child;
The mother's instinct grasps the floating charge,
Together swept away, together close,
In desperate embrace, their forfeit lives.
Some, in full strength, the battle wage, and beat
The foaming surf; in vain, no power it owns
But His, who signed its warrant for these deaths.
The brawny arm, in efforts to escape,
And reach the ark—afloat, but still in sight—
Sinks helpless when upraised, in frantic haste,
To clutch the closèd door—too late!
Sick beds no favor find; the frightened guest
There shrieks for help; no pitying help is near.
Hadst thou, poor suff'rer, in thy days of strength
Despised the warning voice? Did ribald jests
Pollute thy lips? Did Noah's earnest words,
And solemn look, and daily work, provoke
Thy laughter, and tirade of heartless mirth?
How changed! that spectral form more pale becomes;
For death, with cruel creep, has now just reached
The bed-room floor: at length its force prevails.
The room is filled, the vengeful tide intrudes;
And, rising, bursts the tenement, and floats

The couch, and its frail suffering occupant,
On to the watery waste of death without.
A pleasure party plans the morrow's joy;
A bridal pair the nucleus of their mirth.
The setting sun no threat'ning cloud obscures;
Promise of future day, and harbinger
Of dawning good, propitious to their hopes.
Baskets, well stored with thrifty care, their need
Anticipate: their hearts, elate, dread not
Some counter summons calling them away.
Death—a strange visitant where lives prevail
To near a thousand years—they dream not of.
They seek and press their couch with merry hearts,
In promise of more joy with early dawn.
Not death, a stranger visitant than he
Arrests their lightsome steps. The blackened heavens,
The lightning's lurid glare, the thunder's roar,
Appal their hearts, their rebel spirits quell.
The daring bold blasphemer stays his oath,
Remembers Noah's words, his rash affront.
High scaffoldings bespeak the builder's hopes
Of some great mansion, very soon to vie
With that his neighbor builds: envious to rear
Its boastful front, o'ertop the former pride.
He passes by, contemptuous, notes the bulk
Of Noah's ark, finds fault with its design;
Its length, and breadth, and height, not rightly framed;
Its tonnage tells—so jokes his life away.
He hears the warning voice; looks hard, regrets
So fine a man should near to Bedlam dwell,
And not partake its cheer.
The man of pleasure scans th' enormous ship,
And counts it far too large for cruising glee.

Who steers the course? No rudder hast thou put,
The helmsman's toy. Wilt take the ship to sea,
Or bring the sea to ship? A grand device
To frighten foolish men: but foolish work
Bespeaks a fool. So he, and passes on.
　Rain, rain, the beating rain, the foaming surge,
No parley give: for forty days and nights
Their terror pour. The fountains of the deep
Their cerements burst, and overflow the hills.
The buoyant ark upheld, in safety rides,
Its steersman, God; its freight, sweet mercy's charge.
Soon, very soon, a gloomy stillness holds
High empire over all the scene, save where
The plashing waves join chorus with the song
Of those within, safe from the storm without.
All, all is hushed; a dreary wide-spread waste
Conceals the earth. The drunkard's fumy song,
Embattled strife, the fell seducer's wiles,
Ambition's aims, gay pleasure's schemes entombed,
Await to prove their seeds yet competent
To germinate, and yield more bitter fruit,
When lengthened time, and all appliances
Of man's maturer skill, and Satan's craft,
Shall find them place and exercise.
Another deluge of another kind
Will then invade the deep-laid plot, lay bare
The impious schemes imparadised by man,
With much pretence of good, and arrogance
Of comely show: then will sin's coverlet
Be torn away; and then will beauty find
No service forced by guile; but, free to range,
Her skill will multiply the joys of all.

CHAPTER II.

THE ARGUMENT.

EGRESS from the Ark. Noah's drunkenness and curse. Slavery. Noachic laws. Nimrod and Babylonish idolatry. A fancy sketch. Abrahamic covenant and history. Israel in Egypt, and deliverance. A glance at the progress of the nation of Israel. Babylonish captivity. The four kingdoms of Daniel: the fourth identified with the last great foe of God and man: his doings: his end. The final consummation.

THE World is young again: fresh cast, it floats
Buoyant, and weighted less; for guilt and sin
Have narrowed exercise: the ark alone
Exhibits actors on the waste-wide stage:
It finds, at length, firm anchorage, high up
On Ararat; its inmates issue forth,
And seek again the perils of their state.
Their sustenance miraculous has ceased.
The thirst for blood once more sets in: again
The Lion's roar bestirs the quiet herd;
And querulous, the interrupted song
Is supplemented in the sheltering nook.
Man's works are buried deep; incumbent rocks
Conceal deep down all they have done; themselves
Float on the angry deep, and furnish food
For tenants there. Disruptions vast have torn
The solid rocks apart, laid them athwart
Tables unrent; constructing there huge books;
Depositing, between their leaves collapsed,
Crushed spoils of many forms; inanimate,
As trees and plants; and animate, as beasts,

And birds, and fishes; there, as specimens,
Preserved by careful skill, they lie to shew
Their great Creator's awful ways,. when He,
In wrathful mood, o'erthrew His earlier works.
Men have, at length, discovered these, laid bare
Impressures there, deduced a science thence,
Unwarily denied God's great design
To chronicle man's sin, its power t' effect
This overthrow, provoking by its kind
And prevalence God's justice; wearing out
His patience to the uttermost.
Had God a quarrel with the beasts, the birds,
The monsters of the deep, the mountain tops?
Did He in wrath scatter th' enduring hills
And make them bow? As when a King comes down,
Sits in the dust and mourns; his subjects too
Assume his state; his grief is theirs, his joy
Theirs too; so man, creation's lord, brought death
On all that lived, and dismal overthrow
Throughout his realm. An immolation great
Attended man's great death:—the loftiest hills
Depress their heads, sink down as if amazed,
Conscious of woe: incarcerated depths
Pierce through their prison-house, and in their stress
Force upwards bounds imposed. Thus sites are moved;
The ocean beds exchange their place; valleys,
Submerged, receive the eager tide; and hills,
Hurled from their heights, bear, in their headlong flight,
Their mighty base, and madly fling themselves
Into the frightened sea: there uproar reigns,
For from below commotion springs; upheavings thence
Displace the yielding flood; the mountains' plunge
Adds terror to the scene. The waters flee,

And seek in haste the frightful chasms left
Where late the mountains stood: all nature groans,
Bursts with her throes. But now the crisis comes:
The Architect of all, who built the hills
And sunk them low, and made the sea repose
In ordered depths, now interferes, and stays
The dreadful rout. Vengeance had done its work;
Order returns: the overflowing rain
No more descends; the fountains of the deep
Restrained, are sealèd up, no more to wreak
Their fury on mankind. Noah steps forth,
Becomes a husbandman, a vineyard plants,
Lies drunken in his tent, the sport of Ham.
Paternal wrath is roused, the curse descends—
The curse of slavery no doubt, but did this give
Licence to trade in man? Here men have erred,
And outraged much th' inflexible decree.
The curse must be sustained; but why should man
Add chains to those already forged?
"Servant of servants thou shalt be:" this law,
Severely just, needs no severity
From them who claim the hapless race of Ham.
Nay, God would have them mitigate and smooth
The rugged path they tread; mercy prefer
To sacrifice. But men, who wear a skin
That gives predominance, anticipate
The bondage term; make cruel raids, and steal
The husband from his wife; the father snatch
From those who need his care; and disregard
The lover's frantic grief, the maiden's broken heart.
Then they a household build, give time to raise
A doomèd progeny, and buy and sell,
Maltreat and mutilate, and kill; yea, worse,

Debase themselves and them in shameful lust,
And abnegate the claims of decency.
Is this God's institute, just as it stands?
He will avenge, is now avenging much,
The cry of those oppressed; yea, even now
His inquisition sits, and search is made
For blood, for rifled homes, for outraged hearths.
The mother's cry ascends; her wailing babes,
Her blooming sons, her daughters fair to her,
Lift up their voice for vengeance to that God,
Who treasures up their wrongs. " Vengeance is mine,
I will repay." Does God excuse the theft,
The middle passage woe, the sales, and all
The horrors of the whip, and manacles,
And gyves, and brutal lust, and murder foul?
" Prepare to meet thy God !" see even now
He meets thee, He confronts thee there where thou
A specious, bad immunity hast claimed.
There face to face He charges thee with crimes
Not to be named for turpitude; the soul,
With shudd'ring, hears the wrong, the filthiness
Abhors. Thy iron heart must quail before
The horrors of the cup He fills to thee.
Take, see, 'tis blood; for thou hast shed much blood.
Thy homes are rifled now; thy father's heart
Is stricken in thy son; thy daughter's form,
Now outraged, sketches out some by-gone scenes;
Thy tender wife lies at thy feet abused.
These are but samples of His holy wrath;
Be wise, and read, and learn that He is not
An unconcerned spectator of thy sin.
A fast do ye proclaim ! What is its kind?
How will ye order it? Have blows enforced

Their logic on your heart ? Have they supplied
The needed euphrasy to clear your sight,
That you may see your negro is a man,
Whose liberty is dear to him—a sacred right
Defiled by you ? Now is it your resolve
To make a restitution just, of this
That first you took away, and then denied ?
Hear how the Judge of all the earth defines
The fast that He accepts—" To loose the bands
Of wickedness, to let th' oppressed go free,
T' undo the heavy burdens, and to break the yoke."
The inward fast from that, the heart debased
Delights to revel in, is God's demand:
And not to bow the head, just for a day
Afflict the soul, refusing daily bread.
Hear God's rebuke as well—" Behold the day
Whereon ye fast, your pleasure still ye seek,
And all your labors still exact. Behold,
Ye fast for strife, debate, and eke to smite
Yet with the fist of wickedness, and make
Your loud pretentious voice be heard on high."
Have ye forgot the law—"Thou shalt not steal ? "
And that to steal a *man* was death ? How then
Can ye expect that God will smile upon
Your valorous exploits—whilst yet you grasp
Your cruel whip, your chains that gall the limbs
Of crushed humanity ? First leave your sins,
Then God may listen to your humbled suit.

   A great calamity sometimes preludes
A patent good. The flood sweeps off the curse.
Such is the power of faith; for Noah builds
An altar to the Lord. Jehovah owns
His servant's act; with him re-institutes

The primal good. This might be brought about
By that which hurried to their doom mankind
And all that lived: or it might be set up
Miraculous; either by fresh assay
And complication of the soil, attained
By intellective skill; or else, removal thence
Of disability imposed by sin,
And its sore advent; thus accomplishing
The resurrection of the good interred.
A grant is made to Noah, and a law
Is passed interminate: all that had life
Was sanctified for food, by God's entail,
Except the blood. This law is not repealed,
Th' exception too is unrescinded yet.
God gave a valid reason for this clause
Restrictive—"blood is the life thereof:"
A fact not altered since that day.
Again—"if any shed man's blood, by man
Shall then his blood be shed." Is this repealed,
Or can it be? for man was made by God,
In God's own image; and, although indeed
This image has been marred, the fact remains
That gives this early law its cogency.
Man strives t' invalidate this law
As barbarous, unsuited to the light
Of these our gentle times: where fits the act,
And how, of him who, lawless, takes a life?
The light that dissipates this gloomy deed,
Will negative the vengeance too.
 Again men multiply, and soon forget
God's awful check, when He submerged the earth,
And all therein. Fresh claims anon arise;
Fresh disputants enforce their adverse claims:

The right of might prevails. One man appears
Who quells these petty feuds; and he began
To be a mighty one, Nimrod his name:
A rebel—so his name imports—before the Lord.
Hereafter, when from Heaven's eternal heights
The spirit scans the past; as in a glass,
Beholds ages now rolled away; reviews
Receding scenes; then Nimrod's rule will rise,
Despotic, stern—yet welcomed, sovereign sway.
His name, suggestive, speaks of adverse ways—
Molk Gheber, mighty king, in earliest times
Great Nimrod's name, assumes the later form
Of Mulciber, Rome's god of fire; and Molech,
King of men, whose rites the fire performed.
Bol-cahn, hence Vulcan too, a name he took,
That is, interpreted, great Baal's priest:
Accepted such, nor did he seek aught more,
Yet at his death was deified, and filled
Great Baal's throne, the *Only One*, * denounced,
He and his rites, by rapt Isaiah's zeal:
And, as th' eternal Father, swayed the heart,
The idol heart, of Babylon. Ere long his son,
Adon, Adonis, or El-Bar—Tammuz †
His name in Holy Writ, whose fate they wept,
And Israel's daughters too repeat the shame—
As Phaeton, by his rash request, went nigh
To set the world on fire. The God of Heaven
The crisis viewed, and dashed him headlong thence
A lifeless corpse. This tale, stripped of its dress
That classic taste has wrought, reveals that man

* The original term is Achad, admitted by the best scholars as meaning "the Only One," idolatrously worshiped in Babylon: this Israel copied.
† Ezekiel viii. 14.

Who taught the world to worship in the heavens
The glowing Sun, and on the earth enshrine
Perpetual fire. Large statured, graceful, strong,
Excelling in the arts of peace, and good
That men prefer, he taught mankind t' enjoy
The passing hour. So revelry and rout,
And decent sin with gorgeous pageantry,
Enrolled all suffrages, lulled every heart
In soft repose: as Bacchus here he shone.
As Zero-ashta too, the woman's seed:
And Zero-ades, only seed, he won
The Babylonish faith. * The woman first
Received a halo from the son's renown;
But in the lapse of time eclipsed his fame,
And higher worship craved: the heathen mind
Accredited the same. Has Christendom
No counterpart? Mark now the harlot dam!
Well is she Babylon the Great, though yet
An undeveloped germ in full, that bears—
Offensive thought—the keys of heaven and hell:
Whose fasts, whose festivals, whose monks, whose nuns,
Whose shaven crowns, whose celibate, were found
In Euphratean Babylon, and thence they came.
Thus far historic fame; a sample, gleaned
From stores most ample, verifying much
The wide-spread, diabolic scheme, set up
In many lands—in Babylon, in Greece,
In Egypt, China, India, and in Rome;
Whence, in Rome's latter phase, the papacy.

* In the matter of names also, it seems the arch-enemy anticipated this feature in the Messiah's history. Only a few of the names of Bacchus, the Babylonian Messiah, have been given: he is called by Plutarch, Myrionymus—he with ten thousand names.

Here mark the aim; not just a copy set,
And imitations thence; but a fell scheme.
Anticipative of that marv'lous plan
Redemptive; first revealed to him who wrought
Man's first great overthrow: and what to man
Was dark, was to his great intelligence
Most clear. The woman's seed—but not the man's—
Must have an origin divine; and hence appeared
These abstract truths in Babylon of old—
Th' eternal Father, Spirit, and the Son,
The mortal mother too, Semiramis.
But he, the great deceiver, had to please
Man's idol heart, humor its gross desires,
Hide from the view, what none desire—rebuke
Of natural appetites, of pleasures free
From all restraint; and hence Bar-Cush, the same
As Bacchus, lord of all misrule appears.
His scheme was mirth and happiness for all:
All care and apprehension banished far.
A violent death cut short his errant life;
But this was met, provided for, his death
Fulfilled the bruising of the heel, and hence
The bruising of the serpent's head. Most strange,
But not less true, that in old Babylon
These things were known, and thence conveyed
To other and far distant lands.
Bar-Cush has died, where will he rise again?
The world has waited long, the time draws near
When he, who had the deadly wound, will live;
Again take up his wondrous power to harmonize
The jarring elements of human kind;
Afresh propose his schemes to utilize
The ills of life; commingle poisons, hence

Produce a cup of generous wine, intoxicate
With happy madness all the eager crowd
Of aspirants for earthly good.
   Here now imagination importunes
To paint her picture of those ancient times,
When Nimrod ministered as Baal's priest.
A shepherd boy is seen, daring, and bold,
And venturesome, and skilled to throw the lance,
To twang the bow: the wolf he holds at bay,
And makes the lion hesitate, the bear
To quit its prey. Ere long he drops his crook;
The man is grafted on the boy: mere youth,
Ambitious much, leads bearded manhood on,
They brave the lion in his den; assail,
In turn, the shaggy bear. The monster's roar
Affrights the full-grown man; the beardless youth
Withstands alone, confronts the angry beast,
Prevails and wears the spoil. Years glide along,
Honors profuse adorn the brow mature:
Now paramount, he leaves the tented field,
Nimrod, as King; Bol-cahn, as Baal's priest.
Babel, his capital, on Shinar's plain,
Avows Chaldean excellence; his skill,
His energy, here shone magnificent.
A city and a tower, whose top might reach
The heavens above, proudly exalt their pride.
Did he, as Baal's haughty priest, design
A temple for the Sun, so high, the top
Might seem to reach the very Sun itself?
A gorgeous palace too, of lofty height,
Surmounts a hill, by all the city viewed.
High over all, a glittering disc, the same
Wherever seen, bright image of the Sun;

Illumed by night—so magic art devised—
Th' embodiment of him, that now had gone
To nether realms: thus always seen, himself,
Or brilliant likeness, coined by devilish art,
A sensual worship served.
Steps of continuous flight wind round the hill,
Wrought marble, polished smooth; so high th' ascent,
That dizziness was wrought in them who viewed,
And pride in all. The roof, projecting much,
Rested on lofty styles, of height immense,
Skirting a terraced walk. At even-tide
Each pillar shone with skill occult; profuse,
They shed their demon-light with that above.
Around the brilliant show, in dreamy joy,
The underlying city sings its song
Of earnest praise: beholds its god by day,
By night his delegated presence views.
The palace gleams with more than human art
Within: here too bright evidence exists
Of solar occupance, and astral glow.
Pass through a suite of rooms, the inmost seek:
There, high enthroned, Molk Gheber sits in state;
His throne of gold, by steps of marble reached,
Of glittering white; unearthly glory sheds
Its dazzling rays, the courtiers own its power.
Unwonted guests evince th' effect, in look,
In manner, not in dread of aught malign;
For they were confident of good—the good
That circles round the heart of man, delights
And feeds its cravings irrepressible.
It was a tyranny most absolute,
But welcomed much, for all had gladly made
Consignment of their all to him who wrought,

And unremittingly procured their joy.
Behind the throne a door led to the shrine,
Occluse from mortal gaze of all, save him,
The great High Priest, who sought response.
Thence issuing, on his throne he sat; his face
Shone bright from converse intimate within,
And with that god invisible who framed
This idol scheme—the god of this our world.
In weighty tones, which of themselves entranced
The spell-bound soul, and freighted with more good,
Infused complacent joy—prospective mirth—
He gave the order of the day.

  The city traverse now. Surpassing all
Preceding or succeeding monuments
Of peopled sites, devised by wondrous skill;
Behold its lofty walls, its massive gates,
For pleasure formed, protection too from foes
That might arise. A noble river runs
Quite through the midst, where gallant ship
And swift gondola glide. Along its banks,
But terraced high, the noble mansions rise.
Thus Ham and his descendants nullify
Their Father's bitter curse: not slavery
But dominance is theirs; awhile they rule;
All things premise inverted prophecy.
And not the race of Ham alone bow down
To idol shrines: the progeny of Shem,
And Japhet too, are serving other gods.

  So flows the stream of time, but on its banks
A tent is pitched by one who on the plains
Of Ur, hard by the Chaldee pride, bowed down
To gods acknowledged there, Abram his name.
Jehovah visits there, reveals Himself, the True,

The Only One. Abram responds, obeys
The call to leave his gods, his native land,
To go whither he knew not then, content
To walk in that new light; in God's own time
To find the land that He would tell him of.
In Haran next he dwells, there sojourns long.
Has God forgotten him? Has he lost all?
Abandoned gods and kindred, wealth and friends,
To grasp some phantom good? has he resigned
Substantial things for vain uncertainties?
The father of the faithful must be tried;
The friend of God must shew himself a friend,
And trust, when trust seems vain and foolish too.
He knew God could not lie; the sterile womb
Dismayed him not. Faith deals with unseen things
As great realities; God's word alone
Suffices for impossibilities.
So Abram knew; and though Time in its flight
Bore on not only youth, but manhood in its prime,
And left a sere old age, God said, *I will.*
That was enough. Could Faith ask more than this?
But nature speaks—"How shall I know that I
Shall yet inherit this Thou speakest of?"
God condescends; a marv'lous scene occurs.
God's word is pledged, and now He adds His oath—
Two things immutable, God cannot lie.
When God's full time is come, Isaac appears,
The promised seed. The helpless babe now fills
Glad Sarah's arms, expatriates fears that thrive
In soil conditioned for their great increase.
The womb re-energized has warmed the babe;
Its burden posthumous—for it was dead—
Rebukes her unbelief, for she had laughed

Incredulous. The prattling boy recalls
The woman's fading joys: maternal blood
Flows vig'rous through her veins, with youthful strength.
The boy bounds o'er the plain, the father's hope:
The youth begins to understand the sire,
Commune with him of faith and faith's award.
"Take now thy only son, and offer him
On mount Moriah, as a sacrifice."
What words are these? and does the father hear
And live, and not expostulate, protest,
Recall to mind the word, the oath, as though
God had forgotten both; or worse, about
To break them both? Not so, his heart is fixed,
God cannot lie. The everlasting hills
May melt away, the earth dissolve, the Sun
Forbear to shine, but Isaac must endure.
How shall he reconcile th' apparent breach?
He walks by faith; faith does not reconcile
Things seen with things that do not yet appear;
Cares not to understand: yea, more than this,
Has learnt much to mistrust things visible;
And look at things unseen with sure regard.
So Abraham takes the wood, and fire, and knife:
On Isaac lays the wood: they journey on.
The father's bosom heaves with weighty thoughts,
Silent, communes with God.
  "My father," Isaac said, "behold the fire
And wood, but where's the lamb?" The father's heart
Is musing sad; for though he falters not,
Nor doubts the issue of his act, he dreads
The act itself. One greater far than he,
Whose faith had no eclipse, could not endure,
Unmoved, the presentation of that cup

Which He must drink—"If it be possible
Let this cup pass from me, yet not my will
But Thine be done:" the flesh was weak with Him,
That He might sympathize with mortal man.
So Abraham shrank, but stayed not hence his course.
"My son, God will Himself provide a lamb:"
And so they journeyed on. Three days they went
And then beheld the mount of sacrifice.
"My son, God will provide Himself a lamb,
I said; how, if thyself that lamb must be?"
"My father, thou hast taught me trust in God;
And not by word alone, thy ways sustain
All thou hast said. Thou hast made known to me
That I, thy promised seed, shall be thy heir.
God cannot lie. Thy path is clear, and mine:
Thine to obey, and mine to yield my will."
"My son; God's will, not mine, or thine, be done;
That will is good, though I should seem to mar
My own inheritance: though grief, and shame,
Dishonor too, and death, result; and hope,
With all her pleasant themes, withdraw her smile,
Faith still retains her hold on God's own word;
And hence hope too maintains her stable place.
Our act goes far indeed to quench my name;
But though my eyes behold thy ashes lie
There on the altar, raised by my own hand,
Those ashes scattered by the winds of heaven,
I reckon still that God has power to raise,
And give me yet to bear, in aged arms,
Thy seed that God shall give. It must be so:
These hills, though rooted in the earth's firm base,
May be o'erturned; the mighty sea dried up;
The very heavens remove and pass away:

But God's own word remains. In all these things,
I make my boast in God: my faith delights
To put before my God some rigorous test,
And see His solvent power reduce that test:
With God all things are possible.
Thou art thyself a miracle, my son.
Thy mother's womb was dead; thy father too
As good as dead. Conception's limit past;
Nor she, nor I, could hope t' embrace a son;
But, lo! the word—'thy wife shall have a son.'
Due time elapsed, and thou wast born: my age
Was then a hundred years, and ninety hers.
Some years had passed since God at first appeared,
And spake of blessing me in terms so plain,
That even natural sense could not mistake.
Again the Lord appeared, and with an oath
Both sealed His promise, and confirmed my faith.
Impatience ever plucks the unripe fruit;
And hence was Ishmael born, a bond-slave's son.
God changed my name, Abram to Abraham;
Thy mother's too, Sarai is Sarah now.
'Kings shall arise from thee,' God said; 'from thee
And Sarah too, thy wife.' Ere thou wast born
The Lord appeared in Mamre's plain: one day,
When sultry heat and painful stillness reigned,
Three men stood by me, sitting in my tent,
In human guise, but heav'nly visitants;
Jehovah one. Besides the promise made
Once more—thy mother being near this time—
The Lord communed with me of other things.
Towards Sodom now we bent our steps; I went
To bring them on their way; not knowing yet
That, unawares, angels had been my guests.

We paused between my tent and Sodom's gate:
Two went and entered there. Thy cousin Lot
Had pitched his tent in Jordan's fertile plain,
Towards Sodom first; at length he dwelt therein.
The Lord made known to me His awful mind
And purpose to destroy the cities of the plain.
Zoar was spared at Lot's request; I too
Made intercession, and had ten been found—
Ten righteous ones—Sodom had then escaped.
The night closed in on merry-making crowds,
And guilty revelers; the morning dawned
On embers of the fire from heaven; their smoke
Went up, a fearful token of their end.
Ere this, thy cousin Lot had made escape:
He would be rich, and honored too; so sat
In Sodom's gate. Two angels met him there,
The same that left me on the plain: Lot saw,
And bowed himself, and sought of them
To sojourn in his house; they entered there,
Immortal guests. The Sodomites soon swarm,
And make demands intensely bad, most foul.
Infatuate, they had no presentiment
Of further ill, when blindness fell on them;
For God had blinded first their minds, imbued
With most debasing lusts: they madly sought
Forgetfulness of God and all His claims:
Success was theirs; so all restraint was gone.
Lot held Sodoma's doom: whilst he remained
Within its walls, vengeance retributive
Forbore to strike. But wickedness o'erflows;
Hence Lot is urged: he seeks his sons-in-law;
Derisive, they decline t' avail themselves
Of his safe escort, for they could not leave

Their joys behind: he seemed as one who mocked.
So Lot departs: his wife and daughters, steeped
In Sodom's guile, accompany, but bear
Degenerate hearts away; still coveting
The luxe of Sodom's state; discrediting,
Or else commiserating Sodom's fate,
They, ling'ring much, withdraw. While on the way,
Lot's wife, with guilty zest and sad regret,
Looks back, and thence becomes a monument
Of pillared salt. The rest press on and gain
First Zoar, where Lot feared to dwell; then seek
The mountain's drear retreat, sad home for them."

"My father, does it not appear that more,
Than faith's assay is meant, and shadowed forth
By this our act? No murm'ring spirit prompts,
No recreant dread of pain, or vain regret
Of life so early closed, tempts me to ask.
But that my spirit teems with sentiments
Of good to thee and thine; that this precedes,
And typifies some greater sacrifice."

"It does, my son; God in His grace vouchsafes
An outline of His plan. When Adam fell,
And all in him, God first made known that one
Should bruise the serpent's head: now, couple this
With great Jehovah's words—'thee and thy seed.'
Thou art my promised seed; as such, a type
Of Him who, yet to come, shall all fulfil.
I see the day, for distant ages fixed,
When He, the woman's promised seed, shall come.
His day now dawns on my prophetic sight;
Kingdoms will rise and fall ere He appears.
God hath made known the bondage of my race;
Four hundred years to serve in some strange land;

As strangers there to know affliction's yoke:
At length t' emerge with substance, spoil of them
Who spoil. That nation God will judge; and they,
In haste, will urge them thence.
Both I and thou, my son, shall rest in peace.
This country, mine by word immutable,
Has no escheat, for no conditions clog
The covenant then made, and irreversible.
Heirs, not inheritors, we sojourn here:
The land is ours in perpetuity.
But now, as strangers here, we spend a short
Fragment'ry course of our eternal lives:
Hence thou and I must rise again, and here
Reside in youthful immortality,
That God may verify His word to me.
Ages must roll away, then he must come,
The woman's seed. Deep myst'ry here I see,
More than I can express. Thou, as His type;
And I, as bruising thee, assume the place
Of God, who bruises Him. Not man alone,
As thou; not God alone, as God.
Much I desire to know, deeply I search;
But fail to see, with apprehension clear,
The deep communings of my soul with times
Whose fulness will reveal thy antitype.
The woman's seed! mark well those words, for thou
Art seed of mine; an import deep lies here:
Suff'rings are His of more than mortal kind,
And His are glories too, resultant thence.
Yet more I see. My seed will for awhile
Retain the land, but after many years
Will fail to hold their fief. Vain-glorious, they
Will first assume a covenant of works;

Failing in this, then God will drive them hence.
A cruel bondage they will serve awhile,
Longer and fiercer than at first; then He,
Whose right it is, shall come: He will redeem
Th' enslavèd race. Then thou and I shall prove
God's words—'To thee, and after thee thy seed,
I give this land, an everlasting gift.'
I see the promises, afar, and now
Confess myself a stranger in the land."

Thus they beguile the way. A goodly sight!
Father and son alike their way pursue
With solemn mind, concordant hearts and thoughts.
No talk of flocks and herds, investment rare
T' increase their store. True, God had given much;
But he a man of faith, the friend of God,
Had not reliance on these worldly gifts,
But on his God, who richly gave them all.
And now the tragic scene assails their hearts:
The flesh is weak, they seek for strength in God;
God hears, and both confess their weakness gone.

The father binds his son—how tenderly!
With gentle hands, and throbbing, fainting heart,
He lifts and lays the unresisting one
There on the altar, which consentient hands
And hearts have built. And now he takes the knife
To slay his son. Enough: his God demands
No more, and stays his hand: "for now," said He,
"I know thou fearest God, for thou hast not
Withheld thy son, thy only son, from Me.
Thy seed shall be e'en as the stars of Heaven,
And as the sand upon the ocean's shore."

"My thoughts are not as yours," says God, "my ways
Not yours." At forty Isaac finds a wife,

But not a son. Years glide along, and hope
Forbears to smile. When twenty years have sped,
And hope deferred feels sick'ning at the heart—
For nature's limit is just reached—behold!
The quick'ning womb conceives th' expected birth,
And in due time the twins appear. With joy,
The grandsire's arms receive the precious freight;
His long-tried faith gives place to sight; so all
The objects of his life are met: he still survives
For fifteen years, and then departs in faith.
    Now Isaac's hope through Jacob flows: his faith
Rests firm in God, and much he needs His grace;
For eighty years elapse ere Jacob gives
A sign of hope fulfilled. In foreign lands
He sojourned twenty years, and then returned
With many sons; eleven in exile born,
One on the way, a daughter too: with these
He gladdens Isaac's heart, who thence enjoys,
For thirty years, the travail of his soul,
And then departs in peace. But ere he dies,
Full thirteen years, the charm of Jacob's life,
His Rachel's son is snatched away by stealth,
And sold, a bond-slave; first to serve as such,
And then to rule the land. Now here behold
God's will and man's self-will combined—God's will,
As seen in kind prevenient care; and man's,
As seen in mood and act, intolerant,
Of patriarchal spite. Thus man's self-will
God's purpose served, and wrought His will; while they,
With envy moved, evolved their guilt in vain.
As man 'gainst man stands up, his ruin plots;
By schemes and circumvention keen outwits,
And glories in his shame of deep-laid craft

And subtle guile, secures ofttimes defeat
Of his own plans; with this th' accomplishment
Of all he dreads and shuns; so Joseph foils,
Unwittingly, their maddened aim; and they,
Unwittingly, secure the thing they fear.
Their guilt remains, though they have wrought God's will.
God makes the wrath of man educe His praise,
Restrains it too; makes record of his act,
And writes him rebel to His righteous will.

   Must he who ruled almost with regal power
Be first a bond-slave; falsely charged, then pine,
And waste his youth in penal cells? Just so.
How inaccessible is God to man,
If he draws near in human excellence!
Wisdom is folly then, God's ways appear
Outrageous quite; and so indeed they are,
Judged in the light of this our prurient day.
But would man humbly learn and lowly seek,
This would he find—humility precedes
The honor God bestows; and trials lead
To safe prosperity. The time is come:
Now Pharaoh has recourse to one unknown
In courtly halls; yet in the courts above
Renowned, as one Jehovah has delight
To own and much distinguish by His grace.
Pharaoh has visions of the night; he seeks
The aid of those who claim—not wholly false—
The power to penetrate the future's gloom.
But One has crossed their path, who blights their power,
Arrests their wizard gaze, divests them quite
Of skill oracular, suffered by Him
To serve awhile His purposes; immediately
Dispensed by one who ruled at Delphi,

Delos, and elsewhere: imposing much
His tolerated craft, to blind the minds
Of those who willingly believed his lies;—
Lies in the main, not always such, for when
Truth served him better to illude and fix
More duringly his bonds, th' unwonted shift
Had favor at his hands—he spoke the truth.
Time speeds along; Israel have served their term,
They must be free; so Israel's God demands.
Pharaoh demurs—Who is Jehovah then
That I should let the people go?
Nay, let the bonds press tighter yet; forbear
To give them straw, exact the same amount
Of labor at their hands. Will he provoke
Jehovah's power, th' unequal contest wage,
Measure his strength with Israel's God?
Demented quite, defiant rage invites
God's outstretched arm. Blood mocks the craving throat;
Frogs croak and everywhere prevail; the dust
Supplies, in turn, a scourge, hence lice abound;
Then swarms of flying things invade the land;
The favored race alone exempt, so fenced
By God Himself; a murrain next appears,
And desolates their herds; not one succumbs
Of Israel's stock; then boils and putrid sores
Afflict both man and beast; and grievous hail,
Surpassing all since Egypt had a name;
Fire mingled with the hail smote every tree,
And herb, and man, and beast throughout the land;
Goshen again was spared, where Israel dwelt.
Then in the air is heard a rustling sound,
Portentous, troubling much their frighted hearts;
Squadrons detached reveal a sudden gleam

Of intercepted light, and by that light
Intelligence is borne to them appalled;
A locust band unparalleled is there.
And has.the sun forgot to shine ? 'Tis morn,
And yet no light; a solid darkness seems
To shut them in; deep preternatural gloom
Prevails three days. Does Pharaoh yet persist,
An unconvinced spectator of these things ?
No; "I have sinned against the Lord and you."
Respite begets presumptuousness: again,
The heart, elate with pride, repudiates
All conference; with surly threats, he drives
The man of God away—"Now see my face no more."
Felt darkness shrouds the land; 'tis midnight now,
A wail is heard, a bitter cry is raised—
"My child is dead, my first-born child is dead!"
Does echo mock the wail a thousand fold ?
Does Egypt's heir lie stiff, a lifeless hope ?
In every house death thus discriminates.
Enough; e'en Pharaoh's heart—nay, not his heart—
His spirit yields. God's people gather spoil;
Reprisal just, not robbery, but such repaired:
They take their final leave. But how is this,
For they have sojourned there just half the time
Proposed by God at first? Art thou disposed
To understand or cavil at the seeming mark
Of incongruity? The Scriptures shew
How thou may'st understand, but leave thee still
An avenue of doubt. The learned man
Has found much trouble, much ado to rein
And curb his exegesis by the laws
Which there prevail. This point, though clear to some,
To him is cloudy still; for, truth to say,

The terms are strong and positive; not so,
Except to faith, the explication made.
When God announced to Abraham His will
That his posterity should sojourn in a land
That was not theirs, He reckoned from this time
In which He spake; and so one half had passed
When Jacob went to see his son. That the whole time
Is braced between the covenant at first
And Israel's exodus, is plainly taught;
"For this I say, the covenant confirmed
Of God in Christ before, the law has not
The power to disannul—the law announced
Four hundred years and thirty afterwards."
   Behold th' enfranchised hosts near Egypt's sea,
Hemmed in by mountains on their right and left,
And Migdol in their rear, Baal-zephon too.
"How now? Is this the way to take? Is time
So lavish, that we're come to view the coast,
Disport awhile, and then turn back again?
Is food so plentiful that we may eat and drink,
And gather at our ease indefinite?
Is Pharaoh so oblivious of the use
He made of these our limbs, to let us go
And roam at leisure where we will, and not,
In much regret, our re-commitment try?"
"Be not afraid," said Moses, "and forbear
To judge your God: nor shortened is His arm,
Nor dull His ear. Do you so soon forget
His mighty works? Is aught too hard for Him?
He works by rule above our skill to read."
   Alarm invades the host, for tidings spread
Of Pharaoh's blast and eager shout, as he
Beholds them now entangled near the sea.

"The wilderness has hemmed them in," said he,
"Not yet escaped, they'll serve us yet."
　Now faith can calmly gaze, can ponder well,
And weigh the accidents, and yet rejoice.
Who made the sea? Who made the lofty rocks?
Jehovah, who has brought His people there.
Faith walks the sea, or cleaves it for a path,
Or wrenches from their base the mighty hills.
The murm'ring host upbraid—"so did we say,
And tell thee, Moses, ere we left; and urged:—
'We know the worst, now let us perish here,
And not provoke the wilderness to bleach our bones.'"
"Fear not," then Moses said, "but stand ye still;
Jehovah sees, and ye shall see as well,
How He can work. The Lord shall fight, and ye
Shall hold your peace."
　"Now lift thy rod," said God, "stretch out thy hand,
Divide the sea; My people then shall pass
Dry shod, quite through its very midst."
Faith lifts the rod, the conscious sea divides,
Glad Israel presses on th' unwonted path.
Pharaoh, insensate, slackens not, nor stays
His keen pursuit. Faith lifts the rod again,
The sea beheld and fled: in heaps congealed,
Now to its strength returns. Can Israel doubt;
Or any more withhold credence entire?
Alas! the flesh has just begun to give
Its evidence; to serve its term at large;
Conditioned with a law, statutes not good,
But in themselves; weak, through the flesh, to which
They minister: results of this appear
Throughout the history of Abraham's seed.
Bad, wholly bad, and utterly undone;

And so God wills a way more excellent,
And which indeed it dimly predicates.
   And where is Pharaoh now, his chivalry,
His crowding hosts, his haughty tramp, his might,
His excellence? The depths have covered them,
Sunk to the bottom as a stone: Jehovah's blast
Prevailed; they sank as lead, no more to rise.
Now take the timbrel, dance with ecstasy.
Israel, behold your foes there on the shore:
See, handle them; no more your dread; dead, dead.
Now shout again; ye're free, and can ye doubt,
Now lifeless bodies strew the shore for you?
Within three days they, faithless, doubt again.
No miracles persuade man's heart of truth:
A lie needs scant support; and why is this?
If man is true at heart, as some aver,
Then surely all would much prefer the truth.
As fallen, all good is lost and evil reigns.
If Israel needed more than desert food,
Then why not ask? God loves our confidence,
Delights to grant the much assured request;
Encourages the timid suppliant,
Approves the bold approach when wisely made.
The evils we most shun are those most near;
The good we most desire is further off.
So Israel calls to mind Egyptian fare,
Compares it with the wilderness' supply;
Despises this, desiderates the same
That bondage soured. What made the wilderness
Less than a home to them? What moved their hearts
T' appoint a captain who might lead them back? *
What made their present good an ill; their ills,

* Nehemiah ix. 17.

Which they had left, unthought of? Unbelief.
Consider now their case; for they are set
For our example, lest we lust as they.
We underrate the desert life these led:
Privations great were theirs; no water near
To satisfy their thirst; no bread to eat.
Their flocks and herds alone remained as food;
And these would not suffice a lengthened time.
How should they do? The manna could not meet
The cravings of the host. One article of food
Their constant fare, water their only drink!
Consider this, ye epicures, whom dainty bits,
Culled from the num'rous viands of your lot,
Alone can satisfy, nor always these.
Contrast your case with theirs: their sin and yours
Are much coincident; indulgence yours
Denied to them; but discontent was theirs
With some apology, and yours with none.
Who claims contentment, who the quiet mind?
The millionaire? His zest gains by success:
His need of daily bread at first is changed
To need of daily gain; on this he lives:
A mind diseased craves this of him.
Content is not supineness, though alike
In freedom from sharp-visaged care:
The one desires no more than what it has;
The other dreads exertion, so puts up
With meagre fare. Well then, are none content?
Is it a phantom name? And does it tell
Only of what should be, and not what is?
Was Moses not content, and Aaron too,
Were Miriam and others of that host?
A few, a very few. And are there not,

In this our day, great multitudes who own
Jehovah, God, and call Him Father too,
Content with what they have? A very few.
Not all who trust a Savior's blood, can trust
A Father's love, His wisdom, and His care.
But as of old, when money fails, and bread
Is getting low, the murm'ring heart complains.
The nice observer of God's ways can see
His ordering in the deepest poverty,
In stern adversity; and apprehend
How abject need may sing its quiet song,
And gross abundance sigh its good away.
The one, who every comfort owns, shudders
To think how he should do with frugal board,
And straitened means; and wonders much to find
His neighbor lives on half as much as he.
This reas'ning man but half believes God's word;
He wholly trusts himself, that he can tell
What suits him best; but missing this, he frets.
For is it not a law conventional
That poverty's a crime, and wealth a sign
Of excellence? He truly is content,
Who always trusts in God that He knows best
To portion him good things; and who has learnt
How to abound, and how to suffer need.
   Israel profane had perished to a man,
But Moses prays the prayer of faith, and pleads
God's holy name. No selfish heart preferred
That prayer, or he had failed. He passes by,
Unnoticed, God's design, to make of him
A nation greater, mightier than they.
God's honor only could he see, and hence
His power with God. They, ingrate, reap

The fruit of murm'ring lips: "would God," said they,
"We in this wilderness had died!" God heard
And judged them so, for there they fell—all they
Who, having seen God's ways, believed Him not.
Moses as well; he, through their sin, provoked
The wrath of God. "Ye rebels, must we bring
More water from the rock?" he smote it twice,
And so he damaged then the sacred type;
That rock was Christ. The law had smitten once,
That law impersonate now smites again:
So Moses mars his title to the land.
Could he—the law personified—possess
The promised land? The law no promise gives,
But grace secures the good. Moses, as law,
Is barred; for "if the law be heir, then faith
Is void, the promise made of no effect."
Moses was thus disqualified; but yet
His *sin* excluded him; and so he dies
On Pisgah's top; thence views the promised land,
And then departs in confidence of hope.
Now Joshua, Savior, leads the people on;
Faith cleaves the interposing stream; they pass
Dry shod, and enter into promised rest.

And is it rest that Israel finds? Ere this,
The warrior's cry, the tocsin's shrilly sound,
The flashing sword, the ambuscade, the siege,
The breach, the sanguine strife, the wail of woe,
The victor's shout, deep streams of blood, the moan,
The shudd'ring gasp of death, *must be.*
Why must it be? God wills it so. Now hear,
Ye advocates of peace, for what have you
To do with peace? For such as you who hold,
With fervid grasp, your sins, your worldly aims,

Your rank concupiscence, peace is not yours;
But war—war to the death. Your chief is he
Who is a murderer; nor can he frame,
Nor can you advocate true peace: he has
The power of death, and when he most parades
The show of peace, then grows the deadliest war.
Peace there will be; but He who has His name
The Prince of Peace, rides forth A MAN of war.
Just so; as Captain of their host He came,
Marshaled their ranks, detailed the plan of siege,
Foretold the issue of th' assault, forbad
Appropriation of the spoil, and saved
The harlot Rahab through her faith.
Alas, for them! the wedge of gold was there,
The Babylonish garment, silver too
Of glitt'ring white; for man's cupidity
Too much! the secret spoil of one all rued,
For all had sinned; not in the act perhaps,
But in the heart; and they now stood on ground
E'er imminent, for they had late engaged
To serve the Lord. Time speeds its early course,
And judges rule till Samuel's ministry.
The rule was not republican, nor democrat,
But theocratic, God Himself their King.
Of this they tired, from Samuel sought a change,
"That we may be like all the nations round."
What will not Fashion do! Jehovah spurn,
Dethrone Him for some mortal man—some man
To lead them to their wars, their battles fight.
Had Jericho and Ai, Bethel, Dor,
And Makkedah, the Hittites, Amorites,
The Canaanites, the Perizzites, the Jebusites,
And Hivites with their kings, thirty and one,

Giv'n this advice? What prompted them to this?
Oh! it was Fashion, and the present smart
Of Samuel's sons. What folly that an ill
Of momentary date—a passing grief—
Should urge us to an ill most permanent!
Yet so it is; we flatter much our hearts
That good is yet attainable, and seek
The good without alloy: to our chagrin
We find an evil unassayed, that galls much more.
God in His anger gave a king, in wrath
He took their king away. The time would fail
To speak of David, Solomon, their line
Illustrious. Eight hundred years, or more,
They weary God, until at length He turned
To be their enemy. In Babylon
They serve for seventy years. Short-sighted man!
And dost thou think, because thy righteous God,
In much long suff'ring, seems to tolerate
Thy foul neglect of His most stringent law,
He will not yet exact the utmost doit?
He will. Hundreds of years' contumely
Must be atoned for in proud Babylon.
Here they had crowding leisure to adore
Idolatry. Were they confirmed by this
Close-sighted view? Oh no! see Rome at Rome,
If you would see the very thing; and then
Pronounce your preference. A hideous form,
Foreshortened, may conceal its hideousness.
A brilliant ground may even recommend
Some gloomy shade. A casual dalliance
Commends the harlot's charms; to dwell with her
Is hell itself. The quiet of a home
Is varied charmingly by childish noise.

An acid makes a sweet a sweeter still.
Among these sickened captives Daniel shines,
Greatly beloved of God, admired by men.
In visions of the night, God shews to him
Things yet to come, unveils the future to his gaze.
Israel had ceased to be God's sceptred race;
The first dominion rules at Babylon.
The royal despot has a dream; he sees
An image great and terrible; its head
Of gold; silver its breast and arms; and brass
Its belly and its thighs; its legs were iron;
Its feet a part of iron, a part of clay.
A stone assails it in its complex strength,
Aims at the feet, and thus predicts the blow
At some yet future monarchy—some one,
Uniting in a whole, the head of gold,
The silvery breast, the brazen paunch and thighs,
The feet of iron and clay. What is that stone?
Is it, as most suppose, Messiah's self,
Or Ephraim, as Israel's synonym,
God's battle-axe, to rend the nations' crown?
This phantom image had an import deep
In man's affairs; and God's, through man.
Four empires were prefigured by its parts;
Its substance, products of earth's chemistry,
Of common origin, a common fate partake.
The Babylonish, Medo-Persian, Greek,
All owned of God, as having sovereign sway,
Have spent their terms and waned—yea, they have waned,
But not entirely sunk in Time's great sea,
No more to come to land. The chol'ric goat,
Great Grecia's king, the great horn notable,
Had four horns notable as well, in place

Of that which hurled the ram, the Persian king,
Prone on the ground: these indicate a power
Quadripartite; and in its latter time,
And in the line of one of these, shall rise
A king fierce countenanced, and skilled to know
And understand speech enigmatical;
Self-willed, vain-glorious, high above all else,
And aiming e'en above the God of gods.
Fierce dinotherium, strong exceedingly,
With iron teeth symbolical, diverse
From all before. Rome does not ratify
This symbol now, though it may yet fulfil
The more than mortal type. O rampant beast,
With semblance nondescript! no peer of thee
Has yet appeared. But does th' horizon gleam
With thy still distant ray, thy lurid glare?
E'en now the nations pale, as they surmise
They know not what. Thy glorious reign is short,
But terrible: thy rule most absolute.
Wide thy domain, beyond all former rule.
As king of kings, thy blazonry puts out
All minor spheres of power, beside thy own.
The dragon's time is near; when that is come,
No longer will restraint by him, as now,
Conceal thy full proportions, well-endowed
And meted for his need. He occupies,
As yet, his place, the very midst, th' highway
Betwixt the heaven and earth, by him defiled.
The time is imminent when he will dare
The might of Michael's arm, His prowess prove,
Confront th' Archangel's host with his,
Discomfited, in shameful rout will seek
Earth's woeful plains, with deep malicious rage;

There, standing on the sea's great troubled sands,
He calls up thence, and from th' abyss of Hell,
The agent of his will, till now restrained by him.
This man, the Antichrist, his protegé,
Combines, with subtle art and royal state,
The Leopard's beauteous symmetry and guile;
Leonine majesty; as well the grasp
Of ursine strength. To such the Dragon gives
His throne, his power and great authority.
Here Greece predominates: the lion's head
Predicts great Babylon; the ursine paws
Assert the Medo-Persian dynasty.
To him, as Satan's delegate, the world
Will gladly turn; prostrate, adore their King.
Yet more he claims to be; nor claims amiss,
If more than human power substantiates
This more than human right; for he, a man,
In Satan's energy, with marv'lous signs
And wonders of a lie, confirms his claims;
He calls the heavens to witness, and they give
Tokens confirmative, ethereal fire.
The earth attestive sings his praise; for God,
Retributive, hath put it in the hearts
Of kings decemviral to own his sway.

   So peace prevails, and all has promise now
Of joy unchecked, and happiest times for all.
The lie is much accredited that he,
Who in the earliest times assayed to give
The World, bereft of good, its joyous night,
Cut short in his career by one who had,
At first, brought desperate evil on his race;
Now in due time should, by the potent help
Of one opposed to their great enemy,

Return from exile, ill-endured, to those
Whose earthly good his heart is set upon.
His deadly wound is healed—great evidence
Of what he suffered at the hostile hands
Of him who viewed, with jealousy, his aim
T' emancipate mankind; an evidence
That he had died on their behalf, and now
Has burst the bands of death. The scar remains
Demonstrative: to this, God adds His power,
By sending strong delusion, so that they,
Blinded judicially, believe the lie.
Who, unadvised, when looking at the form,
Quiescent, of the Leopard, could premise
Its awful deadly spring, its fatal guile?
So th' antitype of this rapacious beast
Will charm and lull all fears. His calm repose
Amidst the strife of elemental war;
His disavowal of malevolence;
His elegance in arts of peace, yet competence
In warlike schemes—where these, in fair pretence,
Subserve the general good—will gain him trust,
And time to maturate his deep-laid plot
Of universal power and sovereign rule.

Let busy thought anticipate, and shew
The revelation of this lawless one.
Behold him then a king. Endowments rare,
Unparalleled, are his. All that can charm
Yet subjugate: a despot in intent;
In mode and circumstance gentle to all.
Adept in plotting, wary, solving well
The problem how to reconcile a rule
Most tyrannous, with freedom unrestrained.
Proficient in the art of seeming fair,

Th' exterior guise conceals the fires within.
Ambition there has reared its glowing shrine,
Acknowledges a god, who ere this sought
A man of Galilee, placed at his feet
The glories of this world, but worship claimed.
Resplendent terms, dazzling to human sight,
But insufficient for one more than man.
Confounded thus he fled, quelled by the word,
The written word of God, the Spirit's sword.
Now circumstances favor his attempt;
The times beget the man; his element,
The mystery of iniquity, abounds
Intensive, teems with reeking, rank, foul growth,
Conducive to his full development;
And so the seeker seeks not now in vain.
This latter—name now reprobate—ere long
Will change the current of men's thoughts: though once
The cruel plotter of the primal fall,
A branded liar, murderer, and foe
Of God and man; this very ill will seem
Only defeated good, and all man's good
The veriest ill; and he himself confessed
The principle of good. *   Thus recognized,
He manifests himself incarned in him,

* This is no fancy. The Gnostics taught that the God of the Jews is an evil being—this is one step. Teitan, or Satan was the supreme object of worship in the Chaldean mysteries. Tatan-en, that is "Tatan incarnate," was the pre-eminent divinity in Egypt. Some heretics in the early church worshiped Satan, as the benefactor of mankind. Lastly; the Dragon, the symbol of Satan, was worshiped to comparatively recent times, by the Romanists of Poictiers, under the name of "The good St. Vermine." So too St. Swithin is just St. Satan, for another form Sythan became in Anglo-Saxon hands Swythan and Swithin; and the forty days' rain has a traditional connection with the flood; Noah being identified with Tammuz, and Tammuz as Satan incarnate.

L

Who has already well sustained some claims
Of more than usual magnitude; and him,
Not a mere man, he now inaugurates—
Him and his rule, with prodigies, portents
Of power; conclusive, damning evidence.
All nations own him arbiter; yea, kings
Refer their strength and power to him.
What majesty! all own his gifts supreme.
What dignity! he walks a king confest.
What suavity! he heeds the lowliest cause.
What graceful bend to those of low estate!
Though high, surpassing all, the lowliest one
Feels not his low estate; no jealousy
Of favored names, of courtier garb, of rank,
Sours e'en the meanest satellite, that he,
Recalcitrant, should plot rebelliously.
Nations, oppressed by despot rule, in him
Find refuge, and bespeak his powerful aid:
He rends the iron chain, the captive frees.
To patriots, rotting in the loathsome keep,
He brings glad liberty: a despot, yet,
By subtle art, making much show of good:—
And good it is, did no reserve exist
In plots, not yet revealed, of ultimate designs.
War is not countenanced but as a means,
A *via recta*, to an end. Tyrants before
Have based their tyranny on sighs, on tears,
On prison bars, on cruelly crushed hopes,
On seared hearts, on fortunes wrecked, on crimes
Which minions only could abet, and troops defend.
This man, the idol of all hearts, prevails
To meet the need of man: a god professed,
Acknowledged, he has power, or real, or feigned;

And not the less allowed by men bewitched,
Because pretentious claims enforce demands.
Behold his retinue! himself a god
Incarnate, fiends incarnate form his train.
One Lord; for all have now withdrawn their claims.
One faith; for he has now propounded laws
And doctrines suited to the taste of all.
" As many men, so many creeds," has ceased
To be a liberal boast. Divisions, strifes,
Religious feuds, are brands to stigmatize
The faith once held. Religion of the heart—
Man's heart—absorbs all creeds; a crucible,
Heated with hell's own fire, resolves the whole.
No jarring dogma perils unity;
No rival claims of uncorrupted truth;
No fussy sects professing jealous care,
And watchful guardianship of doctrines pure;
But unity in name, in spirit, sways
The leavened mass. The golden age is come;
Joy fills man's heart, for He appears, God-man,
So long predicted, wise, and having power
To banish discord; things that differ frame
In reconcilement; order fix; proclaim
A brotherhood; acknowledged ills remove;
Deep wrongs redress; transmute the face of things.
Thus wine may still exhilarate, but not debase;
Beauty may still allure, man own its sway,
Indulgence give, but not th' excess that breeds
Sheer infamy and hopeless downwardness.
Foul slavery is changed, the manifest
For that not seen nor felt. And why not have
What nature craves; so self-denial spurn
And thus avoid an obloquy, that brought

Hate and rejection of the former faith?
One seat of government, one code of laws.
One badge for high and low, for rich and poor,
The forehead or the dexter hand receives;
Attesting joyous servitude in all.
Churches and chapels still receive their crowds,
Of earnest worshipers; the pulpit still
Shuts in a staunch declamatist, who paints
The glories of the present state foretold.
But many vacant seats await in vain
Their wonted occupants: enquiries made
Elicit no response of truth; though some can tell—
For they had heard the hope expressed—none say:
The vacancy is ominous—a knell,
A muffled whisper of their settled doom.

 A city worthy of the king is reared,
Metropolis unique; its splendor shines,
Through adamantine walls of tow'ring height,
Translucent. Nature sometimes shews her skill
In forming this material for her use;
Now, art elaborate and spirit-craft
Survey elate their rising monument.
Twelve gates the glitt'ring sameness breaks,
Each honored by a name of royal fame;
But one, with more than common regal pomp,
Admits the pseudo-prophet of the king.
Ten kings their honor bring and enter there,
Each at his gate appropriate: gold forms
Their substance, rich inlaid with precious stones.
One gate surpasses all; a single pearl
Enchased in gold, subtends a lofty arch
Of roomy span. Nature has not supplied
This peerless gem, but alchymy occult

And demon-forge. This gorgeous gate is reached
By masonry of marble steps prolonged;
And on the obverse side the same decline.
A plinth of gold surmounts the arch; on this
An image stands of him who enters there,
The world's great king. Mysterious skill has wrought
This faithful semblance of the city's lord.
In startling tones the image speaks, gives forth
Amazing utt'rances; avows its claims,
Commands the bended knee, th' uncovered head,
Or death's sore penalty. Imbruted man
This tribute pays; and yet not all: some few
Are faithful found; refrain, midst faithless crowds,
This fatal step: swift death their recompence.
No schism here is borne; intolerant,
The falchion smites with keen-set promptitude.
Within unearthly glory shines; a glow
Unearthly there pervades all breasts, surcharged
With ardor unrepressed by any law
Adversative. Their native passions speed
A normal course. Restraints, imposed by God,
And ratified by man, no longer owned,
Withdraw their claim. Mad revels now delight
The giddy herd, inflamed by devils who,
Unchecked, have found welcome and clear access
To all the chambers of the heart prepared.

But where is he who reigns lord paramount?
By magic power his throne is now advanced
Above the clouds, above the stars of God
In seeming height, as if these lamps of night
Had hastened down to meet his royal state:
Like the Most High he makes supernal show.
The gazing crowd, admiring, fondly hail

The coming man, now come, to give glad rest,
And full release from pressing ills; confer
A lasting peace, perennial flow of joy,
To interweave their good in every realm.
No adverse tide repels this prosperous flow;
Awhile it holds its course, and amplifies
The sun-clad day. One like themselves men hail,
But more than man, as energized by power
Survening his, with damning evidence
Of rightful place in him who claims; and them
Who, worshiping, confirm all he demands.
So speeds the time; by day the revel holds,
By night repose avails to gather strength
For repetition foul of orgies gross;
Or gorgeous show, and pomp, and revelry.
The glitt'ring mask maintains its pleasing power,
With promise ever fair of lengthened bout.
E'en Death has signed a covenant to spare,
Awhile forego his claim, withdraw his dread:
In league with him who has the power of death,
And them who break the covenant of life.
No dread of disannulling power invades
Their madly merry hearts; they gather now
The joys of ages past, distilled by him
Who cares to satisfy their carnal taste.

So linger on the days of heedless joy
And pleasure unrebuked: the king above
Beholds the abject city right beneath,
Rejoicing in his rule: they, cased within
The adamantine walls, behold their king
And shout his praise. A lengthened vista lies
Outstretched, devised by fancy's power—sustained
By all that eye beholds, that ear receives—

Of life composed and furnished with all good.
Did miracles attest the mission from above
Of Him of Nazareth? To unchanged hearts
His holy life and stern rebuke supplied
A bitter negative. Not so this man;
Both Jew and Gentile bow the knee to Him,
Messiah's claims award; and he, in turn,
Administers no curb to all their lusts.
Their cup is filled; at leisure they repose
And quaff its luscious wine, the wine expressed
From clusters of the vine, now fully ripe.
Is he deceived who sits above this rout?
The summit thus is gained; awhile he rests
Well satisfied; ambition's aim is reached.
Man's day now beams with all its light; his sun,
Resplendent, gains meridian height, reveals
Resources hid till now; and all believe
The golden age has come; not now, as once,
A fleeting good, just shewn, then snatched away.
Alas, poor man! thou art the piteous sport
Of tyranny and hate. The show is good,
But Death grins harshly at thy side: e'en now,
When joy, hilarity, and health robust,
Course through thy veins, Death shakes his cruel dart;
Forbears to strike, not pitying, nor loath:
But when thy flutt'ring heart is confident
Of pleasure unassailable, and ill,
Transmuted, is installed a good,
Then will his ruthless aim transfix thy hopes.
Peace, peace! thronged halls and avenues,
And crowded streets, highways, and theatres,
And concert-rooms, the ploughman's whistled glee,
The sower's hymn of praise, the reaper's song,

Have for their joyous key-note—PEACE.
Peace is their melody, Peace their refrain:
Peace flutters in the breeze, Peace sails the main.
Peace, peace reverberates, and Echo swells
The Io Pæan of the times.
  O fearful interruption of these joys!
A light, surpassing far the mid-day sun
In more than seven-fold splendor, lights the scene.
The hearts of all are chilled, they eye their chief;
He quails not, but descends in graceful mood,
For gravity suspends its law for him,
Through magic art. He greets the trembling crowd,
Assures their hearts; assuages fears and dread
Of unknown ills. Now he in royal state
His palace seeks; a gorgeous spectacle—
A massive pile, and yet proportioned fair;
Of height so vast, that to the wond'ring eye,
It seems of airy build. Vast colonnades,
Of dizzy height, sustain the shelving roof
Of virgin gold; a promenade projects
Its crystal floor, and tops th' imposing flight
Of pure white steps—a graduate pyramid,
Crowned with the wonder of the world.
Within, a throne not readily described;
Earth has not yet revealed, nor art conceived,
Its substance and its form. The eye is pleased,
The ear is filled with sounds forth issuing thence,
Low dulcet strains, susurrus soft, as though
Spirits there find, commercing intimate,
More than mute interchange of thought.
A perfume too, as though of condiment
Prepared by cunning art, pervading thence
The edifice immense. Of varying form,

As if of spirit mould, the throne assumes
Successive change, as though not permanent;
Yet firmly fixed, held by demoniac power.
Fresh marvels wrought compose the public mind;
And artful imitation there within
Of that which glares without, dispels all fear.
Day after day this light remains: at length
They view it as a common thing; relapse,
With all its aggravated ills, succeeds;
Light-heartedness returns; fatal repose.
The phantom throne above has disappeared;
This too the arch-deceiver reconciles
With future purposes: his fertile skill
Turns to account this first of overthrows.
Again the pleasure-seeking crowd, immersed,
Enjoy the passing hour. All care is hushed:
Gay revelry abounds—the whirling dance,
The showy train with pompous pageantry,
Voluptuous chords attuned to charmèd ears;
A fated gladness wraps the sodden heart,
And pleased oblivion's dream holds on its course.
A shout now rends the sky; th' Archangel's voice
Appals all hearts; the city shakes; the frightened crowd
Demand the cause. Again their wily chief,
With air composed, but much misgiving heart,
Ascribes it to his god and theirs; to test
Their trusting hearts, and make some further show
Of what must come—his contest with their foe.
E'en while he speaks, the trump of God removes
All doubt; for, with the lengthened blast,
Bright, in the clouds of heaven, with flaming fire,
Appears that MAN, who owns the throne of heaven.
    But stay: look back; another aspect view

Of this most wilful king's misgovernment.
Gentiles admit his claim, all bow the knee;
The Jewish nation too receive as King,
This "idol shepherd,"* who was once foretold
By that rejected One, their lawful Prince,
As he who yet should come in his own name;
"And him," said He, "ye will receive."
A few are faithful found, a little band;
All else are ardent partisans; forsake,
For him, the ancient covenant, remit
The sacrifice, and in the temple set
The foul abomination that the king suggests.
Others "do valiantly," reject his claims,
Defy his power, oppose his impious lies.
No parleying here; yet does he still conserve
His courtly guise and show of gentleness;
He needs no more: the brethren of the few
Who brave his rage, display a deadly hate;
Apostates, persecute: and who, as they,
Vile renegades, can frame the cruel death?
The vengeful sword, slow torturing fires, lone chains
Clanking across the dank cold dungeon's floor,
Whose walls drip as though weeping sympathy
With captive sighs. The furnace, heated not
In hasty rage, but by deliberate hate,
Ensures a ling'ring residence. The stake,
With all appliances for speedy death,
Is duly shunned; the ring and bolt secure
The hapless victim; and the fires around
Glaring with cruel leisure, scorching, breathe
Remorseless on the fainting victim there.
A writhing form bristles with poisoned barbs,

* Zech. xi. 17.

Venomed with subtile power to fire the veins,
Pollute the fountain, slowly permeate
The burning frame; conduct grim, ruthless Death
Through avenues remotely to the goal,
Which he would reach much sooner, but that they
Retard his more commiserating aim.
The head, compressed, throbs in a metal sphere:
With cool precision nice, its power is watched
T' adjust the finest mark; to agonize,
Yet shun excess, in which the soul might find
Unmeant deliverance; the body rest.

   Seek now Jerusalem, the holy place
In God's intent, the city of the King,
The great I AM. Sodom and Egypt now
Habilitate their names in that fair place
Debased at this set time with bitter wrong,
Unprecedented ill. There spirits lost,
There unclean rites, there crimes yet unannounced,
Abound with loathsome virulence; the times,
In kind and measure, once foretold by Him
Who wept o'er Salem's doom, now culminate.
Another there usurps His place; disciples foul
Mimic His state, but not in lowliness
As He once held. Follow the drunken crowd,
Inebriate with Sodom's wine. Great Babylon
Has filled her cup; the nations of the earth
Have drunk; Jerusalem as well is steeped
In filthiness. Praises resound, and shouts
Of revelry, the noise of them that sing.
Mad Bacchanals, voluptuous forms, leap high;
Actors entranced, enchanted crowds, sweep by.
The temple now is gained: there high enthroned
Is he who, baited with the promise of all good,

Ensnares unwary ones; and he himself
Is netted in the hellish gossamer
Of pride and worldly glare. There now he sits
In courteous state: the summit reached, smiling,
He welcomes all; receives their eager vows
Of loyalty, of faithfulness, of love:—
Yea, love; the world will love its own; a kind
Dissimilar to that which warms the heart
Of patriots, parents, children, husbands, wives;
But yet most potent, for it welds the whole,
And of discordance makes accord.
Meanwhile, as hitherto, two witnesses
Protest against these things, and testify
God's righteousness, and His award for such.
Their term—twelve hundred threescore days—
Has run its course. Till now invulnerable,
They fall before the might of him who boasts
Power irresistible. Who shall make war,
The people say, with him who quells all rise,
All turbulence; who greets all appetence
Adverse to his, with secular affront;
All opposition to his despot will,
With speedy death. Now in the street are thrown
The bodies of these two, who in their days
Of testimony held their enemies at bay.
Fire waited on their word to scorch; the heavens
Were shut at their command, rain was restrained;
Waters were turned to blood; and other plagues
As they might will, burst forth. Their sackcloth garb
Provoked derision first, hatred ensued, and fear:
Now merry-making takes their place, for they
Are still in death. As many years as bore
The loathèd freight of protestation urged

With holy zeal, so many days they lie,
The scorn of all, in that great city where
The Lord was crucified: but after that,
They stand upon their feet; life animates
The martyred forms; they scale the heights of heaven;
Their enemies behold. An earthquake decimates
The city's frame; engulphs seven thousand men;
The rest give glory to the God of Heaven.
 Another aspect of these times observe—
The opening of the seals. No man was found
Worthy of this. The Lion-Lamb prevailed.
The first is broached; then a white horse goes forth,
His rider crowned, and in his hand a bow;
Almighty conqu'ror yet to wear the crowns
Of those despoiled. The second seal reveals
A horse of sanguine hue, precursor sad
Of rest disturbed: the rider wears a sword,
An emblem of his work. The third presents
An ebon steed: there follow in his track
Gaunt famine, lamentation, woe: the hands
Of him who rides hold balances; and these
Premise God's righteousness: although He smites
The nations with his rod, He yet preserves
The wine and oil for those who fear His name.
"The wine that maketh glad man's heart, and oil
That makes his face to shine."
The fourth seal shews a horse of sickly hue,
His rider Death. A horrid train attends
The monarch of the tomb. There Hades spumes
Its loathsome guests—scorpions of hideous form,
Subhuman; dragon-shapes, engendered where
Hot darkness broods, and rears a progeny
Of livid things, abhorrent spectacles,

To greet th' avertent view of men—men who,
Ere this, preferred the darkness of the pit,
When modified with Satan's potent skill.
The fifth seal manifests expectant souls
Awaiting God's full time, retributive;
Hence they are Jewish martyrs manifest.
The sixth seal introduces woe to man,
The day of God.   Heaven weeps its glist'ning tears,
Then rolls away as if in dread amaze;
The Sun wears mourning, and the Moon puts on
A bloody suit.   All nature now complains:
The lab'ring earth, in throes, is rived with pangs;
Gapes with affright: demented crowds rush there,
Where chasms yawn, and shew poor nature's grief,
To hide from Him who sits upon the throne,
Whose day of wrath is come.   And who is He,
Whose frown confounds all hearts? an angry Lamb!
A sight without a precedent, portending ill
Strange, inconceivable.   The seventh seal brings
The awful crisis on: a doom impends
So drear, that God's right arm, when raised to strike,
Arrested seems; for silence holds the front, *
Suspending in its course th' avenging bolt.
Now the strange work is stayed; mercy delights
To view the ceasing of the tramp of Death;
Some respite for the guilty ones.   Justice resumes,
For they are gathered in who caused this lull;
As Lot, who by his lingering held the hand
That rained Sodoma's fires, and raised her mound.

* Silence, in Scripture usage means—a suspension of judgment or contention, as in Psalm xxii. 2, "O my God, I cry in the day-time, but thou hearest not; and in the night season, but there is no silence to me" (marg.) viz. Thou ceasest not to contend against me. Here is a forcible antithesis lost in the text.

The prayers of saints have ceased, the smoke ascends—
The smoke of incense offered there—to God,
There on the golden altar; and its glowing fires
Fill now the emptied censer pans, and these
Are poured down on the earth. That which consumes
Acceptedly the offerings of the saints, consumes
Avengingly their enemies and God's.
Ill-omened voices fill the air; thund'rings
And lightnings crash, and rend nature and art;
Light up the scene now horrible: and last,
Not least, an earthquake duplicates the woe.
Seven angels then prepare themselves to sound
Their trumpet blast. The first sounds his alarm;
And hail, and fire, and blood commingled pour
Destruction on the products of the earth:
A third thereof is smitten with the storm.
The second sounds, and hurls a mount of fire,
And drops it hissing in the sea: blood curls
Around its plunge, the circumambient tide.
The third thereof, is thus defiled: the ships
And tenants of the deep, so far succumb.
The third utters his note: forthwith there falls
A star absinthian to the earth; rivers
And fountains of the same, embittered, give
A bitter death to men. The fourth is heard;
Sun, Moon, and Stars confess his mighty power,
And in the third thereof forbear to shine.
Woe, woe, woe. Oh! words calamitous!
And must it be? Man's sins have countersigned
The bond of life and death. Persistent, he,
In lax effront'ry, risks the fatal strife;
Hardens his heart, rejects most patent signs,
Wraps up his soul in expectation fond

Of good to be. The heavens and earth till now
Have furnished weapons for th' avenging arm;
But now the regions subterrene are broached.
Another angel sounds—the fifth: a star,
Already fallen—Abaddon, Hebrew name,
Apollyon in the Greek—unlocks th' abyss;
Thence issues smoke, a noisome pest, dark'ning
The Sun and all the regions of the air.
Locusts emerge, discriminating how
And where they strike, so as t' avoid a wound
Inducing death; yea, rather they prolong
Men's bitter lives—a loathed continuance.
Of equine shape, they wear a man-like face,
And woman's tresses trail beneath their crowns
Of golden cast, with teeth as lions' teeth,
Their breastplates as of iron, and scorpion-tails.
Earth has no like of these, hence they are ranked
Symbolical: outrageous utt'rances
Have gone from learned lips; and pens, dipped low
In theologic ink, have made large drafts
On credences; as thus, the Saracens
Have been advanced to notoriety as such;
The Arab hordes were locusts in their day;
And, later still, the pealing cannon holds
This dark celebrity. Most clever tricks
Are played with some anomalies, which all
May see if they will look: the common ruse,
That this and that are entered to complete
The filling up, surely had origin
Where these fell locusts issued from—the pit.
By this ingenious sophistry, something
Is changed to nothing; notabilities
Become nonentities; and much is little soon.

The sixth now winds his awful blast; at which
A voice speaks to the angel, bids him loose
Four angel fiends; these marshal close their ranks,
Two hundred million combatants on steeds
Of hellish breed. The horsemen nondescript
Wear breastplates as of fire, of jacinth hue,
Candent with brimstone from the reeking bed
Beneath the mystic Euphratean flood.
These to an hour abide th' appointed time;
Then issue forth to do their hideous work.
The hybrid horses ramp with lion heads;
And serpent tails that, hydra-headed, wave
With cruel hiss: fire, smoke, and brimstone, pour
Their fetid death on men—a third thereof.
One woe remains, one trumpet yet to sound;
Consociate these: whene'er the blast is heard,
The woe begins, God's deep-set mystery ends.
Meanwhile a mighty Angel, cloud-enrobed,
Graced with a rainbow diadem, descends
From heaven; his face refulgent as the Sun;
And in his hand a little open book;
His feet like fiery pedestals: he stands—
Imposing attitude !—his right foot placed
Upon the sea, his left upon the earth.
Then with a mighty voice he cries, as when
A lion roars, and spreads dismay around.
Seven thunders give response, and utter things
As yet sealed up. The Angel lifts his hand
And swears by Him who made the heavens
And all therein; the earth and sea, with all
Their varied store, that time is now run out—
The time of mystery. Such has it been;
For God has *seemed* incompetent, unjust,

Intemperately kind, unreasonably severe,
Unwisely taking from the child those whom
He constituted guardians of the same,
Stripping the house of its best ornaments,
And leaving others, *whom we think* He might,
With better reason, have removed instead.
The villain oft escapes; the honest man
Is troubled with the obloquy of shame.
The murderer avoids the penal noose;
The innocent, protesting, takes his place.
Mistakes occur,—so men, in witless haste,
Have oft averred—as when continued rains
Have flooded lands, all nature, over drenched,
Calls loudly for the genial Sun; and drought,
When thirsty fields and sickly-looking plants
Pant for the shade and cool refreshing shower.
All these are mysteries, and thousands more.
Antagonism works, avails to mar
The goodly show of order, wisely planned;
Subverted oft, but not destroyed; the mode,
The medium, all are set awry; suffered
By Him who watches over all; who will,
At length, gather all up and manifest
His end, though interfered with, yet secured;
Not less complete because of adverse powers.
Under this woe the witnesses appear,
The crisis dawns: the Angel sounds his trump.
Portentous voices high above proclaim—
"The kingdoms of the world have now become
The kingdoms of our Lord and of His Christ."
The heavens impend with death—the vivid flash,
The thunders' deaf'ning boom, artillery
Forged in the heights above; the earth responds;

Disparted, shews deep down a frightful gap;
So nature pleads her sympathies with righteousness.
 Mid-heaven another angel wings his way,
Having a Gospel to proclaim: the first,
The one of grace, has held its term; and all,
Who gave it welcome and enrolled their names,
Are gathered in. But, everlasting, this
Will still enforce its terms, when time has ceased,
And God has framed the everlasting state.
Another angel cries that Babylon has fallen;
That Harlot dam, drunk with the blood of saints,
And martyrs who have spurned her poisoned cup.
The nations that have shared her impious joys
Will share, with respite short, her awful doom.
A gorgeous spectacle this woman shews:
Arrayed in purple, decked with glitt'ring gold,
And precious stones, and gems, she vaunts herself
The arbitress of earth's best joys; she holds
A golden cup, symbolic of her drunken rage.
Awhile she rides the beast; awhile he bears
Th' imperious harridan, ere long to be,
With ten confederate Kings, her bane.
This many-headed beast a symbol serves,
And somewhat complicate. The heads and horns,
In *number* as the dragon's seen before,
Have yet one point dissimilar; and this
Is most significant. "The dragon gives
His power, his throne, and great authority."
To this inservient, this intensive man:
The *horns* are crowned in *this;* the *heads*, in *that.*
"The heads denote seven mountains where in state
The woman sitteth on them;" * kings as well

  * Such is the translation of Rev. xvii. 9.

Are notified: and thus the very site
Of this symbolic whore is pointed out,
The city reigning over subject kings:
Rome unmistakeably revealed, although
Transferences may yet take place, conserve
Her character but not her site: as yet
The mystery holds, the veil is not removed.
Five kings had fallen, one held th' imperial reins
At that set time; the seventh must briefly hold
The regal power; to him the eighth succeeds—
This lawless one. The dragon's heads were crowned,
Denoting power immediate in his hands.
The horns are crowned, when in his delegate.
He vests this power: the heads remain; crownless,
For they have passed away as kings, but shew
A power resuscitated, confluent
In this eighth king. His crownèd horns denote
Ten kings confed'rate, having pledged their power,
Consonantly, to him: they spring from him
As do his horns; he gives them prominence,
And they sustain th' accursed unity
Of Hell's great chief.

Seven angels, woe-commissioned, do their work.
The first pours out his vial on the earth;
A grievous sore results on those who bear
The mystic mark, and number of the name. *

---

* Much controversy has arisen on this subject—the number of the name of the beast. Many names have been proposed which in some way apply to the Papacy; these are well known to students of prophecy. This solution is adopted by such as fix the Savior's advent at the close of the Millenium. Another has been proposed, claiming a living monarch as fulfilling in his name the conditions of the problem: he must doubtless feel complimented, if aware of the honor, for the prospect is a glorious one—to be "cast alive into a lake of fire burning with

The second vial turns the sea to blood.
The third effects the same on fountain heads,
And rivers of the earth; retributive,
For men had shed much righteous blood,
And it is fitting they should drink the same.
The Sun receives the fourth; he lends his rays
To smite with scorching heat. O righteous ways!
In this is deep significance. Man, friv'lous man,
Is now concerned to shew that in the Sun
We live and move and being have; depose
Him who has power to cause His Sun to shine
And give us genial light and heat; or hide,
Behind th' arresting cloud, his quick'ning beams;
Or give it force to scorch; or negative,
With thick-ribbed ice, the regions of the deep.
The creature which man views with reverence,
That to the Maker and His might belongs,
Is made the cause of wretchedness and woe.
The fifth pours out his vial on the throne
Of this infuriate beast—the wilful king.
The darkness of the noisome pit precedes
Th' experience of the pit itself: in rage
Men gnaw their tongues for pain; nor glory give

brimstone." Those acquainted with this latter theory are aware of a disturbance in the quantity of the vowels, and other nodosities of no trifling nature. An accomplished analyst has proposed the name Nero Cæsar, as making up the number; and also answering other terms of the description: the only confirmation yet to be given seems the actual resurrection. This is not so baseless an expectation as some might suppose: besides the plain declarations of the Apocalypse; we may adduce the fact that from the remotest ages such a belief has been cherished. This resuscitation was fondly entertained for Bacchus, for Nero, for Napoleon I. Other names answer to the number 666; thus Teitan or Satan, the *invisible* head of the Chaldee worship; and Saturn or Bacchus, the *visible* head, both make the mystic number—the former by the Greek computation; the latter by the Chaldee.

To God, nor does repentance stir their hearts.
The sixth Euphrates seeks; its rolling tide
Is checked; a way is framed right through its midst,
By which the thronging hosts of Eastern kings
Press eager for the fray of God.
 Madness prevails. Nations are roused; they sound
With energy, the battle cry; sullen,
Morose, with angry haste, accoutred grim
In war habiliments, they pant to face
Their great relentless foe; blaspheming, dare
The further prowess of His might: inflate
With pride and obduracy, blind with rage,
Deluded by the miracles of him
Who heads their host, and righteously bereft
Of heavenly light, they rave impatiently
To rush upon their doom. The gathered hosts
Are viewed with fateful pride by him who leads:
Complacency sits on his brow, and breeds
A kingly smile. Has he not told them oft
That they are gods, and they responding, say
That of all gods he is the chief?
Yes; man is now supreme—that puny thing
That shrinks spasmodic from the nettle's touch;
That blanches at some sudden news; that bows
Before the wintry blast; that faints beneath
The sultry ray; at last, with all his means
And wise appliances, sinks down a wreck.
Aghast they stand awhile: an angel pours
His vial out, the seventh; the air receives
The weighty ill. Thunders and lightnings fill
The mighty void; and from the temple rings
That awful utt'rance—*It is done.*
 Yes; now the myst'ry clears; God's wrath is come,

The time to judge the dead, to give reward
To those who, for His sake, have served and died;
And those destroy who have destroyed the earth.
A fearful earthquake, such as ages past
Ne'er witnessed, rives great Babylon in three:
The cities of the nations too fall down.
Heaven's ordnance peals; and, charged with heavy deaths,
Pours a continuous stream of monstrous hail.
Nought can uncere men's eyes and hearts: they rave,
Tumultuate, still heap up blasphemy.
Confed'rate hosts—ten here parade their strength—
Arrange in phalanx deep, in solid square,
With hellish implements, còmpared with which
Our longest range and best projectiles seem
But serious toys. The monarch's practised eye
Well weighs his work: some thought of untried strife,
Of powers unknown, may occupy his mind,
Do not arrest his stern resolve: he eyes,
With desperate bent, his rival in the air.
He, KING OF KINGS and LORD OF LORDS, holds high
His blazonry. Faithful and True, He rides;
In righteousness He maketh war.
He reins a horse of purest white; His eyes
Shed streams of fire; His head hath many crowns;
He hath His vesture dipped in blood; His name,
THE WORD OF GOD; proceeding from His mouth,
A sword of empyrean temper gleams,
The nations' scourge. On horses like their chief's,
Armies attend, in linen white and clean;
For such attests their righteousness.
   The trump of God prolongs its awful roll
Of startling echoes through the vault of heaven.
The hosts below return their mocking shouts

And mimicry of heaven's loud clarion;
Led on by him who knows his time is come,
Incarnate, whom the heavenly powers detect
As Satan, Devil, that Old Serpent which
Six thousand years ago projected then
His frightful homicide, and laid the train
Which now is fired. The very horses snort
And champ their bits, impatient for the fray:
Vain chivalry, yet adding to th' imposing sight.
Not long they wait: they level high their tubes,
Not by the law of tactics exercised
On gory fields of earth's reluctant plains,
But much obtused. How confident the front
Of these misguided men! assured that he,
Who marshals them, leads on to victory.
Impellent confidence! no joyous show
Of peace within; no righteous cause upholds.
What contrast to the fulgent hosts above,
Attendant on their Chief, a MAN OF WAR!
No weapon in their hands, cuirass, nor shield,
Not coat of mail: one sword throughout the host,
But this with vengeance gleams, surcharged
With wrath and fierceness of Almighty God.
Again the trumpet with an awful crash
Forbodes impending ill. A hurtling storm
Of missiles, forged by devilish art, attests
Their mad expectancy and rash pretence.
Each missile, fiend upborne, invades the ranks,
The serried ranks above. No horrid gap,
Nor sanguine track occurs; for, spiritual,
These warriors own no law corporeal;
So readily admit the hissing orb.
Beyond it speeds its course; outside their ranks

It spends its force; recurrent, drops;
The shower descends, assails the ranks below.
In blank amaze they view the vain assault :
With fruitless haste, they shun descending deaths.
Among them now th' infernal bombs evince
Their hideous power: abortive when they meet
With unsubstantial things, but when they clash
With corp'rate forms, infolded deaths escape.
Confusion roams; dismay and rout prevail.
The leader, where is he? The prophet too?
The both are seized alive, bound hand and foot,
Committed to their foul abode, the lake of fire.

How art thou fallen from heaven, O Lucifer!
Son of the morning! how art thou cut down!
Hell from beneath is moved for thee—for thee
Great Potentate! Thy coming signals it
To stir the dead for thee. Earth's mighty ones,
In glory laid, in marbled sepulchres,
In mausoleums, royal tombs, are roused
To greet thy low descent from loftiness.
"Art thou become," say they, "like unto us,
Weak like ourselves? The grave defiles thy pomp,
Thy minstrelsy; the worm thy covering,
Thy loathsome bed." No feller now distrains
The cedared Lebanon: the earth now rests;
And, singing, celebrates at once thy fall
And her release—thy ruined state, her joy.
"Is this the man," shall thy observers say,
"That made the earth to tremble, kingdoms shake,
That made the world a wilderness, destroyed
Its cities, and that opened not the house
Of those imprisoned by his cruel wrath?" *

* Isaiah xiv. 12, &c.

Light-bearing prince! thy rapt credulity
Has entertained immortal certainties—
To scale the heavens, exalt thy throne above
The stars of God; above the cloud-piled heights
Assume imperial state, like the Most High.
On earth as well, whither the tribes go up,
To worship there—there thou wouldst arrogate
A kingly state, and sit enthroned upon
The sacred mount—hill congregational;
The northern slopes—Jerusalem's bright cliffs.
No; all is lost to thee. Thy caitiff hope
Is ruptured at a blow; thy destiny
Is not above; but far below, in depths
Of infamy, of death; eternal fires
Await thy overthrow, complete thy shame.
No more will nations tremble at thy frown,
Nor trust thy vain pretence. Self-gratulant,
O Lucifer! thy pseudonym records
Thy rash temerity, thy false conceit.
Lie low—no more invite such mightiness.
Thyself deceived, and others by thy means;
Rest thee content with proofs that thou art man,
And not a god invuln'rable to death
That men do dread. Henceforth Hell's travesty
Shall complicate thy woe:—"Thou too art come,"
The fretting crew shall say, "to bear thy part
In this dark world. Chief wilt thou be of us?
What is our war? and what our battle cry?
Who are our enemies? Now bear thee well:
Cuirass, and shield, and spear, and glitt'ring blade,
Assume again; and let Hell's wide domain
Resound with thy exploits and chivalry."

The war above has ceased—its cry is hushed.

The armies remanent are slain by Him
Who rides triumphant now—THE WORD OF GOD.
  An angel then descends, and in his hand
A chain and key—the symbols of his power,—
Binds the arch-fiend, commits him to th' abyss,
And shuts him in; no more to be at large
Until a thousand years have sped their course.
Thus ends man's day till then. This time run out—
Millenium's happy course—he must be loosed
A little while. The nations lie to Him—
THE KING OF KINGS:* their hearts are still estranged
Though outwardly submiss; unconsciously,
They bear a heart unchanged; hence his success
Who then will tempt afresh, and circumvent,
And lead them up once more against heaven's King;
Besiege the city, well beloved of God.
God's fire descends, invades beleag'ring hosts,
And burns them up. The arch deceiver then
Is cast into the lake of fire, his final bourne.
  And now behold a great white throne;
One sits, of everlasting ages, Sire.
He frowns—earth flies amain—Heaven rolls away—
Their noise is great—their bruit is spread.
The mighty Gabriel hears, and humbly bows;
In solemn adoration shrouds his head
With seraph wings, and worships God.
A vast array is there of those once dead,
And now recalled to resurrection life:—
Grim Death gives up his dead; the sea and Hell
Regorge their slain. The books are opened; each
Beholds his own, writ by himself, when he,
Unconscious, in his mortal state, deposed

    * See Psalm xviii. 44.

His evidence. Things done are written there:
Men's words are graven deep; their very thoughts,
Their fleeting looks, have impress made; and thence
Their judgment comes.
Another book is seen—the Book of Life.
Records of grace are there; and there are found
The names of ransomed ones: there shine their gold,
Their silver, precious stones—asbestine works,
Constructed while they sojourned here below.
These are not works of drear incertitude,
Nor procreative of eternal life.
This life inwrought at first, these works result
A normal flow: the fountain Grace, and Grace the stream.
Insatiate Death and gloomy Hell are judged,
And doomed confinement in the lake of fire—
The second death; th' eternal ward of those
Not written in the Book of Life.
 New Heavens appear; the earth is cast afresh.
For those which heretofore admitted sin
And foul rebellion, are no longer found.
All things are new: the sea has disappeared,
For as a type of death, it finds no place.
And now true life and immortality
Are brought to light: ere this to faith, but now
T' unclouded sight.   O Death! where is thy sting?
O Grave! where is thy victory?

BOOK III.

CHAPTER I.—REDEMPTION.

THE ARGUMENT.

I.—THE PRIMAL CAUSE—THE LOVE OF GOD.
  i. Irrespective of the creature.
  ii. Therefore not afterwards affected by it—
    a. By the creature's goodness.
    b. By the creature's naughtiness.

II.—THIS LOVE, AS FAR AS WE KNOW, WAS SIMPLY WILLED, OR SELF-EXISTENT, FOR THE FOLLOWING REASONS:—
  i. Because God is not the subject of emotions, though anthropopathically said to be so.
  ii. Allowing that He is, there was nothing existing to effect this love.
  iii. Nor could it be called forth by foreseen things, for these were antagonistic.

III.—THIS LOVE IS IRREVERSIBLE.
  i. Because God is unchangeable, though
  ii. This love has sometimes this appearance.
  iii. It was unconditional; though
    a. A condition is laid down, but
    b. This condition is secured by God's purpose.

IV.—THE TERMS OF GRACE IN PROMULGATION ARE LIMITED TO NONE; BUT THE RESULT IS A PARTIAL ACCEPTANCE, BECAUSE—
  i. The present condition of man is hostile, and an enemy can only resist.
  ii. God has not met this by an express intimation that He will use more than a reasonable and natural appeal to all.
  iii. A partial reception is secured by a supernatural influence.

V.—The reasons for this diversity of reception.
    i. Two diverse races exist,
        a. The seed of the Evil one.
        b. The seed of the Holy One.
    ii. The limit designed.

VI.—God's partiality is not unjust, for—
    i. Man is dealt with according to his demands, as a reasonable being.
    ii. Justice has its due in all—every sin is expiated.

Redemption's song now sing. The praise of Him,
Almighty King of kings, and Lord of lords,
Jehovah's equal Son; Him who became
A man, and wrought for man Redemption's work.
Angels the song began. The favored plains
Of Bethlehem first heard the joyous strain,
"Glory to God, good will to man;" this strain
Let man take up: to mortal ears most sweet;
In God's esteem the greatest of His works,
If estimated by the great account.
  Man and his history have been our themes;—
How man devised more good than God conferred:
How that became an evil in his hands,
Because he sought it disobediently.
How man—that complex thing, both good and bad,
The good o'ermastered by the bad; the bad
So bad, that wreck and misery succeed
A stormy life; or, should life be a calm,
How death furls up the sails, and sinks the bark.
How man, in conscious need, has made attempts,
By many shifts, evasions, toils, and plans,
To supplement mere life with joyousness.
In measure we have searched and notified
Man's barrenness of thought, or foolery,
In tracing out his origin, his kind,

His destiny; his complicate estate
Of being, offices, endowments, ways;
His capabilities, his waywardness,
Abuse of good, necessity of ill,
To meet existing ill: and with all these
Some glances at a good to countermine
The deadly breach at first; yea too, the train
Of fatal consequents—all these, and more
We have essayed. Man's great necessity
Is God's great opportunity; foreseen,
Provided for, He meets man's rebel act
With graciousness, announcing then a plan
More than restorative: this now unfold
O heav'nly muse! Redemption predicate
In strains oracular; and not as sense,
Or reason might suggest, and so pervert.
Imagination curb; or give the rein
Over the empyrean track that leads
Up to the throne of God. Let reverence hold
The spirit back from rash intrusiveness:
Whilst yet a holy boldness ventures near,
To catch great utt'rances of heav'nly truth.
All arrogance rebuke: let no pretence
Induce unwariness, nor vanity,
So that a snare be set successfully
For wand'ring feet; or that some sore rebuke
Should meet self-confidence, and hurl it down
To painful depths, that meek Humility
Might fence securely for the passers by.
Now turn we to redemption's glorious theme.
 I.—The primal cause was Love—Love, sovereignly
In thought, in purpose; so in exercise,
When, in the lapse of time, occasion brought

The opportunity: then Love appeared
In all its power and grace. The curse fell not
Where Justice might have launched its flaming bolt.
There, in the very track of sin, Love set
The woman's seed, which in due time should be
A counterpart of that humanity
That man defiled; but sinless, pure,
And undefiled, and *so* dissimilar.
God's everlasting love desired, His wisdom planned,
Deliverance for the race whom He had loved,
Without a cause beyond Himself: He loved,
He willed to save, ere good or evil wrought;
Ere He had given being to that race.
Man seeks an object for his love, educing it;
Nor then endures, unless that object serves
His heart with loving ways; his longing eyes
With winning sights; his ears with dulcet sounds.
    i. In this the creature had no part assigned,
In counsel or in deed. Had man's estate
Moved God, as man moves man, by what he does,
Then must the outrage on the fencèd tree
Have caused abhorrency: no curse on man
Evinced God's wrath, although displeasure fixed
A mark continuous—on man was his,
On woman hers: yet such is God's deep love,
That these administer much joy to all
Who, sorrowing, endure the penalty.
    ii. Here is security. God is not moved,
By what man does, to alter His set plans,
His plans determinate: these, in due time,
Are all unrolled; nor does the creature stay
Th' accomplishment thereof, nor expedite.
    a. E'en as at first man's goodness had no claim—

For that had fallen; so neither has it now—
If such exist. The gift was not to help
The failing strength; but for those dead in sin
To furnish and secure eternal life.
Now as at first the fashioned mould remained
A lifeless shape, but lived when breathed into
By God Himself; so in the death of this
A perpetuity would hold, did not
The same Almighty Maker breathe again
The breath of life. Then there is holiness—
The holiness of God, conservative.
   b. But evil still is there, and all around
The same is prevalent. The Evil one
Is unremittingly at work; provokes
Man's enmity; and, in default to crush,
Defiles the work of God—some, clean escaped,
Entrapped once more, bring obloquy
On God's sweet grace. If these blaspheme, it proves
A spurious work at first, and so they fall
From *simulated* grace. But genuineness
Sometimes puts on a foreign garb, consorts
With glib pretence, or open worldliness;
Forsakes its wonted haunts, and oft frequents
Conclaves of enemies; with these allied
It entertains some schemes of double guise:
One view presents the world a partisan
Of virgin good; another shews a mask
Concealing rottenness, known to be there
By those to whom experience has conveyed
Intelligence. Yet, notwithstanding all,
God knows no change. No creature loveliness
Had charms for Him, and no deformity
Can mar His love. It suffers reticence

Through faithlessness in those redeemed:
Thus though the love of God always remains
A constant quantity, man apprehends
A vanishing.   As food most nourishing
Assails our palate with some foreign taste,
Still nourishing, yet gives us gastric pains;
The cause is in ourselves: just so God's love
Seems variable, but truly not, since He
Has not the shadow of a change.   Our fears,
Arising from our conscious low estate,
As children of His love; our wretched doubts—
Engendered by self-contemplation, hence
Deducing sheer unfitness, just as if
Our best condition could e'er justify
A confidence—our fears, our doubts, beget
A questioning.   Oh! fear Him; fear the rod,
He spares it not when worldliness demands;
When disobedience mocks the Father's voice.
He loves His child, not for his loving ways;
Nay, but because he is His child, and needs
The rod corrective, not retributive.
If love in God's own heart had origin
From something found in man, then man,
So mutable, might next present some form
Of stubbornness, self-will, brute appetites,
And sundry ways, to peril love in God.
This love might be regained: well, granted, yet
Again it may be lost; regained once more,
Once more prevened; at length, this random game
Is played quite out, the suit foreclosed.
And what prevents?   Does man at last secure
The costly prize—eternal Life ; or lose
Just as he will; or is it Fate decides?

If he secures, how so? Does he resolve
The issue of his will, and play at I and Thou
So wittingly, as that his mood of grace
And Death's last summons move coincident?
Can he determine that just one turn more
May not adversely plunge him into Hell?
Is God thus weak—He who devised the plan?
Was He constrained to steep it in uncertainty?
Or had He power, but chose to abdicate,
Write *may* instead of *shall;* Himself remain
In ignorance of that about to be?
 II.—God willed His love, He willed its exercise.
We cannot frame a reason for this love,
Which had existence ere its objects had,
Except that "God is love."
 i. God unimpressible, devises things,
Their means and end. Emotions flow outfrom,
Tend to an object causing them: as love
Beams brightly on one loveable; hatred
Scowls bitterly on some inflicting wrong,
And still more bitterly on some one wronged.
Pity weeps over suffering need, or pain,
Or sickness, or distress; and all the more
Do these emotions grow, because restrained
By creature weakness and infirmity.
With God no admiration fondly scans
Some beauteous form, invading suddenly
The wondering eyes; no bitterness surveys
The unexpected foe; no pity warms
O'er sorrow irremediable: He knew—
He caused the whole, always conserving guilt
For all th' opponents of His sovereign will.
 ii. But granting that th' Immutable may feel;—

May love as man, may hate, may meditate
Revenge for wrong, and pity sorrowing ones;
These had no exercise, for they were not
Who might call forth these streamings of His heart.

    iii. And had they been; the best—and at his best,
Would breed but loathing in the heart of God.
Man at his best estate is failing, naught,
And altogether vanity; and dead
To all appliances of good: the good
He loves not; and his heart makes great demand
For that which only grieves the mind of God.
This God foreknew, for all was plainly graved
On unwrought tablets where, dispassionate,
He read the whole. Did He not write it there?
And had He not full prescience of all,
Ere He built up man's form magnificent,
And gave that form a great life principle,
A soul of wondrous power? It will not do
To glance from man to God, and say our state
Moved His compassion and induced His love.
We strive to apprehend God's love by man's:
And so His light ineffable, by that
Which cheers our world;—inadequate the both.
Approximation only can educe
Some premonition of those peerless things,
Which God avers are ours—ours, if by faith
We claim these glorious gifts, yet to be given,
But purposed long ere Time began his flight,
And in his course confirmed and sealed with blood.

    III.—God's love is irreversible. Man's love may fail:
The object of that love, provoking it,
May wear another phase, the opposite—
A facile change—and thus provoke his hate.

Or death may intervene; forgetfulness
Succeed, and wither quite the goodly flower,
Leaving a quiet saddened memory.
A hundred things may interfere, and stay
The current of man's love; for all around
Is changeable, as well as he himself.
Eden received this law, and ministered
This change in all its hues, in perfumed bowers,
In lights and shades; the open sunny walk,
The glen retired, the glorious mid-day sun,
Its morning rise, its evening chastened glow;
The river's noble swell, the little rill,
The gorgeous bloom on trees, aspiring flowers,
Or the meek daisy, or the violet;
The rush of fragrance, or the faintest flow
Of scented wealth. There man and woman walked:
The varied same, a like diversified;
A parted whole, each part an integer;
Complete apart, yet separate incomplete;
Two hearts, each competent to throb alone,
Yet joined, made up a better whole.
In all this great diversity and change
No consternation crept, no sere decay,
Or not, at most, offensively: the leaf
Was not immortal, so it fell; not till
Its purposes were served: the constant change
Was seen rather than felt; or felt, to praise
The great Creator, and His law enjoy.
Sin has defiled this law, and introduced
A pungency for all. The noble stream
Delights us still, but death is there; how oft
It bears its argosies of wealth awhile
In graceful friendliness; but, treacherous, strands

The trusting guest upon its foreign shore!
The murm'ring rill has yet attractiveness;
But some lone pool along its course upbraids
The gloomy suicide. The flowers alone
Seem not defiled; and yet they too, at times,
Moan, as in pain, a mute complaint; the head
Droops low while in the prime; a worm
Is at the root, or revels in the bloom.

   i. God is not so; He changes not: the Sun
Brings back no day to Him; the night no gloom:
The seasons nor relax, nor brace His frame;
The thunder's awful roll, the lightning's flash
He marks unmoved, for all are His, and He
Has ordered all. His hands grasp all His works,
Intact but by His will: He comprehends
Things seen, unseen, unknown; nor e'er entrusts,
To agencies beyond His reach, aught of His plans.
And so because He, changeless, changes not,
His love wears ever an unvarying garb.
Much like an evergreen: the summer heat,
The winter's nipping cold, denude it not
Of verdancy. Or, as the constant Sun
Gives forth its beams, and shines uncompromised,
Though clouds forefend; so God preserves His love,
In spite of all the ways of wilful men;
And all th' ingratitude of those He loves.

   ii. This last suggests God's love as variable.
But as on some bright day, the Sun above
Gives light and warmth, and gladdens nature's heart;
All evidence their joy—the skimming bird,
With joyous twitter, takes what God provides;
The grazing ox; the nibbling sheep; all rest
In busy quietude, or thoughtless glee:

Then gloom obtrudes; clouds thicken o'er the Sun,
Arrest his rays; winds moan and mutter threats;
Sounds ominous appal; and other light
Suspends the cloudy dimness all around.
The face of things is changed; then confidence
Is changed to fear; joy to alarm; and all
Seems hushed, save nature's strife: *yet all this rout
Is from below;* for one beyond the clouds
Might look above, and see the Sun unchanged,
Unshorn of beams; look downward and behold
The ill beneath his feet. So God persists;
He loves e'en though the less He's loved: His thoughts
Are not as ours: He loves because He will.

   iii. Not only is God's love immutable,
But unconditional. Not so the Law—
The law of Sinai; that had a clause
Of shudd'ring import to the heart of man—
"The soul that sinneth, it shall die:" this was
A dismal comment on some stringent laws
Without redress of hope, but sad reserve.
This institute of God appealed to man,
Demanding strict obedience or his death.
True, grace had exercise; but this obtains
With all to whom is yet the term of natural life.
Love is diversified—the love of God
As well as that of man. He sends His rain
Both on the unjust and the just; His sun
He makes to shine on all alike; He feeds
Young ravens when they cry; the bleating lamb
Knows where to find its nourishment, placed there
By hands all-provident: and this is love.
But such must fail, because the objects fail,
Th' occasion temporal must pass away.

But love redemptive has eternity
Its ample range; and wise, makes no demand
That might imperil much its gracious aim.
We must exalt man very much; or else
Depress the Godhead, ere we tolerate
The thought that merit can assign its rights;
Or He, who gives, acknowledge such.
A distance infinite suggests no ground
On which to stand and pre-arrange some terms
For future fellowship. There was a time
When fellowship prevailed; one party broke
And canceled every bond; thenceforth he walked
Apart from Him he wronged, and lengthened out
His wand'ring course; nor ever could he frame
Return to Him he left, for he had left
As enemy to Him and all His ways.
Love is not baulked; it takes the lead, brings near
The wand'ring foe; tells out its wondrous tale,
Unburdened by—*This do and live;* but speaks
Of all the paid-up debt, the canceled bond
Of life and death, redrawn, and signed afresh
By One who dipped His pen in blood—His own.

  a. Believest thou? This one condition binds
The roll of life, but such has no constraint;

  b. For He who made it, made provision too
For its full exercise; uncertainty
Is banished from the scheme that frames for man
Eternal life. Faith is "the gift of God:"*
He gives to whom He will, and "not of works,
Lest any man should boast."

  * Ephes. ii. 8. We acknowledge the difficulty which the Greek text sets up here, in identifying this gift with Faith: a question that may not now be discussed. The position, however, is proved by other texts, especially 1 Cor. xii. 9, unless, in this text, one would claim the assertion on behalf of the *gift,* as distinguished from the *grace* of faith.

IV.—God limits not His word. "Ho! every one,"
Is the life-cry to all. As when of old
The serpent-bitten murmurers were told
To look and live, some turned away, perhaps,
In hopeless pangs; and unbelieving, some
Refused the way of God; or, wise, despised
The foolish means: so still, a num'rous class
Hear the same words, the invitation mock;
Unmoved, they hear the tale of marv'lous love,
Misread its terms, or doubt its power for good.
   i. Only a few receive the joyful news
Of intercourse renewed, of hope revived.
The hostile mind shuts out the friendliness
By this proposed; turns, sick'ning, sheer away;
Prefers the doubtful game of life-long works,
Determined at the close; if e'er at all
They give *hereafter* any room 'mong things
Which occupy their hearts' affection *here*.
   ii. The means employed are not intrenched by terms
Exclusive, but the same to all alike.
Men hear one like themselves proclaim to all,
What he himself has found—*the way of life*.
He tells them how they stand: if faithful, warns;
He speaks of danger now; the judgment-seat;
The hopeless prison-house; the grace of God;
Of justice satisfied; the Father's love;
How He beseeches—"Be ye reconciled;"
Commands—"Repent." All nations stand around,
Invited by the sovereign voice to hear
What it may say. Some marvel, some deride;
Some cleave thereto, some walk away; yet all,
In the free exercise of God's great gifts,
Have heard alike; and all have made their choice.

Deliberative some, impulsive some;
And some of this have spurned, and some, of that;
Of that, some gladly take; and some, of this.
What is the diff'rence then? Why should one spurn,
Another take? The former loathes the way,
Esteems it gloomy, and the end not worth
The irksome means; the latter sees the road
Is narrow, but beyond it widens out
In heavenly plains. It may be that he sees
No more than that he has at length resolved
To choose the better part: this is most true,
But more he has to learn.

  iii. Now all God's means had failed, had He not willed
Effectual calling too: all had refused,
But that He moves unknown to us, unfelt,
Unrecognized, but by intelligence
Of after growth. The child has cognizance
That he has life, not how he lives, nor when
He drew his entrance breath: his opening mind
Some information gains. Much like to this
Is he who, born again, just knows he lives:
The time of birth he *may* define, but how
He entered life is not so clear, till years
Have rolled away; and then he rather knows
Than understands. That which we know, and hear,
And feel—the breeze, the stormy wind, has points
Not clear, though not allied to doubt; just so
With all born from above.

  V.—i. Again; the Gospel deals with diverse kinds;
All have a common human parentage,
But some have also antecedently
A darker type: so One premised of old,
T' account for blank rejection of His words.

   a. " Ye therefore hear them not, because ye're not
Of God, but of the Devil, and his lusts
Ye do; ye cannot understand my speech,
Because ye cannot hear my words."
Now this would be illogical and gross—
With reverence we speak, as fallible—
If such condition were th' effect, and not
The cause: it was their parentage that caused
Their opposition to the truth, and made
Their minds incapable to entertain.
Said Jesus—" I do that which I have seen,
And ye do also that which ye have seen;
I in my Father's house, and ye in yours."
Mysterious, yet most true; diversity
Is stamped most legible: hatred and scorn,
Contempt and wrath, fire up their fiendish hearts
E'en to the last, or black despair, or else
Most fatal quietude. Though it be true
That some display the same conformity,
Who yet forsake their evil ways and live;
Here's no disproof : their earthly parentage
Accounts for this. Ofttimes indeed we find
A foreigner begets a citizen,
Who in due time forsakes his father's house,
His father, mother, kindred, all; and takes
The name and freedom of another state.
An heir of grace lies in a mortal womb
With one who is a scion of another stock.
The pen with trembling writes this solemn truth;
The heart has sad remembrance of its joys
With some who since have shewn hostility,
Despised, reviled, and died impenitent.
   b. With some their heavenly destiny awaits

Development. Ere the Creation's dawn,
When blithe the morning stars sang silently,
And all the sons of God shouted for joy;
They were the joy of God, His well-beloved:
It pleased Him in the myst'ry of the fall
To fold them up, and complicate their state;
And by their means unfold His wisdom, grace,
And justice unrebuked; though sinners, share
The glories of His state; for He has made
These sinning ones His heirs, joint-heirs with Him,
God's equal Son. The theme is wonderful;
For they were first children of wrath; as such
Bore condemnation on their front, and lived
As others in th' indulgence of their lusts;
Thieves, covetous, idolators, unclean,
Effeminate, extortioners, unjust,
As any in the human roll: estranged
In heart and life, yet certainly reclaimed
Ere Death could seize his prey; yea he refrains
If yet no change has taken place in them—
A change necessitous; for, unrenewed,
Their death would be an everlasting ill,
And yet such cannot be: th' eternal plan
Braces the two—*hereafter* endless life,
And *here* that life begun, regenerate.

 ii. Hence the restricted force of common terms:
Their import meets the case of God and man.
God had a purpose hid in mystery;
Man had a need coincident with man.
Wherever man is found, there he requires
Some palliative scheme for current ills.
Sooner or later man finds out his sore.
Varied opinions bear on this; some think

That God is merciful, and will not judge,
Too strictly, erring ones: some think Him kind,
Too good to ill-effect the future state:
Now this is anthropopathy run mad.
But some suppose—and 'tis a growing thought—
That man is as a sort of chrysalis,
Struggling to disinter himself; that he
Has made advance, and has in view a state
Exemptive from the ills he here endures.
Not for himself he plans development—
For this is all, some metamorphosis—
It is the race that he exalts; he thinks
Instinctive energy is close at work,
And will at length present a perfect type.
But for himself, who lauds this theory,
What does he hope? that he shall live again,
Again revisit scenes of present ill,
For ever flourish in the good set up?
This is philanthropy grown imbecile.

 VI.—But God is not unjust, although He make
A diff'rence manifest: although He claim,
And exercise a right to cut, rough-hew,
And polish stones, with which He purposes
To build, to beautify them for His work.

 i. For man prefers the ground God takes with him;
His reason justifies the mode: he scans,
Examines every point; if he detects,
As he conceives, some lurking weakness there,
He challenges that part, though as a whole
He gives it currency. "This do and live,"
Is not objected to; man has no doubt
Of his efficiency: "incline our hearts
To keep this law," is orthodox; but yet

His mind misgives him not, although the law
He asks the power to keep, he spends his life to break.
 ii. Nor can it be alleged that one escapes
The dread award of sin, while others bear
The penalty, and so justice foreshame.
If man will own himself incapable,
Another takes his place, suffers instead:
Yea, *this* is done, though *that* remain undone.
Those who escape avail themselves betimes
Of this provision for their need; believe
What God avers, that He has found a way
Still to be just, and yet to justify
The guilty ones, without their righteous deeds.
This to the Greeks is foolishness; to Jews
A stumbling-block: both try it by their skill,
Decide against its verity, in that
It shelters ignorance and folly too.
The dupes alone are safe: for if the tale
They have believed is not quite genuine,
They are at least a courteous race, and stand
Where others stand at last, before their Judge;
There at His judgment-seat advantaged thus,
That they believed what they supposed God's word,
Coupled with disavowal of all claim
As compensation for their loss of time;
Of character—as fools, for letting slip
Good opportunities for worldly gain;
For works of charity and faith, which cause
Unmeaning sacrifice and wretched waste,
If in this life alone they fix their hope.
They're safe as others, but with prestige great;
And if words bear a natural sense in God's,
As well as other books, what they now sow

Will ripen on eternal plains; and there
They, confident, will reap.
God's plan provides for all demands made by
His justice e'er inexorable; for that
No pity knows, the utmost doit is claimed.
Man pardons as he will, without regard
To turpitude; the only way for him
To imitate God's mode of grace to him,
In his deportment to his fellow men.
He may condone without regard to guilt
Or innocence: yea he may treat a foe
As though he ne'er had wronged him, or provoked
Hostility, and thus commend himself
To God and man: the holy God can not.
He pardons not whom He receives, as though
They ne'er had sinned: or *they* must expiate,
Or *other* in their stead, their every sin.
Sweet mercy prompted in the mode devised;
With that the heart of God was filled; with that
He purposed to delight the sons of men.
But justice smiles when one who, steeped in sin,
Seeks refuge in the arms of God, *just as he is*.
Some men of God—such men of science too—
Object to terms asserting God's great power
As infinite; as thus—He cannot lie,
He cannot pardon sin; but this is gross,
A pass at words: He cannot will to do
What he wills not to do: God cannot sin,
For that He cannot disobey Himself.
So if to will and not to will; to do
And not to do, contemporaneously,
Involve some limitation, then we grant
That God is limited. Nay, God conserves

His attributes; Justice is satisfied;
Mercy, large-hearted, calls to erring men,
"Why will ye die?" And Love, warm-hearted love,
Beseeches, "Be ye reconciled to God."

Oh! the rich grace, and Oh! the depth thereof!
His wisdom and His knowledge, Oh! how great!
Unsearchable His judgments, and His ways
Past finding out; for who hath known His mind,
Or who hath been His counselor?
For of Him, through Him, to Him, are all things;
To Him be glory evermore, Amen.

CHAPTER II.—THE REDEEMER AND THE REDEEMED.

THE ARGUMENT.

I.—THE INCARNATION.
    i. Its nature.   ii. Its prophetical indication.
    iii. Its fulfilment.   iv. Its purpose.

II.—THE ATONEMENT.
    i. How available, not in the sense of a human substitute merely.
    ii. The extent of its application.
    iii. Its results, different
        a. On those who receive. *b.* On those who reject.

III.—THE OBJECT OF THE ATONEMENT—THE CHURCH.
    i. In time.
    ii. In eternity.

I.—THE great Redeemer and His glorious Spouse
Be now the burden of our grateful song.
Say how the Son of God, moved by His love,
Laid by the glory of His heavenly state.

Stooped to become a man, in mortal guise,
Though not in verity: for, though He took
Our likeness and infirmities, He shunned—
He could not otherwise—our lapsed estate,
With all its mortal consequents: as thus,
He knew the frailties of our state; He slept,
He felt the need of bread; and, thirsty, sought
The ministry of one who came to draw
At Jacob's well, where He then, wearied, sat;
Was tempted much to sin; but, sinless, spent
His sorrowing pilgrimage; He sympathized
With those who wept; He pitied those who sinned;
He wept Himself o'er sin's sore mastery,
And blind indifference to offered good.
The cup of carnal good He never sipped,
So Death had no authority o'er Him;
But waited His permission e'er He struck
The sorrowing heart, and drew the life-blood forth.
  i. Incarnate God! The theme is wonderful.
No mortal mind could frame; and if it could,
No heart could dare to entertain the thought,
At first, that God should be a man and die.
No pen, tipped with enduring adamant,
Could last to chronicle the mighty theme.
The virgin womb must bear th' immortal fruit;
The virgin breast must yield the aliment
Of infant life: so truly man was He,
Yet not man's seed, though his reputed son;
His line traced farther back than when man first
Appeared in innocence in Eden's clime.
Yet though th' Eternal, He began to be,
A helpless babe in Bethlehem: His bones
Had not consistency to bear His frame;

That frame evinced its power progressively
To grow as those around, for He increased
In stature; and His mind gave evidence
Of power to open out and learn; as thus,
He learnt obedience by the things He bore;
Not how t' obey, but what obedience is—
What it entails upon obedient ones.
His human soul—for such He had, as well
Th' Eternal Mind—this soul observed
The proper guise of listless infancy;
Of childhood waking up to things around;
Of early youth; of manhood in its prime.
No rare precocity, nor senile ways
Disfigured youth in Him; yet He was wise
Above His years; surpassed His teachers all,
For He had made the honored word of God
His meditation all the day; the night
He often spent in prayer. He daily grew
As men—whene'er they do—in wisdom, grace,
And favor both with God and man.
His was a soul most capable, but not
Replete at first: endowed with wondrous power
To germinate, to ripen in a varied soil
Of good and ill; the good He chose, refused
Th' abounding ill. Not as the first-made man,
In charge at once of ripened intellect;
The second Adam, He fulfilled His course,
Acquiring sympathy for old and young.
And still—O wondrous perpetuity!
He can be touched with our infirmities.
Though presciently He knew, yet in His grace
He would become most conversant with men,
And so became as man; not raised above

By clear immunity from all the ills
Which crowd man's state, but made most capable
To taste them all: and not the ills alone
Which man, unfall'n, might have—as such not ills,
He was in all points tempted just as man,
But yet a sinless one, for He had nought
Corroborative of the dark assault
Of Satan's power; and so the tempter fled,
Before the two-edged sword, the word of God,
Wielded so mightily by him, the Son of God.
A man of sorrows, in the plenitude of grief
He wore an aspect much beyond His years.
The drunkard's song, the bye-word of His race;
Yet He despised the shame for joys to come.

 ii. First God Himself proposed the remedy
For Eden's grief, a yet incipient ill.
The germ He planted there in memory's soil,
To spring and bud and bloom; but bear its fruit
When suns have ceased. The prophets since have told
What they were moved to speak of by the power
That wrought in them: not knowing then themselves
The import of their words; yet, diligent,
They searched, and made enquiry resolute,
To find what things, also what kind of times,
The Spirit signified; for It foretold
Great suff'rings, but far greater glories thence.
Moreover, they were told of some to come,
To whom they ministered this mystery;
Not to themselves, wards of an earlier grace.

 iii. Ages had rolled away; still God forbears
And hides yet in Himself His purposed grace,
Not suff'ring by delay: but in due time
He sends His Son to test the reverence

Of those who claimed to be God's favored race.
Yea, so they were, but nothing takes the place
Of holiness. The temple blazed with gold;
Silver, and costly brass, and almug trees,
Cedar of Lebanon, and all that art
Could cull from nature's store, and cunning skill
Devise to frame, were there; there God Himself
Deigned to respond, and there was pleased to set
The symbol of His presence too. Alas!
Defilement came: then came an enemy
Who spoiled the treasures of His house.
When Christ appeared, those who professed to build
Rejected Him, the Corner Stone; for He,
In their esteem, was without comeliness,
Unsuited to their need. This recusance
Fulfilled the word of God; inimical,
Yet most conducive to the very point
They shunned, with deep malignant scorn.
They could not otherwise: instinctive hate
Plotted abortive schemes; but He who fell
A victim to their rage, arose again
Triumphant over all. Some, malice led;
Some, ignorant; and all by wicked hands
Fulfilled the counsel, deep, determinate
Of God; not only in the penal death,
But in the very mode of prophecy.

iv. Thus God would carry out His gracious plan
To rescue from her lost estate His Church;
That Church so implex that no seraph mind
Could frame to disentagle it, or find
A mitigation of the penalty.
God ordered so that in the course of time
Not only should the object of His love—

His special love—find full deliverance,
And all th' abundant treasures of His house;
But Jews and Gentiles, nations all around,
Should share His grace. The mystery of His will
Is such, that He will gather into one,
Under the headship of His Christ, all things
In heaven and in the earth; and this He calls
The dispensation of the fulness of the times.
God's wisdom manifold is thus made known.
Angels, and principates, and powers desire
To learn from this, and this contemplate deep.

II.—God would reverse estrangement; rectify
The mischief sin had wrought; and reconcile
Those who, though His in love, both hated Him,
And mocked the whole provision of His grace.
How He might still conserve His rectitude,
By granting Justice all its proper claims,
And make these claims exponents of His love,
Was a great problem only to be solved
By wisdom Infinite: precisive terms
Restrained mere mercy in its human phase.
Justice relaxes not; persistent, seeks
Full satisfaction for its mangled code.
While Love, unquenchable, seeks nothing less
Than full enfranchisement; yea, more than this.
Scant pleasure would the heart of man enjoy
To see a much loved one at liberty;
This would not satisfy; he seeks for such
An honored place. One near his heart must be
Most near him too; partake with him his joys,
And share all that is his. Could God do less?
He longs to pour His love in a full tide
Upon His Church, in distant solitude.

i. He has a Son, an only One: to Him
The Father makes proposals of His grace:—
"Wilt thou assume man's likeness, and with him
Experience such proclivities as he,
In sinlessness sustained; as hunger, thirst,
A need for sleep, and all th' infirmities
Of unfallen man—to him unfallen, a good;
But, in th' event of sin, with sin enyoked,
Become an ill—wilt thou partake
And know their sorrowing power? Wilt thou accept
The place of tempted ones; subject Thy state
To Satan's wiles, and know his potency
For ill; the more effectually to curb
His range not undefined? thus being touched
With all the feelings of man's race—his grief,
His tendencies, his imminent distress,
Thou may'st acquire efficiency to meet
And succor in temptation's hour?
And further; wilt thou satisfy—thou canst,
And thou alone—My righteous claims, My law
Outraged by man; endure My outpoured wrath
For man—the vengeance of My holiness?
If thou wilt so, I further state My terms.
Thou knowest well that 'mong the race of men
A people dwell, now earthly, but by Me
Destined to higher things than they can frame.
I give them Thee. They are not of the world;
The world has not for them sufficiency
Of sphere or destiny. If Thou assume
Their form and state, then Thou mayst give to them
Thy form and state: the glory which is Thine,
By such redeeming right let that be theirs:
And where Thy presence is, there too let them

In personal conformity be found.
As I and Thou are one; so Thou and they.
Be Thou the Bridegroom of My love; and they
The Bride. Th' adornment of Thy grace be hers;
And hers, th' endowment of my love, be Thine.
Much beauty hers, Thy great delight, Thy joy;
And Thou th' eternal object of her love."

"O holy Father! terms like these forestall
The deep desire; and, prepossessed, My heart
Makes quick response. Most joyfully I take
The sinner's place; despise the shame; endure,
Not listlessly, not unimpressed, Thy wrath,
Which none, if unsustained, could bear: whilst I,
By righteousness upheld, might underived,
And Justice satisfied; others will bear
Upheld by none of these, but by Thy power
Creative, so inalienate; and thus ensure
A penalty as endless as the joy
Of those who welcome Me with trusting hearts.
Not a mere substitute I go; for that
Would be a bleak reward of sorrows deep,
Unparalleled: not just set free, no more;
For that were incomplete: beyond all this
I give eternal life, and put on them
The glories of My state. Father, I will
That where I am, there likewise they may be;
And see the glory which I had with Thee
Ere yet the worlds were framed."

ii. "O Son! well-pleased, I give Thee more than this.
In the first place, the primest seat of love,
I set My Church, Thy Bride. I lavish much
On her My richest gifts, so to endow
And make her worthy of Thy peerless grace.

Thy throne is set above all other thrones:
Her dowry is proportioned to Thy state.
But while the heavenly heights shall be adorned
By Thee and Thine, I would retain below
A holy race, and make them too ascribe
Their holiness to Thee. Abram, My friend,
Holds still the title-deeds: I gave to him
And to his seed—his seed supremely Thou,
But not exclusively—to him and his
I gave the holy land—holy for that
My eyes and heart are there perpetually.
An oath I gave in pity to My friend
And his infirmity; that he might give
Full credence to My plan t' establish there
The chosen race. Thou knowest all their state,
Their contrariety, their great defect;
How they preferred their lusts, sought other gods,
And sad affinity with nations round.
How I assigned them lessons in the land
Where they in exile served, the land of Ham.
Delivered thence, they murmured, caused a breach
Of confidence; at length I scattered them,
And made them strangers in their own loved land.
These shall be Thine, and Thou shalt be their king,
When I have purged their rebels out; and these
Shall leave their name a curse: the faithful few
Shall be Thy heritage, and Thou shalt reign
Accepted for Thy rule. Yet more I give:
The nations of the earth shall all be Thine,
As Thy inheritance; the utmost parts
Under the whole heavens Thine too.
Rule Thou, and gird Thy sword upon Thy thigh,
And in Thy majesty ride prosp'rously:

Suppress the risings of opposing crowds.
Thou lovest righteousness and hatest guile;
Therefore Thy God anointeth Thee, O God,
Upon My holy hill; and Thou shalt judge
In righteousness. From sea to sea Thy rule,
And peace shall meditate her constant good.
A thousand years shall spend their happy course,
Ere yet again the foe disturbs the rest
Which subject hearts alone can quite secure.
Afresh will he deceive; effect his aims,
Thus most effectively: yet, spite of this—
Yea, by such means—shall all My will be done."

Thus has the mind devised fragment'ry speech.
The theme is infinite: the gracious terms
Most recondite—the unbought love of God
Who owned the Bride, who gave her to His Son:
The love of Him who in His jealousy—
For love is jealous of the least assault—
Devised and, all alone, wrought her release.
This love burns as a most vehement flame,
That many waters cannot quench—waters
Cold, trickling, slow, a slight recurrence oft;
Or rushing floods of worldliness or doubts.

iii. Th' effect is disproportioned to the cause—
So reasoning man would urge against God's plan.
This estimate is formed amiss; a view
Inadequate is taken of the whole.
The range of time suffices not to shew
Its great efficiency: it bears on all
But not on all alike. Whilst some aspire
To mansions in the Father's house, above
Sublunar things, and there behold His face;
Others below, all holy, sing His praise;

Outlying nations chant Millenial rest;
And all creation joins in great Amens.
   a. Ere this a life is spent diversified,
A mingled, troubled course of good and ill.
Some choose the better part; a genuine good
Accrues to them, though plenteous ills remain.
They have a remedy for grief, for care,
For all things critical which oft recur;
Not to prevent; nor, present, stay their course;
But modify, assuage, sometimes remove;
Or, what is better still, increase their strength
To bear, if God so wills, increasing ills.
A burden is but relative; heavy
Or light as it may be; that is, if one,
With lightsomeness of heart, proportioned strength,
And willingness, bears wittingly, 'tis light;
But if he frets, nor balances his load,
So bears it much awry, he wastes his strength
And then a feather added makes him groan.
Some understand their joy, and seem as if
Smiles in their face had found a proper soil
To germinate and hold perennial life.
In others, tears wash out the joyous bloom,
And thick'ning furrows carve the early face.
How should it be? Is man man's arbiter?
Shall one man smile, another weep, a third
Condemn the both; and all be orthodox?
It cannot be; there's ample cause for both,
The child may smile, because he knows that love
Dwells in his Father's heart inviolate;
And he may weep because he is aware
That in his natural heart all evil lurks,
And in his life some episodes of wrong

Against this Father's love defile the way.
But weep not for a Father's love estranged:
It is not so. With tears confess thy sin.
" I love thee not the less," the Father says,
" But I am grieved: thy sins dishonor Me,
Procure thee grief, and shame, and wretchedness.
I cannot, if I would, disown thee now;
I would not, if I could, forego My love.
'Tis not thyself to lose that thou shouldst fear,
But loss to thee *here* and *hereafter* too.
Reward I promise thee, not merited,
But yet obtained whilst in My house below."

 b. Some check all overtures, despise the grace
Which beckons man away from earthly joys,
And substitutes a solid heritage
Of heavenly good: their eyes are closed; their ears
Prefer the soothing tones of him who gained
The ear of Eve; their hearts are occupied
With present things. Objections vary much:
Some Jews of old objected to the place—
" Can any good thing come from Galilee ?"
Some saw objection in the parentage
Of Him who urged Messiah's claims; and scorned
The carpenter, that from his line should rise
A king for them. Some reason on the mode,
And some despise; some shew its fallacy,
And some take credit for their ready faith
In all the priest declares, leaving to him
The weightier things, whilst they to passing cares
Give all their time; a moiety to joys
Which, though they leave a sting, have sweets
Which they must cull. Yes, time is bandied so
By reckless hands, and so insulted by

Defilement gross, no marvel that at length
It takes offence and suddenly forsakes
The witless, foul wrong-doer in the midst
Of pleasure's plans, or business well arranged.
Time is not all the gift that God has made,
Not all the sphere of life's continuance:
And yet men live as if no sequel met
Its last forged link.   Here let man crowd his joys;
Let him determine that to-morrow's good
Shall be as this day's cheer, and even more.
Go on; add house to house, and land to land:
But God will bring thee to account at last.

   III.—Great sacrifices made bespeak great worth.
Worth may reside where worthiness is not.
The diamond sparkles with a radiance pure,
Unique; hence worth and excellent regard.
The rarest gem but rarely finds a purchaser.
Nature may yet reveal one so supreme
That size and brilliancy may disappoint
All purchasers, because of worth unmatched.
But worthiness must have a residence
Where claims unquestioned meet.   The Son of God
Saw worth, and competence to give Him joy,
Wrapped up in that much tarnished thing—the Church.
No worthiness was there; no beauty shone;
For it was then unwrought.   First He redeems
By paying all that Justice stern demands:
Then extricates, and then adorns, brings out
The beauty of this costly gem; imparts
Power to reflect His light, reveals in it
The glory of His state; and on His throne
Will blazon forth in fond parade that which,
Judged by the price paid down, were priceless else.

The royal treasures suffer no decrease
Through this profuse expenditure; they grow
The more: He who before was infinite
In each department of His realm, in this
Makes increase; or, at least, brings forth what else
Must have remained shut up inextricate.

i. The Church holds here no prestige of the joy
And glory yet to come. Time has no power
To manifest her charms, nor her delight.
Just so her Lord declared—"ye shall lament
And weep; the world rejoice." Contempt and shame
Are here the proper lot of those who wear
A foreign garb, and speak another tongue,
Most strange to those around: a certain mark
Of gross fanaticism, weak intent,
If not of stark insanity; hence hate,
Or pity, or the meaning shrug, makes light
Of former friends; dismisses with a stare;
Or shuns, with studied courtesy, the changed,
Frail being of their former love.
The world will love its own: break from its bonds—
Its theatres, its balls, its concert-rooms,
Its innocent relays; assign your cause—
Their insufficiency to fill your heart;
That heart's preoccupance with other joys,
Antagonistic to these same, which once
Gave you their charms; with much significance,
They touch their head, and wonder at the change;
For they had thought that Mr. So and So
Had firm good sense, and strength of intellect.
True; persecution is the proper mark
Of godliness: now in our day 'tis rare,
For godliness is rare. Conformity abounds;

Though non-conformity, with blatent speech,
Asserts existence strong. 'Tis not to creeds,
Endowments, and the like, nor regnant smiles,
That Christ denounced conformity; these all,
And many more, are bad; too bad indeed
For some who yet enjoy life's luxuries,
Oblivious of the suff'ring poor around.
Nor is it merely non-conformity,
However closely urged, that satisfies
The law of Christ. The law of Moses made
Demands imperative, but never aimed
To renovate the heart. The Christian's law
Applies to hearts renewed; on such enjoins,
"Be ye transformed;" and, "Be ye holy, for
That I am holy, saith your God."
Faith is a lawyer studying deep; immersed
In meditation grave; searching, with zeal,
The pandects of his ancient creed; that he
May plead with more efficiency, approved
By God and man. An operative too,
And not a thing of lordly ease at home.
Most practical, he is not satisfied
That he has knowledge of his art; he seeks
Some application of his skill: such finds
Ever some work to do. Life is made up
Of woof and warp; man is the artisan,
But God gives all the power—the skill to plan,
The art to execute, the taste t' adorn,
And finish with the grace of perfectness.
"Hast thou beheld," said God, "My servant Job,
A man perfect and upright, fearing God,
Eschewing evil, and none like him in the earth?"
This grew not as a weed, that needs no care,

That springs spontaneously: much care had wrought
Such great consistency; and faith in God
Had knit the whole. If you would see a man
Most noble, you must search, with diligence,
The rolls of heavenly fame: there you will find
A ruined thing restored. That which was good
Is better now; the second Adam shews
His likeness there. And yet not all who own
A change of heart, construct a change of life:
They're weak in faith; and this, in ignorance,
They plead as their excuse: let such confess
That they sin much; self-judgment suits them best,
Not pity for themselves. If we lay claim
To be esteemed God's pensioners, then let
His bounty raise our aim to use His gifts,
And so increase their power: let thriftless moans
Cease quite their senseless waste of strength,
And godly sorrow take their place; confess
That weakness is our own; acknowledge too
That though it is our sin to fail in faith,
Yet in our desperateness we look to God.
Some, self-condolent, cry—*a lowly band !*
Lonely we grant, but lowliness is scant;
And lordliness is not monopolized
Entirely by the mitred head; lawn sleeves
Are coveted increasingly; and silver cups
And goblets grace the sacramental board,
Where once plain earthenware presumed on much
Now scandalized as primitive.
Chapels are Churches now—a higher mark:
And those who once, in much simplicity,
Put up with intramural exercise,
Must now be comforted, and at their ease,

'Mid labored ornament. Outside appears
The architect's great skill, the builder's art:
Coined buttresses; the Gothic arch, single
Or interlaced; the carver's monument
Of his ecclesiastic zeal. A gabled arch
Sometimes parades the entrance way, pointing
To heaven, as if its treasures there, not here,
Were rioting; a steeple crowns the whole.
Inside as well, the architect has left
Some traces of his talent formative:
But here the decorator reigns supreme.
Mouldings and bas-reliefs, and jutting coigns
Do here and there appear as ormolu.
We know th' apology—that God is pleased
And honored thus. Oh! say not so! forbear
Such sland'rous advocacy, nor assert
The lowly One as honored; nor presume
Thus to rejuvenize the temple form:
When that is done, then will God's people too
Sip of the dew of youth. Again, you claim
Credit for giving to our artisans
Labor for bread: this plea is always good
If too the object of that labor is.
Redemption's song gives forth a jarring sound
As sung by voices half attuned on earth.
For though love is the key-note and refrain,
The harps are oft unstrung; and, hastily
Set up, send forth discordant notes, harsh sounds
Most dissonant; incongruous passages.
Another cause is manifest:—some have declared
As masters in the art of song, who are indeed
But driv'lers in the gentle craft; silence
Becomes them best: their variations grate

On ears refined, that much prefer the strains
Of old church music, grand, magnificent.
But yet they have admirers who aver,
Each for his chief, that he is the great man.
"I am of Paul," says one; another cries,
"Apollos is the model of my thoughts;" a third
Claims Cephas for a faultless type.
   ii. Come, flee away! anticipate that time
When, in the realms above, beauty shall reign,
And ornament abound, without relapse
Into unmeaning use. There countless hosts
Raise loud, and clear, and firm decisive notes,
In diapason sweet: there melody asserts
Its power to ravish even angel ears.
There then will Gabriel stay his rapid flight
To catch the dulcet strains, unparalleled
Since he began to be: creation's song
Was meagre—though grand harmony was there—
Compared with the rich song of those redeemed,
Translated to the music halls above.
There the Chief Singer raises in their midst
A song of love most sweet; its title runs—
"The Rose of Sharon and the Lily of the Vale;"
With symphony, "Thou, Thou art worthy, Thou alone."
The Leader guides the choir as of one heart;
One channel takes the flow of living praise;
A mighty chorus swells th' immortal strain.
One word acquires a solemn emphasis—
BLOOD has a thrilling power; e'en heavenly ears
Acquaint the heart with something deep, untold,
In all its magnitude; its eminence
To cleanse, transform, create anew—at least
Enact a part in this great agency,

Which else were not available.
There, clothed in white, the righteousness of saints,
Put on them by their righteous Head and Lord,
The heavenly hosts handle, with dignity,
And graceful bearing, harps of God; raise high
The strain—" Thou hast redeemed us with Thy blood,
And we have washed our robes and made them clean."
Deep stirring chords burst from the countless throng;
Praise never ending, never wearying praise:
Eternity its stretch, and space its bound.
The fabled music of the spheres is now
A grand reality. All in their course
Abound with interludes of wondrous sounds;
Responsive, greet the joyous choristers,
Who need no pealing organ to affect
Their ardent song: th' immortal harps trill sweet
In rich accord; and these revolving orbs
Boom with harmonious mirth.

    Thus, O Almighty Architect! Thy works
Shall praise and celebrate Thy skill.
Insensate things shall find a tongue,
Give forth their melodies, descant upon
Thy grace, Thy wisdom; and, with great acclaim,
Still furnish in themselves Thy sphere of good.
All things redeemed—all in the heavens and earth—
Shall praise the great Redeemer and their head.
For this hast Thou made known, O righteous God!
The pleasure of Thy will. A ruined world,
By Him restored, shall ever chant Thy praise
In praising Him: such is Thy will, avowed
By that command, "Him worship, all ye gods."
The great redeemed who sing redeeming love
Shall in the heavens perpetuate their song:

On earth, as well, redeemèd ones will swell
The glory of earth's King—Israel restored
The first dominion hold: the nations too,
Outlying pensioners of God's great good,
Complete the universal hymn.

> Praise to the Highest, praise and glory give;
> In whom we move, and being have, and live;
> Praise for redeeming love when all was lost;
> Praise Him who died, not shrinking from the cost.
> Praise Him above who hold the highest place,
> Praise Him on earth, ye greatly favored race:—
> Ye in the heights of heaven who see His face,
> And ye who on the earth partake His grace.
> All in one bright and glorious song unite,
> For life and immortality are brought to light.

CHAPTER III.—THE WORK OF THE SPIRIT

THE ARGUMENT.

INVOCATION.

I.—THE NEW BIRTH.
    i. What is it?
    ii. What is its design?

II.—THE NEW LIFE.
    i. In what does it consist?
    ii. How does it bear on its counterpart—the life which is to come?
    iii. How does it exist Godward?

III.—THE GRACES OF THE SPIRIT.
    i. Faith, Hope, Love.
    ii. The results of Faith—virtue, knowledge, temperance, patience, godliness, brotherly-kindness, love.
    iii. Of Hope—patient waiting.
    iv. Of Love—an abiding in light, self-denial toward God and man, freedom from fear, with perfect confidence and boldness before God.

O Thou! who in Thy all-creative power
O'ershadowed first the mortal womb, and there
In embryo placed the woman's Seed; there made
His bones and uninfected flesh to grow;
Mortal conformity assume, but not
Subjectedness to sin's harsh terms! do Thou
Inspire; not with inventive excellence
Of doubtful kind, but with a truthful view
Of all Thy work; a recollection clear
Of knowledge gained, amassed, approved by Thee
These many years:—alas! what scanty fruit
Has fed the needy soul, through little skill,
Abounding waywardness, and sloth, and thought
Of self-sufficiency! Do thou secern
The evil and the good that in the soul
Of one who owns Thy ministry, are found.
Winnow the chaff, nor let its husky motes
Darken the air of thought, so intercept
Thy heavenly light. Give earnestness, give zeal,
Give tenderness of heart, give love; nor let
Discreetness suffer in the somewhat bold,
Adventurous meddling of the mortal muse
With heavenly and immortal lore.

I.—The living oracles declare, in finished type,
"Ye must be born again." Uncertain sounds
But beat the air: here no uncertainty
Beguiles the craving heart. Does it resolve
Its wretchedness, and has it found, at length,
Its need of other agency? Has it,
Despairing, yielded all its fondest claims
And great expectancy of future good
Through nature's help? Here is the remedy,
Here a glad overture of grace.

i. And what is it? how is it brought about?
How did the natural child bespeak its cast,
Its origin? Did its own act project
And fashion being, corporance, and thought?
Or was it wrought unconscious, framed and knit
Through others' agency mature; such agency
Devised by Him whose infinite resource
Meets all His infinite designs?
He gives the germ, He shelters in the womb,
He brings to birth, He gives the needed strength,
And parturition shews the mortal fruit.
And so again; the wind blows where it lists,
The sound is heard, but who can predicate
The very spot it sprang, or where its blasts
Smite sullenly aspiring things? the trees
Stoop petulant, stiffly resume; beyond,
There still they bend graceful, but moodily.
Here it has passed, *there* still it shews its place.
Men have devised set laws, defined the range
Of stormy winds, death-dealing hurricanes;
They laugh at him; careering, baulk his pride.
The unchained child of death, the awful rush
Of air displaced, puts out man's reckoning.
Sometimes, as if in playful mood, it curls
The product of his mead, lands it elsewhere;
Upsets his fragile corn-field stacks, and whirls
The covering from th' astonished heads of those
Who labor there. Again, with roaring soughs,
The tempest strews wrecks all around, as if
An angry ministry were much at work.
Anon the zephyr fans with gentle breath,
And scarcely woos the glowing face.
Just so the heavenly birth: so every one

Who, of the Spirit born, emerges from
The realms of death and enters into life.
Some tell the very day, the hour, and some
The minute too, when they were born again.
It may be so; but gravest doubts may rise
Of misconception here: their *consciousness*,
It may be, is with them the turning point,
And misconstrued. Some strangely linger near
The threshold of their former godless home;
Do not desiderate re-entrance there,
But breathing much the fetid air, cannot
So readily throw off old nature's scum,
As those who wander farther off, lured by
The rose of Sharon's bloom, the citron grove,
The myrrh and camphire balm, the asphodel,
The singing birds, the turtle's loving coo.
The mind obtused, the head with fumes oppressed,
Find relevance in rural air and sounds.
The child is long a child in actual state,
Ere he has drawn supernal air; wrapt up
In yet unconsciousness, he waits the time
Of entrance on his mortal course; passive,
He gains the outer world; and all the strife
Is with the bearing womb: an occupant
Of time's brief lot, the child has not progressed
To consciousness, till months have sped along.
Just so the family of God: the first faint move
Portends the pregnant change. The birth-throe past,
The heir of light then enters into life.
Not to the detriment of others who
Are later born; joint-heirs are all; and all
With like propinquity, will share alike.
If one would judge aright, let him not seek

To fix the era of his birth, but search
His title deeds; if he believe in Christ
Then is he born of God: a present life
Proves incontestibly a previous birth.
As with the natural, so the spiritual.
   ii. Is it proposed—Whence this necessity
Of being born again? Why must it be
That one who craves an entrance there above,
Must here below endure an utter change,
So radical, that he, who once was dead,
Is made alive again; who blind, receives
His sight; whose ears must be unstopped, ere he
Can listen to th' account of verities,
Of such a kind that eye had not yet seen,
Nor ear had heard, nor had man's heart conceived
Their character? The question indicates
A fair response; an answer to the point.
Stark imbecility requires new strength
For other exercise than it can make.
The tree, denuded of its foliage
By nipping cold, would so remain, unless
Some much restoring agency gave back
Th' arrested powers, and so its rifled dress.
The palate lost must he regained, ere that
Can revel in the savory dish: the broken limb
Reset, consolidate, ere it can find
Its usual occupance. So he, whose heart
Makes its appeal to things inimical,
Whose earnestness is spent in foreign climes,
Whose thoughts, whose words, whose ways, are all inclined
In adverse mood, is utterly unfit
To change his residence, himself unchanged,
For that where dwell the very opposite.

Persistent in his course, he may, he must
Accept the gloomy sequel of his life.
An unchanged heart and life predict
A frightful counterpart: a life renewed
Receives the promise of the life to come.
Thus it is not an arbitrary will,
Intolerant alone—though this is true,
For it can not endure the evil thing—
But strong necessity makes this demand.
The dead would wear his grave-clothes still;
The filthy revel in his filthiness;
The hating heart would hate; the scowl would grow
And furrow deep; and all the pride of life,
Immortalized, would blaze with horrid glare.
These have their place, not where th' Eternal reigns,
But where darkness supreme shuts out the light.
A new creation then alone can meet
A state entirely new. While man remains
A denizen of this old world, in him
The old man lives, a tenant much at home;
But here he dies: a struggling exigence
Defers the sentence passed, that nullifies
All future ill. The new man pants, aspires,
To realms above, his happy portion there;
Awaits the time of change: meanwhile attempts
To frame his character, and ways, and thoughts,
By that new code of laws which God has called
A covenant of grace, and not of works;
And new, for He hath made the first one old.

II.—And does the old man crucified, no more
Complain of outraged plans, of hopes deferred,
Of disappointments, losses, and the like?

i. Oh! these have just begun an endless course,

Or ending but with death—the tomb's relief.
Uncompromising now, the new man fronts
His unrelenting foe. They both reside
Within the precincts of the earthly house:
There in the council-room they fence; the one,
In open warfare, smites his wary foe;
The other lurks, trepans, and circumvents;
Nor risks a stand-up fight on equal terms.
Both have abettors, able seconders,
Who watch th' eventful strife: both lend their aid,
But do not disengage the combatants.
Sometimes the new man trips, and wails his fall;
His enemy exults, redoubles blows,
And by the might of him who aids, would quell
And conquer utterly, but that the friend,
Who never leaves him nor forsakes, takes up
The prostrate one, from whom all comeliness
Seems gone, corruption seemingly restored.
His touch is strength; erewhile the stricken one
Regains his knees; and on his palms, his mouth
Sheer in the dust, he grasps his sword again.
His shield is raised, his helm adjusted fresh,
His tarnished breastplate burnished yet once more.
Ah! he is valiant now, for he is armed
From head to foot, needs but the watchful eye,
All prayer besides, and strict conformity
To tactics of the fight: he lays about,
Makes earnest use of strength obtained,
And shouts his battle cry—*Christ and His cross.*
The foe shrinks back, forbears, assumes a front
Of peacefulness, as if he wearied of
The mortal strife; or else, in feignedness,
Lies low, as though in death. Beware, new man!

The ancient fable here has much approach
To verity: that spoke of one who, felled,
Found strength as he embraced his mother earth.
Here is a foe more dangerous oft, as he
Is vanquished, not destroyed: he, grov'ling, leers
With vengeful hate, his second urges on.
Th' unwary lounge, the drooping lid,
The grounded sword or shield, the unlaced helm,
The self-complacent smile, invite amain
The well-poised shaft, the deep malicious thrust.
Or should the new man shun by vigilance
The open fight; then as the wolf is said
To fawn and imitate the faithful dog—
Where he has learnt to fear the vengeful horn,
That, fond, protects the threatened calf—until
The guardian's fears are lulled, then bears away
The bellowing prey; so much the old man acts:
Allurements gain when fierce attacks might fail.
A golden cup is held with dainty hands,
A smiling aspect lends its winning aid,
A syren voice invites—" Come, let us take our fill."
There deadly poison lurks: no compromise
Is safe for thee, new man. Be vigorous,
Be stern; dash down the proffered good; suspect
All that thine enemy may do; he smiles
But to entrap; he frowns and threatens war,
But when his smiles are understood, for these
Do serve his purpose best; he much prefers
Thy quietness. But when thou rousest up,
And shak'st thyself from earthly dust, he too
Assumes th' arbitrement of strife and war;
Thou'rt safer in the strife than in the lull.

ii. Life is a fragment here: its counterpart

Blooms in another soil; there it expands.
A seedling here, transplanted, there at home
Becomes a noble tree: no fading leaf
Distrains its verdancy; an evergreen,
It bears perennial fruit. A royal stream
Flows from the throne of God; water of life
Its channel fills, sustains the bordering trees;
Yet is their vigor there dependent on,
And measured by their growth on earthly plains;
If stunted here, retarded by neglect,
Or forced unduly, so advanced in haste,
To sickly growth, thence some delay ensues,
Just to regain its proper thriving point,
Whence it may make uninterrupted way.
Time breeds th' eternity of mortal man:
His every act is generative of
Immortal issues in th' eternal state.
Both positive and negative effects
Result to those who sing and those who wail:
The last will lose all good they may have done,
Through gross neglect of terms exemptive of
All future ill; besides woe positive
Through their abounding sin; the others lose
Through their neglect, whilst yet in pilgrimage,
Of ordinances there. These may have built,
But unenduringly; and so the fire,
In trying all, consumes, retributive,
Their works; leaves them untouched. The state is fixed
By God's decree; connatural with that
Borne by th' eternal immigrant from realms
He first inhabited. The unreclaimed
Remains a stranger still: the prodigal,
Returned, stays ever in his Father's house.

Eventualities are influenced there
By antecedents of an earthly type.
Nor is the record lost of good and ill.
The act, the word, the passing look, the thought,
Spontaneous, or unrecognized, compose
A registry, on nature's tissues set
And photographed. The heedless youth that flings
A pebble on the surface of a pool
Takes no account of lasting consequence:
He sees the circling eddies coursing on,
Concentric from the spot where he had plunged
His missile plaything; but he ne'er suspects
What he has done beyond the idle throw,
The impulse of unthinking boyishness.
No thought employs his mind of earth, and air,
And water—matter all affected by
His vagrant act; yet so it is: nor do
The precincts of this world limit th' effects;
All space, impinged by waves too delicate
For mortal nerves t' appreciate, record
Th' effects of causes small in man's esteem.
But who shall weigh or measure time's amount
Of units aggregate; and tell the sum
Of sighs, of heaving breasts, of gentle hearts
Profuse in sympathy; the look of love,
The glare of hate, defiant rage? these all
Make increase always; and unceasing growth
Will strew eternal plains with lavish fruits
Of happiness or woe. Not only minds
With conscious registry, but matter too
Will at the judgment day its tablets rear;
Then judgments framed shall need no witnesses,
No formal sentence of award; but each,

Self-judging, will assign himself his place
Of habitude, in endless joy, or ceaseless woe:
The former grace, the latter justice owns.
Of sounds, kind multiplex—the note of praise,
The voice of prayer, the song of mirth, the shout
Of fierce embattled hosts, the groan of pain,
The victor's clarion, retreating hoofs
Of vanquished steeds, the thunder's roar,
The bellowing of Vulcan's fires, uproar
Of wasting storms, the atmosphere conveys,
Pulsating each, in proper kind, to ears
Attuned most fine, with apprehension keen.
Light too, celestial, or of other spheres
Intact from sin's foul touch, has cognizance
Of acts terrene evading grosser sense.
Effects, interminate in space and time,
Their record make: e'en darkness has its cast
Of special type, its duplicate secures.
Light for the righteous sown will yet reveal
Its broadcast seed of thought, of word, of deed,
Matured to an all bounteous crop of joy,
When God shall manifest His scheme of grace.
Darkness—appalling thought!—is graven deep
With lines of guilt, a horrid chronicle
For hopeless, shrieking, shudd'ring woe to read;
First at the judgment seat of Heaven's high Judge,
Then at its frightful leisure, through the lapse
Of countless years. No hoped for end consumes
The hateful task: the lesson deepens much;
Each look its sequel breeds more evil still.
Commencing lines are formed each moment there;
The ebon palette occupies its place:
To write and read supplies a dismal work.

Unnumbered ages roll away; the work
Has hugely grown; the woe expansive spreads,
And deep'ning still, prevails; the guilt keeps pace;
Each paralleled by each.
And when the lustral fires their part assume,
Will they destroy th' effect of time? blot out
All traces of man's agency, and use
Of sensual gifts? Or will they only purge
All sequent cause of ill; and introduce
An age of glad effect from gladd'ning cause?
Nature is full of causes and effects,
Which from their commonness escape our ken;
Yet do they send their consequence afar.
An acorn drops—the oak less bend assumes,
From minished weight. The bee, on business bent,
Impends its weight on some inviting flower;
The air is cleft by its slow-nodding bloom;
The busy pilferer abandons this,
And this, resilient, cleaves the air again.
Intelligence is borne away to those
Who occupy far distant spheres; they feel
The busy throw of nature's shuttle, true
Throughout her loom.
And should a fiat of th' Almighty Will
Consign a sphere to primal nothingness,
The whole creation starts as if amazed;
Each orb assumes an altered course, traced out
By that set law, which the Almighty framed,
And watches o'er intent; for space is left
To be accounted for, and influence is now
To be re-balanced in the vast array,
For each attracts, each one repels; and all
Unite harmoniously in nature's hymn.

And who shall calculate; unerring, fix
The site of each; and mark the foci of ellipse
Peculiar for each orb; or other form
Impress on tracks pursued by errant worlds?
Who but the Architect of all can sum
The series infinite abstruse, and tell
The number of the stars; their residence
Most apposite? .   .   .   .   .   .
     If we have here digressed—
And we admit some small discursiveness—
A kindred theme has lured us on:' our mind
Has been impressed with what the crowd deride,
Or fail t' observe. Nature and grace prevail
To give to every cause its own effect:
And we have strayed, not vainly, to adduce
Some causes, trivial as they seem to some
With minds illogical, because these things
May almost rank with things impond'rable.
We would deduce a warning from it all,
And say—Beware, O man! how thou dost feel,
Or think, or speak, or act; for neither thou,
Nor this, nor that, did at the time take leave
Of all effect beyond the moment of the deed.
Hereafter, when the summons shall be served
That cites thee to the awful judgment-seat,
All that proceeded from thee *here* shall seem
Fresh carved to meet thy gaze. None may avoid
To be arraigned; or to rehearse the lines
That each—his own accountant—then transcribed,
A faithful entry of his stewardship.
 iii. In God's esteem, His Church is free from taint.
No spot of damning sin, or guilt, or aught
To move God from His grace can here exist.

"Clean every whit," was said by Him who sees
Whate'er is done, and knows whate'er is thought.
Such is His estimate, He cannot err.
First sanctified, then justified,* as such
God views with admiration this fair thing;
Her garments wrought with gold: the king is pleased;
Her beauty, His desire. Uncomeliness,
Which in her natural state was loathsomeness,
Is turned to great attractiveness and grace.
Hers, not for vanity, but love, and joy,
And glory to her Lord; a mirrored show
Of His great majesty, and moulding taste,
And constitutive skill. Fair as the moon,
And terrible as bannered hosts, she shines
With pure reflected light, light that is His
Who weds the heavenly bride. Her Lord He is;
In Him, her Head, she holds all power that she,
Herself in subject might, will exercise.
With all this dignity, how could a flaw,
Or aught divergent from her purity,
Obtain a place? God is well pleased with her,
The Bride of His beloved Son; and, rich
In all th' adornments of His grace, she fills
The highest place in heaven most worthily,
With Him who shares with her His goodliness.
But in their Father's house the wards of grace
Are fashioned for the courts above; and trained,
By time's vicissitudes, for heaven's great joy.

III.—Faith, Hope, and Love have great ability
To build the Christian fane. These give much strength,

---

* Such seems to be the logical, as well as the Scriptural order —"but ye are sanctified, but ye are justified." Heavenly wisdom will not confound this with practical sanctification, viz. holiness of life.

Consistency, and gracefulness, and show
Of well-proportioned parts. Great architects
And builders too, they furnish plans ornate,
And execute the same in skilful work,
Elaborate. Time-proof materials glow,
Wrought by their skill, with living semblances
To one all-comprehensive type unique.
Life actuates all. The Corner-Stone has life—
Essential life; and all, as living stones,
Are knit by this; each wrought and polished here,
Hewn in time's quarry, fashioned in the mode
Of heavenly workmanship. The artisans,
Conforming to the plan, much beautify
The temple residence of Him who dwells
Vice-regal there, there gives His utt'rances.
Faith is an honored name; its drafts are good
On all the treasures of the unseen world,
As well as earthly stores; yet it would draw
But sparingly from these, for they maintain
A doubtful character at Heaven's high court.
Faith's view of incidental things of time
Receives a coloring from time's effects.
A good becomes an ill, an ill a good,
As it may be from corresponding ill,
Or some attendant good; thus health is good,
But much an ill when in confederacy
With schemes of wrong, that else were left undone.
And sickness is a good, when such arrests
The steps of waywardness: a broken limb
Has saved a life; and even death itself
Has met a welcome as delivering from
A greater ill. So ills compose a good,
When wisely mixed; projections angular

Accommodate themselves and form a plane.
Some acids complicated make a sweet,
And poisons—due equivalents observed—
Give wholesome food, or drinks, or condiments.
Faith is a master hand at things of note.
It closes lions' mouths; denies to fire
Its scorching power; says to the Sun, *stand still.*
Great depths recede, and form a walled pathway
For those who flee; for those who seek their ill,
A fatal snare. The heavens withhold their rain
At Faith's command; again pour down their wealth
When Faith renews its suit. The dead are raised,
Deaf ears unstopped, the closèd eye uncered—
But time would fail to chronicle the power,
The deeds of Faith. Based in eternity,
Its rock is Christ; its permanence, God's word.

Hope smiles expectingly: e'er confident,
It has no fears, lest it should haply miss
The promised good to come: the joy thereof
Lights up the present darksome scene; where sights
And sounds oft fill with instant dread of ill.
With men 'tis but a baseless thing; it may,
Or it may not embrace some verity:
It is confessedly a dubious state
Of longing hearts for some outstanding good,
That may at last eventuate in loss,
In ruin, or in death. This is not hope,
But something like it, that has filched its name;
A mongrel and a sorry counterfeit;
For Hope has no uncertainty; no ebb
Nor flow. It is a broad expanse, where storms
Wreck not, where hapless barks ne'er strand; whose waves
Spread not their terror on the shore, nor roar

With presages of death. But time, most frail,
Can breed only loose frailties, and things
Which imitate, at best, immortal types.
The earthly hope bears disappointment oft;
And when it gains, sometimes the promised good
Is but an evil in disguise: thus sudden wealth
Is oft allied with great embarrassment;
The man who gains a hundred thousand pounds
Loses his intellect, and labors much,
With strange obliquity, to reconcile
The being of to-day and yesterday
In his own self. Another gains his suit
In courts of law: his being seemed wrapt up
In intricacies there; excitement ruled
The tenor of his life: that ceases now,
And he has lost as much as he has won;
And what he wins fails to supply his need,
For he has need of more than wealth can buy.
But genuine hope lays hold of unseen things,
And deems them certainties; well-pleased, awaits
The time most congruous to its ardent state.

Warm *Love!* who shall pourtray expressively
Its grace most sweet? Love is the elder grace,
Though in man's apprehension it has place
Sequent to Faith and Hope. She is from God:
His heart the spring, His grace the channeled course
From Heaven to earth, from earth to Heaven; on earth
The peaceful arbitress of diff'ring claims.

FAITH, HOPE, and LOVE! meek triad intertwined!
Of heavenly stature, Love, with circling arms,
Embraces her bright twins—for she conceived
The sister pair—they walk in wisdom's ways.
Eternal joy illumes, sweet fellowship

Delights. Now Faith and Hope hold tenure here,
Endure time's course, and then give place to sight;
But Love remains: her offspring have respect
To unseen verities; deep-musing, search
All evidence of that not yet revealed;
Not prompted by suspicion of its kind,
But much to serve their growth and healthiness.
They have no part in things that do appear,
But things not seen engage their earnestness,
Whilst Love combines the both: she longs to see
Her absent Lord, rejoices in His grace,
As shewn in tokens of His deep regard:
She well appreciates His long delay.
Eternal growth is hers, expanding heart
And limbs of heavenly mould.
Love had not been exhibited to man
In its most brilliant form, but for man's fall.
Such is God's way; an evil imminent
May traverse plans, and seem to mar them all;
They issue in th' accomplishment; either
By infinite subjection of their ill,
Or that they form designedly a woof
In that great chequered fabric Time has wrought.

ii. *Courage* proceeds from Faith, the soldier's mark
Of excellence; and *knowledge*, skilled to use
The weapons of his art, and to evolve
The treasures of the military store:
And *temp'rance* that conserves efficiency:
And *patience* under toil, and weariness,
And watchings, perils, hunger, thirst, and cold,
And heat, and evils multitudinous.
And *godliness*, which shews peculiar ways,
Provoking much hostility from those

Who count it righteous overmuch.
And *kindness brotherly* springs from the bond
Uniting all in close relationship.
Love crowns the whole; love first, love last.

    iii. Hope, ever bright, waits patiently till Time
Has merged in glad eternity; her term
Is just coincident with that: when Time
Has ceased to roam amid our monuments,
Cathedrals, art repositaries, all
That art, yea all that nature's hand has raised—
When Time has ceased to lay his withering hand
On all these things, Hope's mission then has closed.
Then she and Faith mount up to whence they came;
There, by a heavenly alchemy, they change to Sight.

    iv. Love in its earthly form has many things
Which, integrant, give her a heavenly guise.
Thus *Light*, e'en here below, has her esteem
In which to dwell, her constant habitat.
Not of man's day, for that is gross, contrived
For earthly need, material, suited well
To man's estate: but Love has other need;
With heavenly tendency and heavenly joys,
The light of life alone could satisfy
Conditions of her state.
"A friend at all times loves:" this love would lead
A man sometimes e'en to deny himself
What he desires, that he may thus consult
The good or pleasure of the one he loves;
And thus he proves his love. Did he persist,
Although he knows the loved one would be grieved,
His love would thus be tarnished with the breath
Of selfishness. Self is most surely served
In serving others first: the number One

Of which men speak, and boast their care of it
In precedency of all other cares,
Is truly not our Self: this number One
Is Christ—who once, when with the towel girt,
Washed His disciples' feet—our Master, Lord.
This Self-Denial, which *directly* shews our love,
Doth *indirectly* best secure our good.
Indulgence gross, even of lawful things,
Blunts the keen edge of appetite refined.
A sting accompanies the sweet, and when
The latter fails to satisfy, the sting
Increasingly annoys. Of that which helps
To build and constitute the frame of life
A little cheers, invigorates; excess
Breeds wantonness and much satiety,
And loathing of the joy, or spent control,
Or incapacity to pluck the wholesome fruit.
Self-judgment may renew the terms,
And give fresh excellence; but errors made
Deduct a little from the sum; not hence
Unmitigated ill; nay, rather good
Results from penitent resolves, if made
With solemn rectitude, and quick retreat
From inadvertent or deliberate wrong.
God is well-pleased if we confess the sin
And, prompt, forsake it too; and even men
Admit the gracefulness of such a course.
Anger is thus disarmed, and in its stead
Forgiveness qualifies for intercourse,
Renewed and welcomed cordially: the heart,
Estranged from God or man by selfish ways,
Is much corrected, and prepared indeed
For future exigence, by lowliness

Through apprehension of its waywardness.
Next to the man who never sins stands he,
In excellence and imminence of love,
Who owns a fault: save me from him who hides
In furious blame, or wounded pride, or shame,
The pressing claims that consciousness must make,
Unless indeed the conscience is debased.
I love my race, I do not love their ways,
Their guilt, their folly; these are mine as well.
Why should we add to incidental ills,
Which spring from intercourse of diff'ring minds,
Th' injustice of persistence in a wrong;
And irritate yet more a wounded heart
By harsh continuance in th' unfriendly state?
Oh! cultivate the wholesome, earnest work,
Distasteful though it be, of finding fault
With self; much diligence will give success:
And dropping self-esteem awhile, ere long
Great restitution will repair the loss.
The child that disobeys does somewhat fear
That he imperils thus a father's love;
It may be so; the mother may forsake
Her helpless babe, the sire forget his love:
Not so with God. The child of God will fear;
And if he fears the rod for naughtiness
'Tis well: his love, though not destroyed, yet lacks
The freshness of his early days, obscured
By injury done to One who claims from him
The best that he can give—his heart, his love.
Such a return is not determinate,
And so is fallible; in charge of man
It has his tendency. "Love perfected
Removes all fear:" a sense of guiltiness

Obtrudes unfriendliness, a shy retreat
From wonted intercourse. This state of things
Would but intensify, if left to him
Who wanders in his course; but He who claims
The loving heart provokes it ever with
His own most loving ways, and suffers not
The natural bent t' obtain maturity.
Love does not change its *character*, its *phase*
Is varied much: just as the Moon is fair
And clear, if but the medium of our view
Does represent it so; if dulled with mists
We see a murky thing: or, as our sight,
If inefficient, crowds a landscape thick
With forms obscure, and fails to classify,
Or individualize; a lens gives power:
So we have need of euphrasy divine
To purge the humors of the mental eye,
That we may see what exhalations gross
Have much belied; and seeing what is not,
We fear a natural sequence to the phantasy.
God changes not is writ indelibly
For them who have the eyes to see, and ears
To hear: then let our fears be not that God
Can ever change, but that our waywardness
May challenge some mutation of His mode
Of discipline: yet even this, if weighed
And judged with cool constraint, will much induce
A perfect confidence, for wisdom guides.
This is most manifest; for he who wrote
Sententious wisdom tells us that—" a child
Left to himself will bring to shame the one
Who gave him birth." If God then so disrobes
His tenderness, and for our good assumes

A sternness foreign to His heart, He claims
The more our confidence. Thus *boldness* grows:
And, if our hearts condemn us not, we ask,
Assured that we shall have all our requests;
As they are framed not by our natural sense,
But sanctified by prayer and the Word.

Thus has the Spirit's work been faintly traced,
And more is left unsaid than has been said.
Some may denounce the measure, some the kind:
Dry doctrines may amuse some minds; and some
Delight in works a priori; some few
A due admixture of the both approve,
The works posterior to the faith; for such
Our pages may afford some hints.

Press Education much, this first, this last;
But base it on the text book of our faith:
Then it will lend a powerful aid to stem
The current of those generative ills
That roll in frightful rapids down our streets.
Ah no! it suits not man's estate; he owns
Another guide, the spirit of the world.
Progress, the watchword of the times, ignores
Divine expediency, adopts man's law
And man's development; whereas 'twere best
That wise repression ruled in his affairs.
If ignorance is fruitful in dark crimes,
Knowledge is readier still to plot, and guide
Some meaner hand to execute; so mar
The little social good now left.
But shall we dignify this craftiness,
Give it relationship to knowledge; or,
In stricter justice own that ignorance

Induces crime—the ignorance of that
Which might prevent? or rather more; may not,
In spite of knowledge of a moral kind,
The heart depraved sum up the consequence,
And yet resolve to have its horrid feast,
By unclean courses fed—adultery,
Lasciviousness, seditions, murders, strifes,
Led on and stimulated by the craft of hell?
Conservative, the Spirit wisely draws
His lessons from the written Word of God.
That men, as they have handled this, have left
Some foulings there, is not to be denied:
But He who framed the institutes at first,
Knows how to sift the precious from the vile.
The natural man would rudely deal with this,
And treat it as a common thing, whilst yet
The Deity is there. If one will use,
And safely exercise his mind and heart
With God's most holy book, then let him seek
The Spirit's guidance there: self-confident,
He but ensures discrepancy, and toil
Disheartening and drear.

 Now to the Triune God—the Father, Son,
And Holy Spirit, three in One, be praise,
Here and hereafter; here where evil reigns,
And there where angel hosts and ransomed ones
Shall ever raise their tuneful songs; Amen.

BOOK IV.

THE MILLENIUM.

THE ARGUMENT.

Introduction. The King of nations. Character of the Millenium. Relation of man to man. The walk of Pleasure. Duration of life. Natural changes. The arch of Heaven. Regions of the air. The regions under the earth. Inhabitants thereof. A conclave there—Satan, Beelzebub, Apollyon, and others. Despair breaks it up. A subsequent meeting. Results. Final committal of evil spirits. Time's close.

MILLENIAL rest now sing. Awhile presume
To look beyond this age: and in advance
Contemplate meek the glories of that state.
Visit the unseen world; let Fancy sketch—
But not uncurbed—the doings of that place.
Consistency observe in portraiture,
In converse representative; sweet truth
Maintain, albeit lies should importune
As urged by wounded pride and thwarted views.
If aught is hazarded, depicting means
To gain an end—that end not unrevealed—
Let strict sobriety define its terms,
Nor let the understanding shun its laws.
God uses means, as oft what others plan,
As those which He Himself may plan; and all
To bring about His sundry purposes.
Time, space, and matter—all are conversant

With this decree; and all are building up
This universal frame. The many work
They know not why; nor do they stay t' enquire,
If rational, how tends their endless course.
The issues they propose, it may be, stretch
No further than their present need; content
To find their exigencies met; or if
They go beyond, and tax their current strength,
It is to meet some further, later need.
Their insight does not compliment their skill
To penetrate arcana of the unseen world:
Or how, or why, the Architect thereof,
As well as of this world and its concerns,
Doth work unceasingly. We might conceive
A sole Divinity, a Three in One,
An awful Monos, self-involved, implex
In dread infinity, eternity,
That give no rest to finite minds, if they
Attempt their gauge:—we might conceive of such,
For such there must have been—how long such held
The solitary reign, thought shrinks amazed
From dwelling on: but with the due constraint
Of Sovereign will, the teeming worlds appeared,
From nothing sprang to being at the word
Of Him, with whom to will is as to do.
Then agencies began: insentient, some
His bidding do unerringly; and some,
With mind endowed, rebellion perpetrate.
What may have been ere God revealed Himself
First in the spot where, as His archives shew,
Our common Sire, not ignorant, presumed
To dare His frown, God has not chronicled.
The period is not distant far, when Sight

Shall gaze, and travel unrebuked—look back
And view the past, in earnest retrospect;
Or, unrestrained, investigate the whole,
Both causes and effects, that circle round
Its being and its state.   Then will the heart
Delight and revel in no dangerous joys,
No hazardous employ.   Th' Almighty hand
Will firmly grasp all it has made: and should
The great Contriver e'er again project
Some other state original; its laws
Will e'er prospect eternity: no flaw
Will weaken their extent, or damage aught
Of their design, should post-eternity
Protract their hoar continuance.

   The King of nations now we celebrate;
Who, God and man, unites the claims of both.
Shall it be deemed incredible that He,
Who came the King of Glory, and avowed
His royalty, His heavenly parentage,
His princely line of birth, should suffer men
And devils, in their rage, to work their will,
To banish Him from His domains on earth,
And not successfully appeal at last?
It does not meet the case to say that He
Wrought out Redemption's scheme, the more prevailed
That they so madly sought to nullify
His righteous claims.   Most true, but not the less
They triumphed and suppressed His sovereign state:
For hear His words, "I am a King:" they mocked,
Invested Him with marks of royalty
In rude contempt, as giving Him His rights.
Again admire and wonder, but forbear
To reconcile what human thought may cloud,

Not harmonize. Christ came into the world,
"Was born to be a King," with might t' enforce,
And wisdom to ensure this cherished aim,
This purpose of His will; and yet He dies,
The King of Israel dies; thrust out, He leaves
His heritage to foes, retires amidst
Derisive plaudits, shouts, and bitter taunts,
And challenges to prove what He avers.
Man has his way, and prospers in his course;
Rejects God's present good, but He evolves
A greater good thereby, victorious in
A seeming overthrow. And shall He not
Take up the broken chain, united by
The link of grace, and here much eulogize
His sovereign rule? He will. The day of grace
Endures a little while; its complement
Is short; when that is filled, a thousand years
Will run their course, then Time will close.
A greater good than man has yet enjoyed
Shall fill the earth; and peace and righteousness
Shall meet in amity, the both conserved.
Yet grace will not, as now, allow the mind
To plot, the hand to execute man's will:
All wrong will meet a speedy, strict award.
Excision, holy, just, will vindicate
The righteous King's esteem of righteousness,
And strict subjection to His kingly will.
Then sin will hide its head, lurk in the heart,
And seldom dare to shew its front: not urged
By Hell's great chief, with legionary aid
Of trooping fiends, sin lies a buried seed
Deep in its genial soil, the human heart.
As in the natural mould, seed deeply sunk,

Denied the stimulant of light, remains
In germinating power obtused; but when
Released, and circumstanced with fav'ring help,
It thrusts its rootlet down for nourishment;
Obtrudes its style and leaves, and fructifies
And bears yet other seed, and multiplies.
So usually the heart in this glad time,
Will hold subsidence of its turbid state;
Provocatives awanting, seldom then
Will consciousness of aught malevolent,
Or adverse to the righteous rule, exist.

   Set free from certain dogmas, so esteemed
That to impeach their soundness were to risk
Impeachment of one's sanity, but which indeed
Are fruitful sources of abounding ill;
Set free from these—so tyrannous, because
So self-imposed—the world will freely breathe,
And prove the wisdom of that social law,
"Thou shalt thy neighbor love e'en as thyself."
The *good* will be interpreted aright.
No coffers crammed with gold, and intersticed
With groans and curses of the suff'ring poor.
No vineyard reft by kingly hands, to swell
The royal lot, because contiguous.
No hoarding of the cereal crops, until
The owner reads of high quotations, raised
Up to the point that justifies delay.
No sleekened coat of worn-out steed, worked up
To take the eye, and hide the ruin there.
Content abounds, for need is simplified,
Diminished much; and so demands are met
Most readily. Labor, still good, but free
From bending toil, supplies the daily bread.

War in his gory shroud, lies buried low,
Deep in the battle field; and gentle Peace,
So long o'ercome, o'ercomes at last; and there
A mound is·raised of broken shields, and swords,
And shivered spears, and balls, and empty shells.
Hatred has fled, prime minister of Strife,
And sought and found a residence below.
Ambition lowers now her haughty front;
And Envy shrinks despised. Malice and Rage,
Ashamed, retire, as not enduring smiles
And offices of love. Impatient Spite delays
Its fretfulness, and surreptitious clutch.
Its mannered Obloquy has quite forgot
Its busy ways and thriftless diligence.
Commerce still lives and thrives, but not as once,
Purveying for insatiate lusts. It serves
For happy intercourse, and interchange
Of what each nation yields profuse, and thus
A balance keeps. Nor does it register
In golden characters, on ledger graved,
And on subsidiary books as well—
"In cheapest markets buy, in dearest sell."
This fairest maxim of our days has grown
In disrepute; for when examined well
It makes disclosure of a selfish flaw;
Of base attempts to lower or to raise
The market price as suits the business man.
"He will be rich;" this is most popular;
This great first rule is unimpeachable
In days precedent of millenial joy,
When man declares another's honesty
Imperative; his own desirable,
If so his coffers may be quickly filled.

But when the days of godless rule have passed,
No longer fearing lest his neighbor wins
As well as he, the man of business knows
And occupies his place; and gladly finds
That occupation in itself is good.
   Pleasure still trips along the sunny glades,
Or traverses the streets of busy towns,
Or smiles in warehouse rooms; her garland throws
Around the well-set limbs of laboring swains.
She claims affinity in every house;
And, welcome, joins their cares, excluding gloom
And anxious thoughts; their sports, securing good.
The ox, when at the plough, her visits shares,
And, cheerful, leaves the furrow in his track.
The horse receives her as his charge, and trots
The lighter for his load: the ass its welcome gives.
Nature no longer sighs, her groans are hushed:
This genial visitant, with subtile power,
Has sought all avenues; through all her veins
Infused a joyous thrill. The heavens rejoice;
The earth is glad; the sea its roar keeps up,
Its fulness brings, in happy industry:
There Pleasure trills her lays, instils sweet joy.
The fields, and all therein, trees of the wood,
And hill and dale rejoice; give forth their praise
In living strains: relieved from pilfering hands,
And many foes, fowls of the air recite
Their merry song, and warble out their thanks.
There Pleasure keeps high court; detraction's spleen
Assails her not, though decked in gay attire.
But chiefly in the courts of God's own house
Is pleasure found; there she delights in song,
And minstrelsy; there she presides, intones

Its services; prolongs the organ's swell,
And leads the choral symphonies; and there
The harps of God owe much their excellence
Of heart-felt tone to her inspiring power.

   Ere childhood merges into youth, its term
Has reached a hundred years; and virile strength
Endures to seven-fold this. A thousand years
Will scarce exhaust th' extended span of life.
Trees will their vigor lose and die, ere man,
Who in his childhood set the tender twig,
Initiates the downward path of life.
The vineyard, planted by the owner's hand,
Exhausted, fails ere he himself declines.
The builder sees the stately house he reared
In mouldering state, ere he himself departs.*

   The mount of God presents a wondrous change.
The lion's nature fails, his sanguine thirst
Is quenched: no longer does the calf provoke
Fell, ravening jaws; the fatling's tender flesh
Invites no more; now herding with the ox
The lion stretches out his massive limbs;
The leopard and the kid, in playful mood,
Display disparity; the cow and bear
Greet with soft friendliness: no violence
Can happen there in Zion's favored spot.
The nations all around recline at ease,
Not fearing warlike din, or clash of arms,
Or martial shout; the cause of war has ceased.
Nor does the husbandman in vain pursue
His daily toil; he reaps a full reward
Of corn, and wine, and oil; and harvest home
A grateful offering yields to Him who gives

            * Isaiah lxv. 20, &c.

The springing blade and ripening ear: milk flows
In copious streams; rich apian stores abound
In hives, or crannied rocks, or hollow trees.
The Sun has ceased to scorch, the moon to blight.
The lightning's vivid flash, the thunder's roar,
Forbear to terrify. Nor drenching rain,
Nor drought, nor blight, nor adverse wind,
Nor fouling insect any more oppress.
All nature blooms: springs in the desert rise;
The wilderness, reclaimed, spurns barrenness,
And yields its floral meed.

   Now look above. The arch of Heaven presents
A spacious race-course where the glorious Sun
His journey runs: at night the same is seen
By native light, one vast continuous block
Of granite, quarried by Almighty hands,
And wrought—illusive show—in concave form;
Thus meeting by its span the earth's outstretched
And green convexity; contrives with that
A spheric lune, shifting as oft the foot
Alights on other track. Above, below,
Within, what marvels there abound!
The arch above suggests empyrean light;
Magnificent avowal of the throne of God.
A wondrous screen, dissevering mortal gaze
From uncreated things; glory prevails
Ineffable, and all its ways and means
Of manifesting God supremely there.

   The lune itself survey. Ere now th' abode
Of spirits foul, dark plotters of all ill;
There they have reared their schemes, there counter-wrought
To all God's plans of good, thence poured th' effects
Of malice, rage, and baffled aim, and drenched

Terrestrial plains. Sin, pioneer of Death,
Was their device, to imbricate man's state
With woe continuous, so in its track
Are found griefs wasting, multitudinous.
All life, through them, is burdened with complaints.
The laboring soul is pressed with many cares,
The body with sad complicate distress;
In that are passions raging fatally,
And pale-faced Malady in this contrives
A sore amount of pain. The end is near—
The end of power thus rancorously abused;
Power used oppressively, and ruinous
For all the subjects of its rule—a rule
Not always harsh, but always false: at times
It takes a guise most tyrannous, usurps
The mental state of man, controls the will,
Subjects the mortal part to servitude,
Or throws it helpless on the strand of Time.
But worse than all is that dread power that blinds
Men's hearts, and shuts them up in ignorance
Of that about to be—the judgment-seat,
The great Assize for guilt, the awful drop
That launches into woe, the endless grief,
The sovereign grace that saves.
The sound of war is heard: heaven's legions move
Against the rebel host—those Michael leads,
And Satan these. No foaming steeds are there,
No armaments, or mortal weapons framed
For mortal strife. Impalpable, they meet;
In dread encounter urge their might; the one,
In fateful lunacy, to keep their place,
So long usurped: the other, light-sustained,
In heavenly confidence, to vindicate

God's righteous wrath, and execute His will.
Short is the contest, short the pass at arms
Of those well-ordered combatants: though they,
As spiritual, utter no sounds, yet he
Who 'gainst the man of Uz aroused the powers
Of nature's elements—the fire of heaven
That burnt his flocks; the desolating storm
That overthrew his house, and those therein
Gave to a sudden death; now with his host
Calls up a din and war of sounds that strike
Old Time with great amazement, and premise
Some era in his flight of solemn kind.
Yea, such it is. The day of evil wanes—
Its sun has set—'tis dusk. An omened peace—
A lull unnatural—has introduced
Its evening's short repose; a brief suspense
Derides men's hope, which they have registered
Sententiously—"a good time coming yet."
A glare lights up the scene—all seems on fire—
The lightning's zigzag course, and sheety form,
Express, in deaf'ning tones, their fearful power.
The mountain tops, aspiring domes, cities
That pierce the clouds with pinnacles of pride,
Receive th' electric shock—confess their grief
In bursting throes, and toppled eminence.
The frightened earth quakes with the awful noise,
The heavens themselves are trembling with dismay.
The winds seem marshaled for a tournament;
Adverse they rush, and meet with angry roar;
Then prone descend, dispart the stubborn rocks,
And strew them helplessly. All nature owns
A crisis in her malady—Woe, woe!
Ah! woe to thee by reason of the trumps

Of angels yet to sound. An angel fallen
Removes the hideous cause from heaven to earth.
His power is circumscribed; but more enraged,
That he and his, so long the tenants there
Where He *who is as God* has foiled their might,
Are exiled now for an eternal term.
Yes, Michael's arm prevails: although his foe
Has gathered all his host, and urged the Powers
With subtle arguments; reminding them
How great the stake for which they fight; how great
The shame defeat will bring; how deep the gulf
Awaiting them. Prudence restrains the pen,
Lest it attempt that which would bring contempt.
A contest is involved—two armies meet—
And one at least is yet to be convinced
Of might superior to its own, else why
The issue try? The *fact* is evident; the *mode*,
A mystery. If men meet men in fight
Their blows give pain and death; and these
May cause defeat and flight: but spirits war
Exempt from these sore disabilities.
Sheer might prevails to hurl defeated might
Down from the airy heights—the means are hid.
Imagination might invent some scene
Where warriors of colossal bulk are matched
With foes of kindred height, whose force tears up
Firm-rooted rocks—mere missiles in their hands:
Whose strength drives far the vengeful blade within
The riven side, that gapes with deathless pain.
But such would need deep coloring and skill
To hide the monstrous flaws; art would enlarge
Her claims to that degree which few could meet.
　　Satan is now cast down—great is his rage—

His time on earth is short: this he will crowd
With schemes malevolent; in it condense
The wonders of an age—releasing bands
Intelligent, from regions subterrene.
With this infernal agency he will evoke
Unheard of ills: by other means, evolve
Great intellectual stores. Frail man is placed
Between these two—their forces play on him:
By one he is induced to hail that time
Predicted by man's fond solicitude;
When good that he desires shall be confirmed
Through man's development: the other mocks
His cherished hope with adverse evidence
Of damnatory power—one nurtures hope;
The other breeds despair. Deluded much,
Men trust the lie attested by great signs
Which God Himself confirms; retributive,
For they have had delight in wickedness.
Now Satan's scheme is ripe—to give the world
A risen one, so blend God's plan and his,
That all must be deceived except the few
Who, in the love of truth, that truth conserve.

Now look again, and with the eye of faith.
Ethereal space is occupied with hosts
That hitherto could not inhabit there,
For there impurity was found; unclean
In God's esteem, it was no fitting place
Wherein to bring the objects of His love—
The Bride and Bridegroom of His grace.
Now He, the Son of God, has purified
The many mansions of His Father's house;
Behold the meeting in the air foretold
In early time, and thus fulfilled.

The nether arc, earth's crust, conglomerate
Of rocks, and sand, and clay, and shells, débris
Of former occupants, and skeletons
Of tribes that trod the plains, or cleft the air,
Or peopled ocean's depths, abuts far down—
A hundred miles as some assert—on fire,
On liquid fire, a bottomless abyss:
Roofed in secure, it foils e'en spirit power
To broach, when by a stronger arm immured;
And corporate forms, judicially condemned
To roam the spacious sphere, find nought throughout
Correlative, but to the central point
They tend; yet buoyant, so that in despair
They seek and find the horrid roof, jutting
With crags, and caverns drear scooped by the surf;
Where lurk unearthly monsters, hideous shapes
Of hell begot. All these a welcome hiss
To those who enter there, deep-loathing guests:
Infernal baying too, and echoing roar,
Surprise their ears: again they, shudd'ring, trace
In fiery depths a headlong shrieking course:
Again ascend and find an outlet, tunneled up
To realms above, through which the molten mass
Runs bellowing with a frightful surge.
Sometimes a flaming jet is seen, which once
Mere fancy deemed the vent of Vulcan's forge—
A near approach to stern reality—
This belches out its cumbrous, scorching freight,
Encrusts earth's plains and clambers city walls
With cruel creep—a slow resistless course,
O'erwhelms the fated town, or else it shakes
Its dust of death o'er all, and so entombs
The busy crowd surprised in life's great game.

The Worm is there that never dies, swarming
In countless myriads through the vast abyss.
This tortuous thing, with entozoic power,
Inhabits all who dwell in that dark world;
For ever feeding on consumeless things.
There Death prevails, dread King of all the place,
Cold, passionless, unmoved; with subtile power
To hold his sway; impassive, occupies
All other occupants. Satan himself,
Who had the power of death, his subject now
Is powerless 'gainst his introvenient might.
In him Death holds high court; his ruthless grasp,
Relaxing not, holds him pre-eminent.
Fit usurpation this, that he, who framed,
And introduced, and gave encouragement
To such a cruel lord, should, in his turn,
A forced allegiance give. So Death, immortal, reigns.
There rolls, in sinuous folds, the wily Snake,
Th' old Serpent named; voluminous, his length
A frightful coil; outstretched, pervading far
The sweltering sphere. There the red Dragon too
Parades his scaly pride; with hideous jaws
Still ravening, but restrained; his hapless prey
Is with him there: by him and them these halls
Are traversed as their endless prison-house.
Huge length of tail is his, with which he swept
Heaven's canopy, assayed the stars, and drew
Out of their spheres a third, hurled to the earth.
A foiled antagonist, he still retains
In dread remembrance Michael's potent arm.
The earth received him first smarting with wounds,
And there awhile he urged his hate; but now
The lake of fire re-bellows with his maimèd pride.

Here now he roams with all his vanquished hosts,
A spirit-army, quelled by Him whose wrath they dared.
There Moloch raves, and in a horrid gorge
Awaits, as if expecting victims still:
Eternal vigils meet eternal shame.
There Dagon's truncate form, Jehovah's scorn,
Surmounts a pedestal of jutting rock,
Laved by the fretting tide with ceaseless roll.
There Ashtaroth attempts a winning smile,
That issues in a grin preposterous.
And Tammuz shews his wound, and still invites
The pitying wail; but sobs are howlings now.
Remphan is there, his star sulphureous burns.
Infernal locusts swarm in hellish mail,
And scorpions dire enact their cruel part,
In that dread scheme of everlasting pain.
What drear abodes! what hideous company
For men whom God besought; who, heedless, spurned
Eternal life! who once on earth partook
God's bounty, and despised his grace; who soiled,
With impious feet, that blood which, flowing, met
The tide of hell, and stayed its hissing course;
But which, dishonored foul with gross attempts
To supplement its claims, leaves to the foe
The rash detractor of its worth. Engulphed
And buried in the sea of death, no more
Does Hope relieve; no more are terms proposed;
Nor aught residual of Redemption's scheme
Avails, for that makes no account of Hell.
Each there repeats his contumacious course
That he initiated in the plains above,
In all its purposes, but lacks the power
T' indulge and quench the raging lust within.

The murderer with cruel nerve and cheek
Unblanched; the suicide, with weary heart;
The covetous, with eager greed; th' adulterer,
With burning veins; the liar, face to face
With him that first the subterfuge employed.
And there the fierce oppressor clanks the chain
He welded for his hapless victim's thrall:
Death oft enfranchised such, foully immured
In cheerless vaults, denied the light of life;
He now assumes th' unpitying tyrant's place,
Nor has he relevance of hope: though once
He gave dismissal to the burdened soul,
That cared not to enquire with what intent;
Now in his second sphere of rule, he flings
The suppliant back, mocks the great agony,
And spurns the frantic prayer. Advance of night
Makes no approach of day; for Darkness grim,
Morose, and vigilant, keeps watch, and bars
Th' access of light. There Memory fertile grows,
And reproduces all her teeming store
Of thoughts, of words, of deeds, of vows unkept,
Of broken oaths, of pledges unredeemed,
Of outraged confidence, polluted beds,
Wrecked faith, and all the nameless wrongs
That load the breast with sighs, the heart with grief.
Oblivion has beguilement none in these abodes.
 Th' imprisoned sluggish tide partakes the whirl
Of all th' imposed and ponderous weight without;
But, where the pole impends, there this is small,
And hence recession of the flood which frets
Th' incumbent roof. A cavern hence results
Lugubrious, serving well hell's purposes.
Here then, both roaming fiends and corp'rate forms

Are met; a partial resurrection serves
Satanic schemes.   Cain with his savage front
And mark indelible, and murderous club.
There, tow'ring high, the hybrid progeny
Of sons of God and daughters fair of men.
There Nimrod lifts pre-eminent his head,
That barely tolerates the lofty roof.
There Esau mourns his birth-right once despised;
And there the Pharoah drives his vengeful car.
There Anak's lofty brow defiance scowls.
Goliath too, his gory sword unsheaths,
A phantom duplicate of that huge brand
Wherewith he thought to slay the shepherd youth.
There Rapha's brood parade columnar bulk.
Og, Bashan's king, maintains his stalwart height
'Mid kindred forms.   Belshazzar there conceits
Proud Babel's mimic state.   Assyria's pomp
In Sardan gleams.   Black visaged Haman glares.
Antiochus is there, God's raging foe.
There Herod, famous for his mad attempt
To slay the babe of Bethlehem: and there
Iscariot too, the traitorous friend, still plots.
Additions yet arrive, for they have learnt
That mighty projects occupy the powers.
These all have lost their jargon, and assume
Hell's intercourse of thought.
Despair, sometimes a visitant elsewhere,
Has here her proper home, in Hell's wide range.
A shapeless sprite, approaching human form;
With eyes, whose wolfish sockets roll fierce balls
Of scorching fire; her mouth, a frightful gap
Protruding boarish tusks; within, a crop
Of bristling cruel teeth, and oblique fangs,

With deadly poison charged. Around her neck—
Or where such might be sought—a sick'ning coil
Of nameless things, or Furies hell begot,
Engendered by the loathsome hag; their home
Is there, and all the tenants of that place
The objects of their spite. The monster's hands—
Or what appear as such—grasp poisoned barbs,
And writhing snakes with pliant power to twine,
And bury in their victim's form, their cruel fangs.
No ears relieve the matted hair, profuse
With snaky forms, Gorgonic brood; they wave
Their hissing heads, erect their grisly crest,
And shoot a threat'ning glare. No feet appear:
Impellent rage gives energy of flight,
In hot pursuit of bootless speed.
Hell's terror! none but Death himself can view
The hateful, withering sight, and keep his place;
All seek, in flight, to shun the dreaded thing:
In vain! the victim's speed no refuge finds;
The curling snakes retain their fastened hold.
Now Hatred takes her place, fell arbitress
Of wayward plots, her counsels here prevail.
Consentaneity prevails, and growth
Of energy to frame and execute.

But who is he that, rising, quells and stills
Tumultuous din, unites divided groups,
Silence obtains, and ears strictly intent
On his address? He holds all suffrages;
Both spirit-power and corp'rate might have made
Consignment of their all, their subject wills,
To him; the same, as that on earth prevailed
To occupy the foremost place; Satan
Incarnate then, and still th' embodiment

Of him below. His haughty form dilates
With conscious majesty and lustrous glow.
Infernal emanation with sulphureous stench,
Emitting light beseeming to the place,
Relieves the utter gloom. His fame above,
As Satan's archetype, has reached below;
All know him now as Satan's choice; by him
Elect as medium of his direst works,
As fittest for his deepest schemes: they bow
Expectant, still their fatal trust repeat;
And he, deceiving and deceived, confirms
Their ardent wills. Hate doggedly persists,
And presses on, when all seems lost on which
To hang expectancy. A lambent flame
Distinguishes the head of hell's great chief;
His kingly mien, above th' assembled crowd;
A fiery cincture girds his glowing brow;
O'er all pre-eminent except in height,
Of this beseemingly; for not so low
That some, who frame their notions from that which
The eye can measure, might deduce his worth,
And so might hold him lightly in esteem:
Nor lofty, so that envy might traduce.
But deep intelligence is there; those eyes,
That pierce the gloomy depths where they have met,
Shoot rays of searching light; each glance projects
Illuminating power, as if in quest
Of untold thoughts. No undue haste appears
Prelusive of his thoughts; nor, dominant,
Conveys his words; no hesitancy mars
The urgency of his appeal. Yet, though supreme
In mightiness, as so endowed at first,
And hence continually advancing more

By greater increments; he frames his thoughts
In glozing words, cementing further still
The black fraternity. But when his theme
Involves the great Eternal, deep-set hate
Is seen in furious gestures, heard in tones
Of concentrated hiss.
 "Compeers !" he thus began, "your help is sought
In counsel and effect. Not now do I,
As untried chief of untried hosts, begin
To prove your wisdom and deep prevalence
Of insight into things. Ages untold
Have passed, in which your aidance has advanced
Our deep-laid schemes and efforts to dethrone
Him whom men, flatt'ring, call th' Omnipotent.
Ye know how oft success has met our aim.
I will not now recount your energies,
Your mightiness suggestive of your deeds,
These deeds themselves; nor will I mention how
For Eden's pair, I planned and sought release;
So gendering then, in them and theirs, a breach
Continuous; but rather bid you think
And ruminate on all the past events
And issues of your part therein. What skill
In deep contrivance ! Wary, how ye shunned
The traverse lines ! How plots with counterplots
Ye made abortive ; and defiled set plans
Innumerous ! Six thousand years have passed
In which ye have prevailed and held your way :
Sudden surprise has wrought mishap at length.
Ye have o'ercome, and may, yea must again.
Say peers, shall we remain supine, cooped up
In this abode? Have we no quarrels now,
No great affronts t' avenge ? Have we no plans

To be renewed? Shall we, decumbent here,
Yield up our rights of freedom to the will
And random fortune of the God of Heaven?
He exercises there high power; so let it be.
But then shall we consent to wander here
Inglorious pris'ners and avow defeat
As irretrievable? Ye well remember how
In distant ages I upheld the throne
Of Him who now has dealt us this reverse.
Heaven's highest pinnacle I scaled, and there
Confronted, and ne'er quailed before intensest light—
Now darkness shrouds my gaze.—
On in the lapse of time the rumor spread,
And reached my ears, that other beings framed
Not of pure spirit kind, would be endowed
With residence, some settlement remote,
Yet in the universe in which I moved
In undisputed sway, accepted for
My genial rule. I owned indeed the rule
And lordship of another in my sphere:
Some inadvertency of mine induced
His superescent power, not permanent;
And but for mine, would not be what it is:
Just as the light illumes nocturnal plains,
Which, if the Moon refuse, would come to nought.
Not always he who rules surpasses him
Who suffers rule. Oft had I made essay
To stem the current of another's will,
Deemed unassailable, and not in vain;
Whether as in effect of plans reversed,
Or effort, as precisive of the claims
Of one who would subject all others, curb
And, stern, repress all rightful liberty.

How could we, you and I, coadjuvant,
Sustaining, as we did, the solid spheres,
In wisdom, guiding; prompt, repressing bent
And tendency to oblique course; ofttimes
Evolving good, where fatal ill had grown
But for our prudent care and watchful eye:
How could we tolerate the weak intent—
Apart from agency of such as yours—
Of him who could not slight, and scarcely dared,
The effort of your wills, your powerful might.
This creature man, our lordly foe designed
To have a residence among the spheres
By us upheld, in some conglobate world
Remote from usual habitudes, prepared
For him with special reference to his need,
And appetites of grosser kind than ours;
Disparted from the spirit world by form,
And brute endowments, sentient powers
By organism wrought, and passions such
As we despise, but earnest welcome gave,
As fittest for our need—far-sighted skill !
Ye know that no design of ill we planned
When we contrived th' occasion to disprove
The hollow show—the wisdom, goodness, skill,
Much vaunted of their God. But knowing well
The irksomeness of needless laws, restraints
Illiberal, and harsh requirements, fraught
With peril imminent, then I essayed,
Sustained by your approval good, to stem
The ripening of this pregnant ill: yea more,
I moved therein because of your desire,
And solemn conclave held in other place
Than this; and this the general voice upheld:

No honor do I claim, beyond th' award
Of skill executive, devised by powers
Consentient and unanimous.
  " Ye have remembrance of the primal curse,
Couched in imperious tones and words devised
To wound becoming pride? How has it wrought?
The serpent's head is not yet bruised; nor yet
Is dust its food. The curse in part has told;
In part has failed. What does this argue then?
Infallibility in him who cursed;
Or utter weakness in some adverse power?
Our might is not debased since then, though shocked;
The last foul blow will arm our powers afresh
With wariness; experience rectify.
We know the great resources of our foe,
In part our own; our capability
Will strengthen with our need; occasions serve
Development; our next attempt will shew
Improved acquaintance with our enemy:
Defeat gives lessons good for victory.
Our foe has taught us much; and we do well
To learn e'en from an enemy.
If for six thousand years I have prevailed
To distance him, t' avert the sentence passed,
Unjustly so, upon the thing I used,
That had no power but do my bidding, so
Was innocent of rebel will: have we
No just expectancy of further shift,
Further evasion of this dominance?
Our failure now has been from quietude
And inference of calm immunity,
Forejudged by unsuspecting ones at ease.
When, unawares, and unprepared, harm came;.

The storm alighted on unshielded heads.
Ye have remembrance of the feint, the tree
Of knowledge good and ill; to give desires
And join forbiddance of the fairest fruit
Of Eden's growth. Did this his goodness prove,
Which of itself would surely work in time,
Apart from us, what he indeed designed—
The ruin of the race. Foresight in us
Induced our effort to transfer the fief;
Give them to hold it from ourselves, and so
Avert the evil that might else arise
From accidental breach of law inopportune.
Continuance, hinged on strict obedience to
This arbitrary law, must be abridged;
And hence absolved by all tribunals, save
The one that framed such an imparity.
Now say, could creature appetite endure
The luscious thing, so pleasing to the sight,
And not desire its sweets? If good for food,
Then why deny its use? And if deny,
Then why endow it with inviting show?
Mere gloss was all the liberty conferred,
Since this must peril all—an imperate excuse
For covert purpose of subjacent ill.
Our part in this has been traduced; as yet
We cannot boast the issue of our scheme:
Not all who aim the highest always hit
The highest mark. We cannot hide the fact
That we have failed, for thence our meeting springs;
How we may rectify the adverse thrust,
And make appearance of unvanquished might.
One of our subtlest schemes ye know has been
To throw discredit on man's origin,

Reputed of the dust. It suited not
That we should countenance such theory:
As long as that was held, our foe maintained
A hold on man for his subjectedness.
Aught else would serve much better for our views—
Chance atoms, spontaneity, matter
Eternal, electricity, and last
Variety and incidence of form,
Marking development.

"One other point, my lords. When man was formed,
It was announced that one of kindred kind,
As having moulded limbs and sympathies
In common with man's race, would occupy
The place viceregal due to me; not one
Of man begot, but surreptitious, made
And gendered in abnormal way; and yet
A claimant for the full regard of men
As one of them. He was to plant his throne
Above all principalities and powers,
And fill forsooth the highest throne on earth:
Moreover gain deliv'rance from our hands
Of men, by conquest ours, ere we had proved
Our purpose, and design to remedy
The patent ills defeated aim has wrought.
I dared to question this new thing; I dared
Dispute th' inauguration of this thing,
This novice in the art of rule.
Estrangement had sprung up; and then I left
Th' abode and objects of my earnest care
To foreign rule: reluctant, for I held
In clear remembrance long retreating lines
Of great activities of mutual good,
To ruled and ruler in my sphere. I sought

Th' earth's orbit, and descried the rolling thing;
At that set time, it may be, in its course,
Upheld by some of you. Soon I obtained
The pleasèd ear of Eve, her thoughtful mind
Quicksighted to detect the flagrant law
Unjust, that barred the hand from touching that
The heart desired. She took, and Adam too;
Ye know results. The swift not always win
The well-contested race; nor do the strong
Always the battle gain: the swift to-day,
To-morrow may defer to him now weak.
The advent of this minion to earth's plains
I could not bar. I not alone have failed
In best concerted plans: He too who rules
The heights of heaven and vaunts His greater power
Has often viewed His will arraigned, thwarted,
And made abortive in its exercise.
But still I wrought, and urgent on the steps
Of this supplanter, I embayed Him in
A narrow pass. He, moved by me, at length
Declared Himself a King; and thus provoked
Both Jew and Gentile; raised the fears of this,
In that inspired contempt; or worse, enraged;
For they expected other than this low-born man.
You know how I succeeded and prevailed
To have Him die a malefactor's death.
I might revert to some success of those
Who followed Him, disciples of His creed,
In forced ejectments of some valiant ones
'Mong you who, strong in purpose, failed to hold
Through stress of adverse power. I then came down
Swift on the lightning's train, that I had caught
And made subservient to my will: no more

Were heard the boastings of the Nazarenes.
We now deliberate some speedy means
Of egress from this foul commitment, and
Do you your counsel give."
    Thus the Arch Fiend essayed by any means
To move; and whilst he used mere words of truth
When they availed, yet lies availed him most,
And these he lavished much.
Malicious, full of deadly hate, he strove
To urge them on. Though confident that he
Could best originate, and specify;
Yet strength is added both in counsel and
Reserve of means, by those to whom he makes
Crafty appeal through specious reasonings.
    Beelzebub then rose: his mighty bulk
Upheaved, for he had sought among the crowd
The hugest stature of great Anak's sons:
So high, it seemed delay of weighty things
T' elongate all his height. His princely head
Appeared to penetrate the cavern's roof;
His roaring voice sepulchral seemed to shake
The solid masonry, to startle all around.
A spear and shield he bore, much loved reserve
Of giant form, that trod embattled fields.
The shield a spacious orb of weight immense,
By bare impressure crushing common foes;
His spear finds stinted room throughout the cave.
His fetid breath, to merely human kind
A fatal stench, and in a hundred fights
Of deadly power; now in the courts of hell
A rank endowment fixed.
    "Ye powers!" he said—and more intensive sat
Silence on all—"we are not wont to prate

Of purposed deeds, and shrink when in our way
Great obstacles obvene. Ye know my might,
The prowess of my arm: not mated in
The adverse ranks; whole squadrons shrank dismayed,
Nor dared dispute with me the victor's palm.
But not in daring deeds alone I claim
A foremost rank; for side by side with him
Who first obtained your ear I fought, and now
As heretofore, in conference move."

Thus he, huge demigod, in arrogance
Assumed co-equal fame with him, whom all
Acknowledge now their head and president.
Whilst he, unmoved, maintained his lofty place;
And, conscious, made no protest of mere words,
But looked expressively, as though he sought
Some proof of boasted skill and wise debate.

So he continued—" Here have we avail
Of room and good occasion for the show
And exercise of skill and strength; behold!
This refuge have we, left by oversight amiss.
Not refuge only does it now afford,
But vantage ground whence we may surely work,
At length effect release from this foul place:
For this our first great overthrow need not
Extinguish all attempts to gain yet more
Than we have lost. Skill to devise is here;
Arms used to effort; mighty strength; nor now
Is interruption here from errant tide.
Should we have left, prepared for adverse hosts,
This meeting place, so suited to the need?
Deduce from this him fallible, whose might
We know indeed, and make acknowledgment
That he has now the upper hand: but he

Who now is high may next fall very low.
First let us make this place yet more secure
With walls and bulwarks fitted to resist
A sudden lurch of this revolving globe,
Which yet might render tenantless, henceforth
Untenable, this vasty cave: this do,
Then other projects may obtain our time,
And energy, and strength. We have not closed
Our efforts to confuse our wary foe.
Our purpose is maligned; as though its aim
And agency were adverse to all good.
Now what is good? That which our foe has done
And labeled with this term convertible!
And evil—what is that? a converse mode;
Good, but for this that he, who had a date
Anterior to our race; an earlier sphere
Of exercise; an opportunity,
With no opponent to delay his plans,
Of working undisturbed, resolved his laws
By self-aggrandisement—these he called good.
Had he resolved our plan, *that* had been good;
And his, so cavalierly flounced, had been
The evil then:—so circumstantial is
The guise an action takes. My lords, ye know—
No language is occult to us, nor prescience
Confined to him, who arrogates so much—
Ye know, I say, the record of the ways
Of him who now bestrides our prostrate power;
How he denounces him who takes a life
With violent hands, and brands the fatal act
With obloquy of name; and heaps deep shame
Ulteriorly on all who stay life's course:—
Yet Jael won his praise—if not direct,

Yet by an advocate of his; one who,
As prophetess, delivered all his mind.
And what was Jael's act ? A murder foul,
Foul treachery, consummate tact in guile:
All reprobate 'mong men; commended by
This god, who ranges in his scheme all good.
Again; an enemy will sometimes serve
An enemy; so when it suited him
To seek our aid—it suited us as well—
One from our ranks became a volunteer
To do his will: the more so as we deemed
Th' occasion fitting to besmear his name
With great reproach. If any attribute,
That he doth claim exclusively, is more
Insisted on than others in the list,
It is that he is true. Observe him now—
' Who shall deceive the King, that he may go
And fall at Ramoth-gilead ?' One said this,
Another that: then one of us, astute,
Took up the challenge, and supplied a lack
In all the multiplied machinery.
'Thou shalt persuade him and prevail: go forth,
So do.' We needed not the prophecy
To tell us of success: we undertake,
And we perform. One arm alone—one will,
Of all existencies, has e'er prevailed
To circumvent our aim; *that* turned aside—
Whate'er th' intent—we walk the course unclogged.
Again; adultery is denounced by him,
In laws which, penally confirmed, announced
His great abhorrence of th' alluring crime;
And yet he issues his command:—'Go, take .
A wife of whoredoms, children of whoredoms too

Thou shalt beget:' and this a second time
Hosea was compelled to do. We know
The plea that complicate resource has urged—
The prophet was a sign: what! must he break
The laws which he had made, to find a mode
Symbolical? And is his vaunted rule
So pregnant with this good, that happiness
Outstrips the race of ill? Does it abound
So as to claim a balance on its side
If weighed against the ill? If so, then whence
The suicides, the anguished cries, the moans
Of pain, the catenation death has forged
From man down to the lowest link of life?
Did Hezekiah wrong his god when he
Desired a longer term of life? Or was
That life prolonged that he might propagate
Manasseh, he who drenched the streets with blood:
Thus furnishing—transparent though it be—
A reason for estrangement of the race
From Judah sprung. Perfection is an art
We see not yet: our sun has been eclipsed,
Or we had early proved with certainty
The good we planned. The germ was in its place,
But time had not supplied the needed warmth
That it might germinate: or, shall I say,
The spore had burst its case, begun to shew
Its vigorous powers aspiringly, when trouble came.
With sudden blast the tempest swept amain
Throughout our sphere, where we revolved
Our weighty thoughts: crushed by the sudden bolt,
The effort fair retreated, not to die,
But to be nurtured for another throe.
We will believe the utter uselessness

Of all we may project, when all resource
Is hid from us—when all our power to plan,
All means to execute, alike sink down
In piteous helplessness. When thought is gagged,
When speech is hushed, when agencies decline,
Then may we own a greater than ourselves
Is at the helm. Till then farewell to gloom,
To apprehension of results, to fears;
Till then, as well, let all devices swell
Our store of competence. No mean amount
Of generalship, and wise avail of means
Sustain our foe: these must be met by us—
His mines, with counter-mines; his open force,
With subtlety. Our aim is to retrieve,
Re-institute all that we lost at first,
And more set up. Word-master I am not:
But when the time is come, debate in arms
Will find for me the foremost rank."

   Mis-representative of good! This fiend
Has many repetitions of himself
Among the sons of men. They scan God's word,
His ways, His works; they understand Him not:
Yet wilfully pronounce Him fallible.
If powerful, yet amiss in kindliness;
Or, in His goodness, intricate, infirm.
Malicious, some traduce; some implicate,
In their esteem, the wisdom of His rule.
All who attempt t' unrol His policy
Make havoc and disfranchise common sense.
The compound, fiend and man, surpasses far
In gross default, the undiluted fiend;
For *this* has not a good to negative,
Whilst *that* alone has made His good an ill.

Apollyon then arose, a subtle fiend:
He Nimrod's frame dilates; in stature matched,
And in presuming might, with him last named:
Inferior not, in counsel deeper far;
Second to none but Satan's fatal eminence.
In heavenly rolls his name is registered
The angel of the bottomless abyss.
Fallen wingèd cherub! Nimrod's graceful height
Maintains his volant fame. Vast pinions hang
By diabolic art contrived and hellish skill.
His hands grasp fiery darts of dreadful power,
Well known to those who have forsworn his right,
Revolted from allegiance to his rule.
Nought but the shield of faith can intercept
Their spiteful flight, their burning quench.
And nought, when wounds occur, can e'er avail
But blood—the blood of Christ, to counteract
The sore effect, and heal the piercèd heart.
This mighty prince no weapon fears, but such
As, forged by heavenly art, are tempered so
That use blunts not; but, sharpened by the fray,
Acquire more competence. The Spirit's sword
Makes earnest work; Apollyon dreads its power:
The weakest makes with this effective thrusts,
And parries blow with blow behind his shield.
Apollyon—or Abaddon, such his name
In th' Hebrew tongue—king of the locust band,
In conscious might and majesty, uprears
His courtly frame. Felt silence now prevails,
Waits on his well-tried powers in skilled debate,
Not shrill, nor hoarse, but thrilling tenor notes
Convey his thoughts, impress his influence.

"My lords! it argues great deficiency

Of forethought and ulterior means in one
Who arrogates supremacy, that we,
In spirit power and sinewy strength should here
Amass our force, here congregate where both,
Concurrent, may effect so very much
Against contrivance hasty and precipitate.
Our foremost step has been premised; well said,
Nor let delay endanger aught our plans.
Then, well secured, consentient, let us work
A passage to the realms above.
Ye know how ye have counseled heretofore,
Suggesting instruments of curious kind
In various arts; of deadly power in war;
Which, worked by skill and stalwart frames, produced
Effects ne'er dreamt of in preceding times.
My lords! ye have not yet your limit reached
Of deep device and cunning skill, e'er prompt,
To frame from means abortive in the hands
Of grosser kind, fit instruments to work our will.
My unremitting care has been to thwart
The will of him who, in the wantonness
Of adventitious power, has set us down
As rebels to his rule and government:
Debarred approach to explicate our ways
To supplement his governmental laws.
These had defect, as we had long foreseen,
Prospecting them through far futurity;
As burdened with detail, involved, confused,
Injurious to the subjects of his rule.
This gave offence; and, unforgiving, he
Implacable pursues relentlessly
Well meaning helps and favorers of his plans.
Far-seeing, we anticipated ill,

And interposed counsel unsought; for this
Unthankful, he occasion took to wreak,
On unsuspecting ones, bitterest revenge.
Hostile, he yet pursues with deadly hate;
And we, committed to the same set course,
Make sheer avowal of our firm resolve
To persevere and work our adverse will.
We have prevailed, as ye have heard; and may,
Yea, must again, for that our lordly wills
Know no restraint that we can tolerate.
'Tis bruited that he is Omnipotent:
Not yet we own this overweening claim.
And Omnipresent too; now is he here?
Why not suppress our thoughts, our words, our ways,
Our measures for the still projected change,
Th' establishment of other, better rule?
Do ye consent to fret your time away,
Exclude all means by unavailing grief,
And low despondency? Regret is vain;
Leave that to fools and minds of weak intent.
Let resolution firm, congenerous means
And measures prompt, employ our agencies.
If schism enters, then rude mockery
Will shame our host. Ye all assign to me
No common rank, but readily I yield
The foremost place; and this another fills.
Yet not another, for the three who claim
Your audience first are one—a three-fold one!
But paralleled by other instances
In things of common kind; yea, man himself
Is one in spirit, body and a soul.
Give counsel now, ye peers; if aught occurs
To any, diverse from our utterances.

We claim and advocate your skill, and seek
Your operative aid as well, to plan
And execute. Outlets there are from hence,
But not available: more than myself
Have made attempts, but adverse tendency
Of liquid, ponderous matter, filling up
Those chambered ways, has foiled us hitherto.
Here no such bar exists, unless ye shrink
In timid fear, and quail before the task:
Or dread the boasted might that oft has failed,
In contest with your schemes adversative:
Unless ye suffer pride to thrust you down;
And, dominant, suppress all liberty,
All longings to avow your conscious claim
To take a part in rule and agency;
Arouse and shake this fest'ring coil away
That fetters mind and limbs—is't cowardice?
Is it your liking thus to be confined,
And cabined with no exercise of powers
Fitted to rule and guide aright the spheres?
All stratagems are lawful with a foe.
In ages past we have prevailed to stay
And implicate some well-planned schemes, yet not
In our esteem the best that might be wrought.
Such we have sought to rectify; and some,
'Gainst which we have no damnatory views,
Except as helping to advance the claims
To sovereignty, we have defiled with gross
And adverse ridicule: as thus, I moved
Some men to read the record of the rocks
By wary promptings, not at first with show
Antagonistic to the early creed;
But slow and sure, I caused a line to spring

Small angled from the orthodox; alarm
Was thus forestalled; divergence was so small
That even great divines adherence gave,
And advocated what appeared to them
A help to their divinity; Aha!
At length some took alarm, and raised a cry;
Too late! the ruse had great success; the twig
Was limed auspiciously; the greatest minds
Were charmed with rich discov'ries made, and these
Were facts we could not hide; but well we knew
That some new law would be as charming too.
We knew the facts, and knew as well that they
Would in the course of time be brought to bear
On man's belief; and so, being thus forewarned,
We were forearmed, and well prepared to meet
The evolution of events that time must bring.
Our present aim is to emancipate
This great assembly, now inglorious here,
Eager to exercise their powers for good;
Assured that our designs for liberty
Are more contributive than harsh restraint.
Give us, ye powers, th' advantage of your thoughts."

Thus with deep sophistry, a spice of truth,
And keen provocatives, the graceful fiend—
If gracefulness may be, where all is lost
Of excellence; ruined irrep'rably,
And yet magnificent; for God's great work
Retains the proof of greatness in the wreck—
Thus having spoke, his massive pinions move
In easy curvature: no grateful breeze
Responds; a reeky vapor fills the cave,
Pestiferous, intensely hot, more hot
Through motion thus impressed.

Response of murmuring applause ensued,
The cavern filled. Fell Hatred much inspired,
And urged them on to shame in fruitless toil.
One craven spirit then availed himself
Of Sardan's form, who rose and hazarded
A faint suggestion of contingency.

"How then," he urged, "shall we hereby ensure
Remission of our woe, or aggravate
The penalty already laid? Suppose we gain
The object now proposed—our freedom, rights,
And glad egression hence; an after part
Belongs to us; pre-meditation now befits
How we may meet the further exercise
Of power which we indeed might deprecate,
But that we are as well assured that he,
Who lodged us here, will utterly reject,
As that we rue our part in strife bygone."

Then Discord, pettish sprite with spleeny voice,
Appeared; almost prevailed to spoil th' effect
Of plans, with subtle sophistry enforced,
And impious lies. Her entry wrought in some
Dismay; in others, rage; some, hasty, claimed
At once t' initiate their schemes.
But why do all together cease their din?
And why does silence ominous ensue?
Despair has entered now, that frightful thing.
Close pressing on the steps of Discord, she
Has found the meeting place: all see, nor stay
To face; nor seek to shun the waste of fire:
A rush of hopeless fugitives ensues.
One word from Satan as they madly court
The seething covert which of late they shunned—
"We meet again." He said, and coursed along,

Not caring to confront th' avenger dread
Of Him, who knows the way to take with those
Who slight His word, as well as those who know
And do the just enactments of His will.
Her numerous agents know and do their work,
No bidding wait: instinct with burning rage,
Their victims seek. Her hundred hands discharge,
With lightning speed, their venomed shafts; and she,
The chief avenger, seeks the chief; in guilt
Pre-eminent, pre-eminent in woe.
He, swift in flight, retreats; she equals him,
And fastens on him with her cruel fangs:
The spirit and corporeal power alike
Partake their virulence. Does it seem strange
That they should take this dread alternative?
For see, they plunge beneath the fiery tide,
Invite the horrors of that lake so late escaped,
As they, emerging, sought the cavern's mouth
And respite from their woe; and with th' intent
Of resting there. No rest for such; no rest
For any that deny God's sovereign right and will.
This maddened course is not dissimilar
To numerous instances in earthly things.
The pining inmate of bleak prison walls
Seeks hasty riddance of his burdened life
From these same gloomy limits of his cell;
Against their buttressed strength he rushes, mad
With cruelty and sickly hope deferred.
The disappointed suitor courts the gurge
That murmurs o'er the frenzied guilty plunge.
The broken merchant stems the tide of life,
The fatal noose his rash resort; some seek
The battle field, to close their wearied life.

How many summon death, with helpless hands,
By oaths, demented ravings, and the stings
Of conscience bruted by self-will ! and some,
Not few, the demon Alcohol herds on.
   They meet again, and make attempts to work,
Elaborate their plans.   Huge blocks, dislodged
By giant strength, rest in a bed prepared
By ready might and readier wills: apace
The fabric grows, bitumen near supplies
Strength for the massive joints.
Elate they view the rising walls, well coined
And buttressed, so that space may be retained,
While yet approach is made throughout the void
To solid masonry, as though one block.
A void is left for entry, fitted close
With one vast rock prepared by hands expert.
Vain work, but that the God whom they malign,
Had willed success.   Sometimes the means alone,
Sometimes the end as well, are used by Him,
If by that means or end a greater end
Is thus obtained: He suffers progress, then
Avails Himself of foes to work His will.
What great amazement and perplexity
Await for those who take great pains to plan
And expedite, and find another's will the end !
Chagrin and rage succeed; then other means
And other objects are proposed; the same results.
Eternity will e'er repeat the endless tale,
And disappointment's garb assume, if foes
Still work against: no faculty abeyed;
But unremitting exercise will strengthen each.
Nor men nor devils carry with them hence
Aught to relieve their utter wreck; evil alone,

Most capable of frightful growth, they bring.
Sin, ceaseless, heaps intensity of pain;
And pain evolves more sin. They cannot stay
The hateful dualism; nor could they,
If willing, stay the cause producing it;
Nor, had they power, would inclination yield.

   Eternity! O dread immeasurable word!
Girdle of God, without beginning, end!
No spring nor issue of its course: the past
Is lost in thought interminate; obscured
The more by all attempts to penetrate
The dim recess. The ever-shifting *now*
Indents a central point, between the past
And that to come; this intricate as that;
And saturant with marvelous things that He,
Great occupant, has set, each in its place.
Let thought excursive range, and backward rove;
Retrace the past, the hoary past; adopt
A unit of a million years; make Time
Its increment, and by a fiction let
Time spend a moment in its course; and let
These moments occupy that million years.
How far has thought receded? But a step.
Go on, a million times repeat this step;
The bourne makes no approach, the route
Unshortened, yet extends. Then duplicate
Thought's traversed line, with *now*, th' accepted time
Whence to initiate a forward course:
The goal is reached; heaven echoes with the shout
That marks th' expiry of this little term,
Crowded with marvels of the grace, the power,
And wisdom of that God invisible,
Who filleth all th' interminate expanse

Of space and time. But listen to the sad response
In curtained depths below. The shriek of woe,
The wail of mad despair, there still abound,
There still are heaping up. No beam of Hope
E'er penetrates the prison walls; no joyous sport
Of Spring makes slow expiring Winter smile;
No grateful shade gives e'er a refuge glad
From scorching Summer's heat. No dated lease
Assigns a def'nite term, or gives a thought
Of quittance at some period, though removed
Far into dim Eternity. And do they keep
A reckoning there of ages flitting by?
Do they essay a livid chronicle
Of passing years? Do they a measure keep
Of threescore years and ten? And do they there
A drear rehearsal make of ways, and words,
And thoughts they registered above?
And do they there impeach God's judgment seat;
Or do they justify? Yea, do they not
Inscribe continuously on every wave
Which rolls its sluggish weight, that God is just?
Stay man, forbear thy madly impious ways:
Thy reasonings frail will never satisfy
The contradictions which thy finite mind,
Thy bad declivities, extemporize.
Thou canst not reconcile; but thou canst yield
Thy erring judgment to a greater mind—
An infinite, that offers thee a good
For that which, at its best, provides an ill.
   Pass on a thousand years, a period since
The first commitment to these foul abodes,
By Justice stern, but irreproachable.
From time to time the work had made advance;

Oft interrupted by Despair, resumed
When appetence had grown again.
At length they view the work complete, fitted
For all their purposes. The breach is made,
And all had now escaped, but One kept watch
Secerning ways and means; suppressing some
Intrinsically ill; and suffering some
As apposite. Uncarnate, three escape,
Spirits unclean, and gain the upper world:
A sad proruption for the sons of men.
A slumb'ring advocacy now starts up.
The human heart is no way changed, although
Consummate training for a thousand years
Has wrought effectually to meliorate
The badness there indigenous to all.
The root, the tree, the branches—all retain
Their native tendency; the fruit alone
Has much improved, through careful husbandry
And pruning freely, made imperative
By rank luxuriancy. A spark will fall
Harmless on matter incombustible;
But where a substance fulminant resides
In safest quietude, a brand applied
Wakes up a fearful power, whose candent breath
And detonance spread death and mad dismay.
Or when a foul miasma fills the air,
It takes effect where some affinity
Invites its outrages. So in the last sad time
Of this world's history; when God has made
Most manifest the blessings of His rule,
In full subjectedness to earth's great King,
A last probation He will make, so prove
The dangerous tolerance of hearts corrupt,

A nature prone to germinate, and bud,
And fructify, and yield a poisonous fruit.
Hell's trinity, Satanic triad, roams
About earth's plains again: still more inspired
With hatred, malice, and determined spite,
T" insure the overthrow of God's set plans.
The power is great: and soon, by specious wiles,
Are lured, around the standard, countless hosts.
Then Gog, confed'rate prince of various clans;
Togarmah of the north, and Ethiop,
And Persia, Libya, Gomer and his bands,
And all their glitt'ring train, will move their strength
Against the undefended camp, the land
Of unwalled villages, that neither gates
Nor bars defend: whose quiet rest in God
Provokes Satanic rage; whose natural ease
And plenitude, and wealth—now not a snare
Except to envious hearts without—entice
Marauding hordes. The end is not as when
The Gog of earlier times came as a cloud,
And covered all the land: then jealousy,
Diversity of creed, and fancied wrongs,
Bred mad asperity; the spear reversed,
And gleaming falchion, drank a brother's blood:
Whilst from above, heaven's great artillery poured
Their mingled storm of death. Now fire alone
Performs the dreadful work—avenges God
And those who trust in Him.
Satan is bound in everlasting chains
With no conditioned clause; no respite breaks
The drear monotony. The ceaseless tide
Of cumulative woe rolls on: Despair
Surceases not as heretofore; ruthless,

Pursues her work; fetters and torturing coils
Her bidding do; vindictive, she pursues.
Her aim is one, all share her spleen; yet all
Do not alike partake the grievous pain.
As with a poison coursing through the veins;
In one immunity is found, as in the king
Of ancient times who ruled the Pontic plains:
Or as the brute, with antidotal blood,
Partakes the rankest venom, yet escapes:*
Another dies; something correlative
Gives potency, and so the poison works.
So though the sentence be the same, the same
Is not endured by prisoners in their cell;
One suffers more, because his memory works
In gloomy solitude; unbidden, crowds
His past life's incidents, calls up its sins
In thought, in word, in deed. Select
The merest sinner in the courts of hell,
He suffers least. So in the realms above;
The highest in th' enjoyment of their sweets
Is he, who made God's sovereign will and work
His highest aim. On earth, in heaven, in hell
A sentence has its complements: th' award
Of future good is not the mere entail
Of endless life, an arbitrary mode
Of balancing accounts: nor does the clause
Condemnatory fix th' amount of pain.
But man himself is building up for aye
His torture-room; or else is treasuring up
Great stores of supplemental joy.
Th' initial course its proper sequel finds,
Through all eternity, in its award.

* The hedge-hog; the deadliest poisons do not affect it.

Grim Death, the earliest, latest foe, is seized,
Committed to the lake of fire; and there
Dark sin expresses still the fatal ill
That gives his sting its lasting virulence.
Now deadlier certitude attends his work;
Not one evades its power; all avenues
Of thought and being own the loathèd guest.
    Eternal Justice shuts the door of Hell:
Nought but eternal Wisdom can throw back
The ponderous bars, or burst its casemates, proof
Against the cries of woe. He who has framed
The concrete mass, arching the prison house,
And He alone can broach its thick-set ribs.
    Here Time refrains a longer course: his roll
He tenders to the great Accountant: He
Unfolds the vast array of all; hands each
What each has writ on Time's great book: here each
His writing knows, is cognizant of words
Of hasty wrath, of viperous speech that stings
The guilty and the innocent alike;
Lewd thoughts in vivid truthfulness
Transcribed; the murderer's look of hate;
The miser's gloating gaze; ambition's wrong.
    But blood is there. Deep dyed, some tissues shew
No record left: suffused with that, they yield
The entry of the damning catalogue—
The autographs of countless multitudes.
Of these, a period happened in their course
When they forbore to write in Time's account:
This blood then blotted out all they had writ.
Henceforth the Book of Life, record of grace,
Receives all minutes of their earthly course.
Grace enters there the names of these, their faith

And works of faith wrought by the God of heaven,
And by Him placed to their account.
Marvels of Grace!
 Now to th' Eternal King, invisible,
Immortal, only wise, be endless praise,
And honor, glory, evermore.   Amen.

BOOK V.

THE ETERNAL STATE.

THE ARGUMENT.

Introduction. The New Jerusalem. The earthly Jerusalem.
Jacob's dream fulfilled. Heaven's harmony. God all in all.
Hymn.

MILLENIAL Suns have set. New heavens appear,
In which no Sun has place; the Moon has ceased
To shed recurrent light; the Stars have failed,
Hid in effulgence greater than the Sun.
Fire has performed its work, and ceased to rage
In righteous vehemence; its lustral power
Has justified the holiness of God.
Sin has retired before its wrath; escaped
To where its revels shall endure for aye:
Not unrebuked; yet unrestrained, its strength
Will forge enduring chains to gird itself.
Not less perverse than in the earthly sphere;
But more intense, its virulence will pace
With onward time; its power increase to bind
Th' original decree of banishment
From where it might defile, to other realms
Where it shall ever heap remorseless guilt,
Accumulative woe. Most beautiful
Within its mask, it swayed the heart of man

Six thousand years—a time of mystery.
A heavenly lens alone could penetrate
That mask, reveal th' intrinsic hideousness.
Its history terrene we have essayed,
Exhausted not; then it had power to draw
Immortals down, who saw the mask alone,
Nor cared to look within: men reveled in
Its fatal charms; and in their mad delight
Provided denizens for that dark world
Where woe intensive rolls, despair abides.

But now berid of this impetuous guest,
The Earth, in fearless joy, has spread her feast,
In graceful loveliness, to cheer all hearts.
Excess breeds no disgust; defect, no dread.
Anticipation cowers not before
Some future ill. The eye drops not its veil
To shun some piteous sight; the ear receives
No tidings with regret. The senses all,
Celestially refined, express great joy
Through every avenue, discover sweets
In every exercise, range unrebuked
To distant spheres, investigate their store,
Evoke much good, and minister the same.
The heavens above present a planisphere
Of glory there intyped; the earth responds
A faithful photograph. Man has not ceased
As representative of God supreme.
Deformity that sin had wrought has fled
With that which gave it countenance; but still
Diversity prevails; creative skill
Infused this elegance in all its works.
A diverse similarity still prints
The needed individuality:

But no misgrowth impedes immortal limbs;
No fumes corporeal dull the god-like mind.
Time has no residence on earth, his place
Eternity now fills. Age makes no dents
Of years elapsed; no furrows trace their length:
Perennial youth delights the teeming crowds.
No weariness distracts the purposed flight
To distant worlds. Satiety refrains
T' accompany the good of life, nor clogs
Th' enjoyment of its sweets. A brotherhood
Is now set up that makes no hollow show,
That lays no claim it cannot verify.
Love wanders unrebuked, nor fears to shew
Its tenderness, lest it should weep when those
To whom it ministers may misconstrue—
He who is Love has framed a state of love.
A bright cosmogony elucidates
Creative excellence, Almighty skill,
Administrative power, consummate good.
The senses all refined do not reject
What, not recuperative from decay,
Delights: food there is none, if by such food
Growth is maintained; but entertainment finds
Provision for its claims. Sweet Pleasure roams
Unqualified by etiquette, or laws
Conservative: abandonment prevails;
For stiff-restraint commingles not
Its awkward forms; and in th' eternal state
This law is prevalent. Deep consciousness
Of full security does not beget
A lawlessness, or blind indifference.
Existing evil none ignore; but all
Are cognizant how it has wrought its part

In one great whole; not accidentally
As though a weaker party had prevailed
To negative a Great First Cause, or clog
His laws with hostile ways, that deep resource
Must plan to meet—not unforseen indeed,
But which the Arbiter of all could not,
Or would not exercise Himself to stay.
Poor sterile logic this! rash compliment
To Him who, self-possessed, e'er balances
The two eternities; between the past
And that to come, discrepancy is not.
God does not subsequently counterplot
What has sprung up; He is not pressed with fear
Lest it should mar or interrupt His plans:
Th' eternal scheme embraces good and ill.
The grandest harmony is best obtained
With sounds dissimilar, selected by
The minstrel's art, and wrought consummately
In unison. Two living hearts, alike
In mould, in instinct, sensibility,
In tenderness, in readiness to weep
For sorrow not their own, are not the best
To mingle joys, secure the happiest lot.
All nature testifies this principle
Of all God's ways—inscrutable indeed,
But manifest—that He, all-wise, designed
A varied whole; not merely of the *same*,
Which might evince extensive skill and art,
But deep and complicate diversity,
Demanding calculation nice, to curb
Each agency from undue prevalence,
From interference irretrievable,
Or from excess minute, minute defect.

Th' eternal state presents th' abstruse results,
Not clear to our intelligence; but when
This mortal puts on immortality,
And death is swallowed up in life, then too
Shall sense give way to sight, to clear
Unclouded apprehension of that scheme
Which Time, yet young, had mystified with sin.
Some things inevident we yet allow;
Yea, more; things contradictory we grant,
Because of evidence beyond themselves.
A long continued creed acquires respect,
More reverent than wise, if for its age
It gains esteem: it may be, honored names
Add weight. We would not lightly controvert
Established laws, or doctrines manacled
With theologic bonds; and if our mind
Is prone t' investigate an ancient chart
And finds some new discovered isles not there,
Results will justify th' invet'racy;
For good, not evil, is the purposed end,
That some unconscious bark may not be wrecked
Where heretofore no waves dashed on the shore.
 All things are new. All that was once has passed;
And, with the earth, are classed 'mong things that were.
See first, nobly resplendent over all,
The holy city, new Jerusalem, where reigns
Supremely there, the world's Almighty King.
There is His throne, and there His wondrous Bride,
On whom is lavished royal love and grace,
Beyond descriptive powers. The place is built
For her delight; and ornaments profuse
Adorn this royal residence, this bridal gift:
Prescriptive not for her alone; He dwells

Much in her company. Foundations deep
Receive the lofty walls, profusely wrought
With skilful garniture, and planted by
Almighty hands. A mountain great and high,
Reared by the Architect of heaven and earth,
Springing from plains below, a basement gives.
God's glory there prevails; the Lamb of God
Lights up the beauteous scene; His glory shines
Through pure translucent walls, speeds on its course
In genial prevalence, the light of life.
Not as a creature light that may be dimmed;
Or, in excess, may scorch; or, in defect,
May suffer cold to nip: this carries joy;
Perennial gladness sings its constant song.
Th' immediate vicinage below presents
The earthly relative, beloved of God,
Jerusalem, the earth's metropolis,
Joy of the earth. The nations now rejoice,
Their kings—for kings there are who reign, and rule
In righteousness—do bring their glory there.
Behold the holy mount: here Jacob's dream
Is more than verified; angels ascend,
And some the while descend; but crownèd heads,
Ascending and descending, visit there,
And bring the glory of their state; return
With messages of love. The slope is filled
With happy visitants, who seek and find
An entrance there; whom gates of pearl receive,
To view the wonders of that glorious place.
No night is there, nor gorgeous temple reared
With costly stones; the Lord, Almighty God,
The Lamb as well, its temple are; and praise
The ritual service of the thronging crowds.

Now God fulfils His word to dwell with men.
All tears are wiped away; nor sorrow, death,
Nor crying e'er intrudes; for former things
Are passed away. No more does creature strength
Essay its powers; no more is happiness
In peril found. All things are new; no sea
With boisterous waves and roar, invades the land;
No gallant ship is seen. Eternal day
Has dawned, and night has fled away.
   Within the walls one street pervades its length
A noble river courses through its midst;
On either side the tree of life, with fruits
Of different kinds, one kind for every month.
Its leaves medicinal, not curative,
But by anticipation, warding off—
For God will yet use means—ill that might else
Invade all but Himself, and those whom He
Has made one with Himself and His great Son.
That "there shall be no curse" gives evidence
That sickness will not call for medicine;
But health will seek benign constituents,
Ensuring thus a fair continuance.
God's servants serve—a joyous service too.
They see His face, and in their foreheads wear
His glorious name; they reign for evermore.
Now trace the river's source—the throne of God!
Water of life it bears; onward it flows;
It gains the hills' fair brow, leaps gently down
Its gradual slope; the nations freely drink;
Its myriad channels glide, meand'ring slow;
God's wondrous gift of grace and love to all.
   Now hark! How ravishing! What heav'nly strains!
Lo! Harps of God, ne'er out of tune; their strings

Are fingered by immortal hands, and chord
Well with the trump of God, and voices tuned
For heavenly lays; the burden of their song,
Set for Eternity—the blood of Christ.
It circles still; and, as the ages roll,
Illuminates the records of the blest.
Space infinite resounds the name of Him
Who on the throne, chief singer there, gives forth
The note of praise; for He alone can sing
Without reproach, Himself, and celebrate
What He has done; for He, and He alone
No blemish owns in all that He has done,
For all is well. Yet not Himself alone
He sings, for He and His beloved are one.
His Bride, joy of His heart, is there; equal,
But not in might, nor primogeniture,
But in the heart of God, and near His own.
She sings His praise, among ten thousand chief;
And He responds, her beauty celebrates,
Her peerless majesty admires.

    Now God is ALL IN ALL, Heaven's Trinity,
The Father, Word, and Spirit, Three in One.
The MAN, God's fellow, has sustained God's throne
A thousand years on earth. Mysterious One!
Not less a man than God; not less the God
Than man: the sorrowing man, the mighty God.
Days of eternity were His, but yet He died
Ere He had reached His early prime.
Without an origin, yet born a babe
In lowly Bethlehem: the source of strength,
Yet helped by angel ministry: He fed
A multitude, yet He had need of bread:
All power in heaven and earth are His, and yet

He yields His early life to murderers.
So He prevails, and now for evermore
He shines the light of life, and has Himself
His bright reward. Yea, for this very joy
He sped His course, endured the awful Cross,
Despised the shame. Eternal joy was His,
Yet by a heavenly paralogue, this bears
An increase, for another's joy is His;
And His another shares: increase is made,
The two are greater than the one. Here too
Deep mystery hangs her veil; and thought,
Laboring, can but approximate, and not
Lift up the veil: the longed for time is near,
And immortality shall raise the screen:
Then holy gaze shall penetrate the range
Of Wisdom Infinite; though never sound
Its utmost depths. Whilst making swift approach,
The distance still maintains its primal length:
Infinity has no admeasurement.

Yet one look more. The regions round are filled
With occupants that breathe empyrean air,
Pure emanation from the throne of God.
Angelic beings, messengers of Him
Who has delight in all that He has made.
These still are ministers to do His will;
Still learn His grace by marking well the Bride,
As nearer still; and still more intimate
With Him her heart adores—Him who sets forth
The image of th' Eternal God; His Father, hers.

HYMN.

O glorious vista ! when shall be revealed
The beauties of that state so long concealed ?
When shall Thy ransomed ones, O Lord, behold
That world, the half of which has not been told ?
Shall longing hearts restrain their earnestness;
And wearied hearts rebuke their weariness ?
Or hope deferred renew its hopefulness;
And joy still cultivate its joyfulness ?
Thy faithful ones, O Lord, still trust in Thee;
Thy prisoners of hope still hope in Thee:
The fondest hearts increase their fondness still;
Their weariness of earthly joy fulfils Thy will.
The Day Star is not far, its rising nears,
First in our hearts, whilst yet we shed our tears;—
For sorrow still abides, and wrings our hearts,
And well we know the sore of fiery darts.
But midnight sure is past, the dawn is near,
Yea, see the morning breaks; we'll chide our fear;
For He who said, "Behold I quickly come,"
Is not far off. Our hearts respond, Oh ! come !
The Spirit and the Bride say, Come;
Lord Jesus, come. Amen.

THE END.

PUBLICATIONS OF INTEREST
RESPECTING THE
NEW ORPHAN HOUSES, ASHLEY DOWN, BRISTOL,

Where 1,150 Orphans are maintained; with a contemplated enlargement to accommodate 2,000 Orphans.

ASHLEY DOWN; or, Living Faith in a Living God. A Memorial of the first Quarter of a Century of the New Orphan Houses on Ashley Down. By W. ELFE TAYLER. Price 3s. 6d. (Post free.)

MIGHTY THROUGH GOD. Some Account of the Extraordinary Labours of the Rev. George Müller, of Bristol, as Founder and Director of an Institution for Missionary Work at Home and Abroad, and other operations. By W. ELFE TAYLER. Neatly bound in cloth. Price 1s. 6d. (Post free.)

PHOTOGRAPHIC PICTURE OF ELEVEN HUN- DRED ORPHANS from the Ashley Down Orphan Houses, Bristol; taken at an excursion of the children to Shirehampton Park. Price 2s.

STEREOSCOPIC - SLIDE VIEWS OF ORPHAN HOUSES AND CHILDREN, 1s. 6d. each; Part of Grounds with Group of Boys; House No. 1, with Group of Boys; House No. 1, with two Masters; House No. 1, with Group of Infants; House No. 1, with Group of Girls; House No. 2, with Group of Girls; House No. 3.

FAITH, HOPE, AND CHARITY EXEMPLIFIED: Lines on the New Orphan Houses, Ashley Down, with View of the Orphan Houses. Price 2d., or 1s. 9d. per dozen.

VIEW OF ORPHAN HOUSES, with Printed Ex- tracts from Mr. Müller's Reports. Price 1½d., or 1s. 3d. per dozen. Useful for inclosing in letters to friends, to give an idea of the magnitude of the work, and the principles on which it is conducted.

VIEWS OF ORPHAN HOUSES ON LETTER PAPER OR CARDS. One Penny each.

BRIEF NARRATIVE OF FACTS RELATIVE TO THE NEW ORPHAN HOUSES for 1,150 Children, on Ashley Down. By GEORGE MULLER. Price 6d.

A VISIT TO THE NEW ORPHAN HOUSE, Ashley Down. Price 2d.

THE LORD'S DEALINGS WITH GEO. MULLER. Written by himself. 2 volumes. Price 6s.

FAITH AND PRAYER EXEMPLIFIED IN THE SUPPORT OF 1,150 ORPHANS. A Four-page Tract. Price 3d. per dozen, or 1s. 3d. per 100.

SOLD BY W. MACK, BOOKSELLER AND PRINTER,
38, PARK STREET, BRISTOL.

Advertisements.

THE BELIEVER'S STANDING IN CHRIST, AND HIS CONSEQUENT RELATION TO THE WORLD. By the Rev. S. WILKINSON, Taunton. Price 1d.

PREPARATORY DISCIPLINE; OR, FORTY YEARS IN MIDIAN. By the Rev. M. DICKIE. Price 3d.

THE GOOD WOMAN; OR, THE MODEL WIFE, MOTHER, AND MISTRESS, OF THE BOOK OF PROVERBS. By the Rev. H. I. ROPER. Price 4d.

GO TO JESUS. A little book that should have a large circulation. Price 1½d.

HAPPY JOHN, THE DYING POLICEMAN. By the Rev. D. A. DOUDNEY. Third Edition. Price 2d.

CHRIST THE ONLY SAVIOUR. Price 2d.

A SCRIPTURE CALENDAR FOR READING THE OLD TESTAMENT ONCE, AND THE NEW TESTAMENT AND PSALMS TWICE, DURING THE YEAR. By the late Rev. JAMES SHERMAN. Price 3d.

DOES MASSA LOVE MY JESUS? By the Rev. S. A. WALKER. Fourth Thousand. Price 2d.

OUR TIMES AND OUR CHURCHES. By Rev. S. HEBDITCH. Price 2d.

CHURCH EFFICIENCY; OR, CHURCH PRINCIPLES CONDUCIVE TO CHURCH PROSPERITY. By Rev. H. M. GUNN, Warminster. Price 3d.

OLIVER CROMWELL. By Rev. N. HAYCROFT, M.A. Second Edition. Price 6d.

HEROES & LESSONS OF ST. BARTHOLOMEW'S DAY, A.D. 1662. By Rev. N. HAYCROFT. Second Edition. Price 6d.

REGENERATION BY WATER AND THE SPIRIT: a Sermon. By Rev. S. A. WALKER, Rector of St. Mary-le-Port, Bristol. "Showing Scriptural authority for the use of the Baptismal Service by the Evangelical Clergy." Price 2d.

BAPTISMAL REGENERATION, ACCORDING TO THE BIBLE, THE PRAYER-BOOK, AND THE EVANGELICAL CLERGY. By Rev. N. HAYCROFT. Price 2d.

HOW LONG WILL THE LAITY BEAR IT? A Question for the Sheep against the Shepherds. By Rev. S. A. WALKER, M.A., Incumbent of St. Mary-le-Port, Bristol. Second Edition. Price 1s. ("The design of this Pamphlet is to bring before the Christian Laity the character and aim of that party in the National Church known as Anglo-Catholics.")

BAPTISM IN OLD AGE; OR, OBEDIENCE AND HAPPI-NESS. By Rev. T. POTTENGER. Price 1d.

THE GREAT INSURANCE. By Rev. H. QUICK. Price 1d.

W. MACK, 38, PARK STREET, BRISTOL.

Advertisements.

By the Rev. HENRY CRAIK.

THE HEBREW LANGUAGE: ITS HISTORY AND CHARACTERISTICS; INCLUDING IMPROVED RENDERINGS OF SELECT PASSAGES IN OUR AUTHORIZED TRANSLATION OF THE OLD TESTAMENT. Price 3s. 6d.

HINTS AND SUGGESTIONS ON THE PROPOSED REVISION OF OUR ENGLISH BIBLE, a Reprint from Mr. Craik's larger work. Can be had separately. Price 6d.

THE DISTINGUISHING CHARACTERISTICS AND ESSENTIAL RELATIONSHIPS OF THE LEADING LANGUAGES OF ASIA AND EUROPE. Stitched in a neat wrapper, price 8d.; or, bound in Cloth, 1s.

PRINCIPIA HEBRAICA; an Easy Introduction to the Hebrew Language. Price 10s. 6d.

W. MACK, BRISTOL; BAGSTER & SONS, LONDON.

By Rev. M. BROCK, M.A., of Christ Church, Clifton.

SHORT CHAPTERS ON THE COVENANT OF GRACE. Price 2s. 6d.

INFANT BAPTISM. Price $1\frac{1}{2}d$.

THE SACRAMENT OF THE LORD'S SUPPER. Price 3d.

THOUGHTS ON THE TRANSFIGURATION. Price 2d.

THE OLD TESTAMENT CONFIRMED BY THE NEW, IN THE WORDS OF JESUS AND OF HIS APOSTLES. Price 2d.

DOCTRINES FOR THE CHURCH. Containing "JUSTIFICATION," "SANCTIFICATION," "GLORIFICATION," and "THE LORD'S COMING." Price 2s.

The above may be had in Separate Tracts:—

JUSTIFICATION BY FAITH ONLY. Price $1\frac{1}{2}d$.
SANCTIFICATION OF THE SPIRIT. Price $1\frac{1}{2}d$.
GLORIFICATION. Price $1\frac{1}{2}d$.
THE LORD'S COMING: A GREAT PRACTICAL DOCTRINE. Price $1\frac{1}{2}d$.

W. MACK, 38, PARK STREET, BRISTOL.

Advertisements.

By W. ELFE TAYLER.

HISTORY OF THE TEMPORAL POWER OF THE POPES;
SHOWING THE CRIMES BY WHICH IT WAS ORIGINALLY ACQUIRED, AND AFTERWARDS ENLARGED; WITH AN APPENDIX OF SCARCE AND CURIOUS DOCUMENTS, AND A COLOURED MAP, POINTING OUT THE POSITION OF THE REVOLTED STATES OF THE CHURCH. Price 2s. 6d.

THE END NOT YET. Price 1s. 6d.

The object of this work is to show that the word of GOD affords no ground for the extraordinary theory of Dr. CUMMING, that the Coming of Christ and the commencement of the Millennium will take place in the year 1867. The Author goes on to show, however, that there is good ground in Scripture for believing that the year above specified will prove the era of a great *Crisis* in the History of Europe.

By Rev. S. A. WALKER, M.A.

THE CHRISTIAN SOLDIER READY: TWELVE LECTURES, FORMING PART OF A SERIES OF WEDNESDAY EVENING LECTURES ON THE EPISTLE TO THE EPHESIANS. Price 2s. 6d.

The contents of this handsome volume are as follow:—The Source of Readiness—Necessity of Readiness—Character of Readiness—Difficulties of Readiness—The Girdle of Readiness—The Breastplate of Readiness—The Sandals of Readiness—The Shield of Readiness—The Helmet of Readiness—The Sword of Readiness—Readiness in Prayer—Ministerial Readiness

W. MACK, 38, PARK STREET, BRISTOL.
MACINTOSH & CO., PATERNOSTER ROW, LONDON.

Now ready, an edition of 10,000 *copies, royal* 32mo, *neat cover, price* 2d.; *in quantities,* 12s. 6d. *per* 100.

CHRIST THE ONLY SAVIOUR.

A Christian minister well versed in tract literature, and who gratuitously circulates thousands of small religious publications every year, thus writes:—"Your little work, 'Christ the Only Saviour,' is well calculated for usefulness. When there is so much teaching in our day whose tendency is rather to conceal than exhibit Christ, one welcomes any publication, large or small, whose aim is to give the Saviour, both as to His person and His work, that prominence to which He is justly entitled, and which is universally afforded Him in the sacred Scriptures.

"I have already commenced the purchase of 'Christ the Only Saviour,' and intend to give it as wide a circulation as my circumstances permit."

THE BOOK SOCIETY, 19, PATERNOSTER ROW, LONDON.
W. MACK, 38, PARK STREET, BRISTOL.

www.ingramcontent.com/pod-product-compliance
Lightning Source LLC
Chambersburg PA
CBHW030756230426
43667CB00007B/984